Learning in Jerusalem

Learning in Jerusalem

Dialogues with
Distinguished Teachers of Judaism

SHALOM FREEDMAN

JASON ARONSON INC.
Northvale, New Jersey
Jerusalem

This book was set in 11 pt. Garamond by Hightech Data Inc., of Bangalore, India and printed and bound by Book-mart Press, Inc. of North Bergen, NJ.

Library of Congress Cataloging-in-Publication Data

Freedman, Shalom.
    Learning in Jerusalem : dialogues with distinguished teachers of
Judaism / Shalom Freedman.
        p.   cm.
    ISBN 0-7657-6020-7
    1. Rabbis—Jerusalem—Interviews. 2. Jewish scholars—Jerusalem—
Interviews.   3. Judaism—20th century. I. Title.
BM750.F633 1998
296.6'1'09659442—dc21   98-28050

Printed in the United States of America. Jason Aronson Inc. offers books and cassettes. For information and catalog write to Jason Aronson Inc., 230 Livingston Street, Northvale, New Jersey 07647-1726, or visit our website: http://www.aronson.com.

In gratitude for the sustenance and love
of so many years
and for the *Illuyi Neshama*
of my mother,
EDITH (ZEIBERT) FREEDMAN,
and my aunt,
MOLLY ZEIBERT.

And as a prayer for the health
and well-being of my sister and brother-in-law,
JOYCE FREEDMAN APSEL and DAVID APSEL:
Their devoted care for my mother
and my aunt
through long years of illness
has been a deed of loving kindness.

Contents

Preface

This book is a series of conversations with outstanding teachers of Judaism in Jerusalem. It is the continuation of a previous volume of such conversations that centered too on the subject of *avodat Hashem,* the "service of God." The work's central purpose is to enhance the understanding of this central concept of Judaism.

Among the teachers interviewed are many of the most prominent thinkers and scholars working today. The book includes interviews with: Dr. Miriam Adahan, founder of EMETT (Emotional Maturity Established Through Torah), a method for integrating Torah values into everyday life; Rabbi Nachum Amsel, outstanding Jewish educator and author of *The Jewish Encyclopedia of Moral and Ethical Issues;* Rabbi Eliyahu Avichail, the world's leading authority on crypto–Jewish communities; Rabbi Shlomo ha–Kohen Aviner, Chief Rabbi of Beit El, director of Ateret Kohanim Yeshiva, and popular author; Rabbi Joshua Berman, lecturer in Bible at Nishmat Institute and author of *The Temple: Its Symbolism and Meaning, Then and Now;* Phil Chernofsky, writer of the world's most popular English language Torah Parshah sheet, *Torah Tidbits;* Rabbi Chaim Eisen, distinguished Torah scholar, thinker, and co–founder and former editor of the *Journal of Jewish Thought;* Mimi Feigelson, among the most well–known pupils of Rabbi Shlomo Carlebach *z"l* and pioneer teacher in women's learning at Yakar and Pardess Institutes; Rabbi Emanuel Feldman, author of *On Judaism* and editor of the magazine *Tradition;* Rabbi Menachem Fruman, Chief Rabbi of Tekoah, interfaith dialogue pioneer, and religious poet; Rabbi Mordechai Gafni, among the most brilliant and popular Jewish thinkers working today; Rabbi David Hartman, director of the Shalom Hartman Institute, author of *The Living Covenant,* and twice national Jewish Book Award recipient; Israel Hess *z"l,* profound Jewish thinker and author of *Emunah* and *Drech ha–Avodah;* Rabbi Zev Leff, Rabbi of Moshav Matityahu, author of *Outlook and Insights on the Weekly*

Torah Portion; Professor Israel Levine, distinguished scholar of the Second Temple period and communal leader of the Masorati movement
in Israel; Professor Aviezer Ravitzky, teacher of Jewish philosophy at
Hebrew University and author of *Messianism, Zionism, and Jewish Radicalism*; Professor Eliezer Schweid, among the world's leading authorities on the history of Jewish thought, author of over twenty books,
and Israel Prize recipient; Dr. Daniel Shalit, popular teacher of Torah
and author of *Sicchot Panim* ("Internal Conversations"); Dr. Gavriel
Sivan, expert on Jewish communal life and author of *The Bible and
Civilization;* Rabbi Adin Steinsaltz, the most well-known Torah teacher
of our generation; and Rabbi Berel Wein, author of *Triumph and Survival* (The story of the Jews in the modern era) and well-known communal leader both in the United States and Israel.

The interviews were conducted from May 1995 to January 1997.
A number of the interviews were conducted in Hebrew (Rabbis
Steinsaltz, Aviner, and Fruman; Professors Ravitzky and Schweid, and
Dr. Shalit) and translated by me into English. A number of the teach-
ers chose to correct and improve the transcript so as to better express
their views.

Once again I feel great gratitude to each of the teachers of Torah
for giving their time, and sharing a small part of their great knowledge
with me. My meeting each one of them was a deep and meaningful
learning experience.

As Dr. Daniel Shalit has said, the subject of *avodat Hashem* is an
infinite one, which no person or work or set of works can ever hope
to exhaust. My hope is that this work will bring additional understanding of the concept and, what is most important, will aid each and every reader's particular service of God.

Acknowledgments

First to all, my thanks goes to the teachers of Torah and Judaism who consented to give their valuable time to this enterprise. Special thanks to Rabbis Chaim Eisen, Mordechai Gafni, and Phil Chernofsky, from whose *shiurim* I regularly learn from.

I would also like to thank once again Dr. Yaakov Fogelman for his great generosity and incomparable knowledge of the Jerusalem Torah learning scene. There are no words to thank my friend and continual source of inspiration, the teacher of hasidism, David Herzberg. Weekly learning sessions with him continually teach the joy and love of learning Torah. I also would like to thank Professor Lawrence Besserman whose broad learning and kindly intelligence have increased my understanding of many modern intellectual questions. Moshe Bobrovsky's wide knowledge of many Jewish worlds has given me many insights and much help.

Once again the staff of Jason Aronson Inc. has my thanks. Production Editor Kenneth J. Silver, Copy Editor Steven Sher, and Proofreader Suzanne Lindenblatt Gilad have done invaluable work. My deepest thanks goes to Arthur Kurzweil, not only for his continual faith in me, but also for the whole educational enterprise that Jason Aronson Inc. has contributed to the Jewish world.

I cannot conclude without a word of gratitude to the Creator and Sustainer of all, who has given me so many years of blessing and work to do this work I love to do.

Dr. Miriam Adahan

Dr. Miriam Adahan has devoted her working life helping those suffering from various forms of emotional abuse to lead lives of dignity in Torah. Among her important books are *EMETT: Emotional Maturity Established through Torah, Raising Children to Care, Living with Difficult People (Including Yourself)*. Dr. Adahan's works of *tzedakah* and her wide clinical practice are informed by the idea that each and every one of us is a *tselem elokim* whom Hashem loves, and that this love should enable us to contend with whatever difficulty and suffering our lives may bring us.

Dr. Adahan, the mother of four children, lives in the Ramot district of Jerusalem. It is at her office there that we had this interview.

S.F.: You cite Rabbi Dessler, who says that one great source of *avodat Hashem* is gratitude for all we have been given by God. You in your work inspire others to be appreciative and grateful for the good in their lives. Could you say something more about the meaning of *avodat Hashem* for you in your life and work?

Dr. Adahan: *Avodat Hashem* is loving human beings, loving yourself, and the people around you. It has nothing to do with what goes on in the synagogue. It has to do with what goes on in the home, in business, and in our interactions with people. And here is where we often fail. People make a separation between *avodat Hashem* when they are *davvening*, or learning or in a class, and the way they treat people, which is so often a catastrophe.

S.F.: The Rambam says the greatest love of Hashem is to teach others to love Hashem. I know this is central to your work, and to the Jewish way of seeing the world. Why then is there so much of the opposite, so much pettiness, senseless hatred, cruelty? You in your work repeatedly seek to help those who are subject to abuse and accusations from family members, from those close to us whom we should be helping. Why is there this cruelty, even in the Jewish world?

Dr. Adahan: We all have a severely judgmental side, which makes us think we have the right to put others down. This one is beautiful and rich and learned, so off to the right. This one is inadequate in some way, so off to the left. The physical reality is essentially about separation, fragmentation, *machloket* (dispute): In truth, everyone is different from everyone else. Our essential aloneness is frightening. Only love can make us feel less alone. So we must control our urge to be nasty, to pick on people, because of the differences.

Only throw dirt on others at the gravesite. No dirt, no hurting of feelings.

S.F.: I sense in reading your work that you have had to overcome a burden of insult and accusation, great personal hurt. You have really had to build for yourself a new idea of yourself, a new identity. Do you believe most people capable of such a transformation? After all, you have as a creative person one great advantage over many others, the power to make your ideas and thoughts influence people. Through your writing, your speaking, your helping others, you have a world of creation that is not given to most people.

Dr. Adahan: It wasn't always like this. I had been the victim of emotional abuse from many from the time I was very small. And I had a very unhappy marriage. So I had to figure out how to give myself some sense of value when I had no sense of value. It look a long, long time. I was very depressed for many years about the amount of cruelty and abuse in the world. Now I assume that, before I came into this world, my *neshama* (soul) didn't ask to be loved or understood; it asked for understanding and sensitivity. And for that, one has to go through a variety of losses. But I count the gains, not the losses; it has to be worth it to be able now to give people the tools to deal with loss.

S.F.: And now?

Dr. Adahan: I am still working on it, helping people overcome their basest urges and realize their Godliness.

S.F.: You have helped many people, including myself. One way you have done this is by helping to give us the idea that we are all created in the image of God, that we are loved by God regardless of our success or lack of it in the world.

Dr. Adahan: Among the people I work with, and the people who like my books, are many who have been victimized, mainly victims of *ona'as devarim* ("emotional abuse"). Usually when people say "Miriam I love your books," I know that they have suffered a lot. And that's a good share of mankind. The majority of children are brought up with a tremendous amount of criticism, both at home and at school. In every class, there is a star or two, and many others feel worthless because they are considered "less" than someone else. My thing is to get across to people that you are a success in God's eyes, if you are working on your *middot* (qualities of character). You can't love anybody unless you feel you have values. If you do not respect yourself, then you cannot respect others. And so my job is to help people feel good about themselves as they are, for who' they are, by focusing on their spiritual successes day in and day out, their efforts to be disciplined, loving, patient, etc.

S.F.: What is specifically Jewish about your approach?

Dr. Adahan: You mean between this and a general idea of just loving people? We see historically that Christianity has not done a very good job. Christianity led straight to the Inquisition and the concentration camps, because much of it was built on hatred of Jews, not love of humanity. I think it should be easier for a Jew to have a sense of value because a Jew can be proud of doing God's will all day long. That's where the sense of value comes from. Unfortunately, many have taken Judaism and used it as a hammer to beat themselves up with; if you don't have an IQ of 180, or you are not a brilliant learner, or if you are not the perfect housewife, you're not worthy of respect. Nonsense. We all have a desire for perfection. It's built in, part of the *neshamah*. We want to grow, to elevate ourselves. But the desire for perfection, which is legitimate in itself, can be perverted into a desire for material perfection instead of true inner spiritual connection. The desire for betterment can become a passion for belittlement of oneself and others. So that same craving for betterment just goes off a little bit, and you get this belittlement obsession.

S.F.: Among the people who turn to you for help are those who are going through terrible suffering. When they say to you "Why is Hashem doing this to me?," how do you answer them?

Dr. Adahan: I don't. There are many books, but books can only provide intellectual solace. One outstanding such book edited by Rabbi Bulman is *Longing for the Dawn*. Each person must wage his own long battle to understand how his personal losses can be turned into an impetus for greater Godliness. Basically, there's only one thing that helps people bear the suffering, and that's to have a relationship with Hashem. That's why I have these techniques for creating a relationship with Hashem, and feeling His love. That's why I have people writing imaginary conversations with Hashem, and getting answers back. Not just talking, but learning how to listen. This is a very personal process—I'm here to hold a person's hand, so to speak, to give him courage to go forward, to break out of his personal prison of anger, resentment, bitterness, and fear. The way to begin the process of personal liberation is by turning every encounter with another person into an opportunity to express love, forgiveness, compassion. This is especially important with our family members. This is what I teach. Then, if you feel that Hashem really loves you, you can bear everything. You understand that suffering is a way of tearing you away from the illusions of material reality, helping you create a spiritual reality. That's the gift of pain.

S.F.: Are you almost always dealing with people who have religious beliefs? Do people turn to you who are not religious?

Dr. Adahan: Many religious people who have no connection with God think God is a monster who is out to punish them. What I have to do is help them build a sense of a loving God's presence in their lives. It's Christian to think of God as wrathful, punishing, and angry. That's the way a lot of people see God because their parents were overly harsh. We tend to see God as we saw our parents.

S.F.: I think that's true. And this leads me to ask you something I did not want to ask you during your most recent lecture because I did not want to break the mood and spirit of your talk. It has to do with the exclusive stress on God's loving aspect. There is, after all, the God who speaks out of the whirlwind, who is so beyond us, and whom we cannot help but perceive with awe and terror. You have so much confidence that God is primarily love, that God loves you. How do you know this?

Dr. Adahan: What's our choice? If God does not love me, then I am in deep trouble. I just know what works. A very practical person, I was an atheist for the first twenty-nine years of my life because of the

Holocaust. From the time I was a small child, I read everything I could get my hands on about the Holocaust. Then, I had an experience of God at the age of twenty-nine. I was very lucky. Until that time, I thought that anybody who believed in God after the Holocaust must be an intellectual and emotional cripple. I had two beliefs: one, that there was no God, and two, if there was a God, He was a monster for allowing such cruelty to exist. Then I had an experience, in Berkeley, California. Sitting by myself in a garden, I closed my eyes for a few seconds. When I opened them, the world was gold. God existed. I just saw God emanating out of the entire world. It lasted three days, an unexplainable, unimaginable experience. It was nothing intellectual. It was something super-rational, supernatural.

S.F.: Were your parents survivors?

Dr. Adahan: No. My father, Alav ha-Shalom, was involved in trying to get Jews out of the Holocaust. He was part of the delegation that tried to get Roosevelt to bomb the railroad tracks into Auschwitz. He was in tremendous anguish. So as a small child (I was born in 1942)—I do not know if I was telepathic—I had Holocaust "memories." As a child of 3 or 4, I used to see people packed together in a room and hear people screaming at night. I used to be terrified of the sight of striped pajamas.

S.F.: As a small child—I was also born in 1942 and grew up in upstate New York—I knew survivors who came to our town. One of my best friends, Sammy Rozines z"l, was a survivor of the camps. But I never had the kind of experience you are describing.

Dr. Adahan: It was very real. I saw Nazis all around. I have very vivid memories from the age of four or five, of what went on there.

S.F.: So these experiences naturally raise the question of a kind and compassionate God.

Dr. Adahan: I couldn't fathom how a kind God could do this.

S.F.: You have written how Hashem is with us in our pain. I have heard this idea from others, and yet have difficulty understanding precisely what this means.

Dr. Adahan: I can't explain it. All I can do is say is that, if your deepest desire is to grow from your experiences and contribute to the world because of them, then you will feel His Kindness in many ways. I haven't had much experience with love, so I had to create it from nothing, ex nihilo. I started keeping a list of the nice things that happened to me. I actually kept a list. Any nice thing I wrote down, and as I focused on the positive in my life, more and more positive things happened to me. And nice people came into my life. Little by little that began refocusing my mind from all the trauma, pain, and rejection. I had to reprogram my entire brain, component by component. Once I knew that there is a God, that this world is essentially spiritual and that our job here is to make this truth real, I had to integrate what happened into my daily life for times of great disappointment and grief. I had the awareness that the world is essentially spiritual, and that we are all going through trials and tribulations here for a purpose. Though I dropped back down many times after that, that seminal event, the religious experience of God, kept me alive.

S.F.: And did your academic studies help you in this?

Dr. Adahan: Nothing. Nothing. It was intellectual garbage.

S.F.: So your formal training is not at the heart of your method for helping others?

Dr. Adahan: I know people need to feel loved. My next book, if I have enough time to write it and if it ever comes out, will be called "How to Love If You Were Not, or If You Are Not Well-Loved." There are a lot of lonely people in the world, a lot of singles, a lot of very lonely people. Most marriages are not happy ones. Statistically, the majority are not.

S.F.: But there are many good marriages and loving people who really do help each other. I can here see a criticism of your approach. One might say that you do not work at helping create such relationships, but rather on consoling those who are not loved. You tell people who cannot find human love to be consoled with the love of God.

Dr. Adahan: Anybody who is dependent on someone else for making him happy is in big trouble, because if that person dies or rejects you, you are devastated. Statistically, studies have been done in Japan, Sweden, Israel, all over the world, showing that about 20 percent of marriages are what we call "best friend" marriages. These marriages are those in which people have a really deep understanding of each other, considering themselves to be "of one flesh."

S.F.: Reb Aryeh Levine's famous "My wife's foot hurts us."

Dr. Adahan: Exactly. But that means that eighty-percent are in various degrees of loneliness. Most people are not going to get divorced, especially in the *frum* world. So what do we have to offer them? If you live with an emotionally cold person who cannot love, how are you going to get your love? From giving, contributing to society—then you feel Hashem's love in return.

S.F.: You know as well as I that our sources of love are varied: spouses, children, parents, siblings, wider family, friends. And yet there is often one member of the family who seems to take the burden of all the others' sorrows and griefs, the *noseh oll* (bearer of the burden). I know you are that person for many people whom you help, whose stories you listen to, with whom you sympathize. Do you have someone who does this for you, or is it through the process of helping others that you feel that you yourself are most helped?

Dr. Adahan: I like giving. I have not found anybody with whom I had that kind of relationship on a steady basis. No, I have not had that experience.

S.F.: So your deepest personal relationship really is with Hashem?

Dr. Adahan: That's right. Just Him and me, which I think has in a sense been a big gift. I have been forced to turn to Hashem.

S.F.: I have at times felt a parallel experience. Someone like yourself is somehow better prepared to be in that situation of being alone than most people are. You have your writing, your work with others, creative action.

Dr. Adahan: I am very lucky. We all have a special mission, something to offer that no one else can give. I think that everyone has a gift to give the world.

S.F.: Even those who are greatly limited in intelligence and ability?

Dr. Adahan: Everybody has a gift, even if the gift is in letting others take care of them. We have that opportunity of giving others a chance to do *chesed.*

S.F.: Where do you want to take these people when they come to you? Is there some special point you want them to reach?

Dr. Adahan: To a relationship with Hashem: to feel God's love, to feel that God is a reality. And they have the strength to become a person full of love and appreciation for life, independent of anything that happens externally.

S.F.: I know a person, very kind and good, yet filled with guilt and depression, without any faith in God. Can you help such a person?

Dr. Adahan: What I do with these people is have them talk to the higher power within themselves. I ask them to draw a picture of themselves with their non–dominant hand: as they would like to be, with the qualities they would like to have. I say "This is your essence." The qualities you would like to have are your essence. Then they will talk to their own *neshamah.* Everybody wants to do that—rich, poor, intelligent, unintelligent, creative, uncreative, religious, non–religious—everybody.

S.F.: And when they talk to their own essence, what does this give to them?

Dr. Adahan: They have someone to talk to twenty-four hours a day. Then they connect with the godliness within them. Next, I teach them how to let this loving part take over and control all their thoughts and actions. It takes time.

S.F.: I am just thinking of those who by their nature are so negative as to make it doubtful that such a discipline will work with them.

Dr. Adahan: Some people do not want to grow. There's no way to help. But everyone who does come to me does so because he wants to change. If he's not lazy, then he'll change with the exercises I give. I have seen very depressed people who within an hour are smiling because they made a new connection with God. Whether they are going to keep it up is another matter. It's work. You know the old joke: someone on the street asks how to get to Carnegie Hall. Another answers "practice, practice, practice." So to reach joy and love, you have to work at it. And this is my work. I try to do a *chesed* a day, try to do constant acts of self–discipline. But I have to work at it because I don't have the foundation that some people have, which makes them more joyous and loving.

S.F.: Do you have a sense of the collective *avodat Hashem* of *Am Yisrael* in *Eretz Yisrael*? How do you believe we are doing?

Dr. Adahan: We are not doing so great. The second Beit Ha–Mikdash was destroyed because of senseless hatred, and we are still in that. We need a lot of love, abundant love. If you have love in your heart, then you are connected to Hashem. If you do not have love in your heart, then you are disconnected. My job is to connect us again, to teach people how to love. It's wonderful work. You saw in the handwriting workshop how people were writing with their left hands, and getting those love letters.

S.F.: I sensed many people are helped. But you again and again made the point that it does not end in one meeting or group of meetings, but rather is a continual day–by–day struggle.

Dr. Adahan: That is the big point. People want to be spiritual, but they don't always want to work at it. We know Reform and Conservative people often say, "We will do just that which is convenient for us." But *frum* people too have to discipline themselves to love—it requires forgiveness, giving the benefit of the doubt, being silent when you are hostile, and giving when you do not necessarily feel like giving.

S.F.: And what kind of "learning" is essential to this process? Must it be Gemara learning?

Dr. Adahan: I think learning is very important, but I see a lot of people who are learning and yet not integrating what they learn into their personality. Learning should make us more loving. We should bless everyone and everything—it's all a teaching, all part of God.

S.F.: Do you feel many people are forced into "learning frameworks" who do not belong there?

Dr. Adahan: Absolutely. Most men should be learning a trade, should be both learning and working. It's a disastrous situation if, to avoid the Army, or to make a *shidduch* (a match for marriage), boys often lie. Not all are born to learn exclusively. Not everybody has an IQ of 180. A quarter of the population has some degree of learning disability, so forcing kids to sit and learn morning to night usually creates emotional problems. It's cruel. We treat children in a very cruel manner, and then they become cruel adults.

S.F.: In this failing of individuals is also a social failure of responsibility toward *Clal Yisrael*. Where do you stand in relation to religious Zionism?

Dr. Adahan: I love living in Israel. But I am not a *gadol*, so I want to leave these kinds of questions for *posekim* (Rabbinical decisors). I define myself as a *Chardal* (*Haredi* religious Zionist). I was very close to Habad, but I did not agree with the *Mosheach* campaign. The Haredi world is closed to me because my kids are not big learners. If I could have lived in one place, I would probably have loved to live in Hebron, but we live in dangerous times. We're in danger of losing our precious country. All I can do is remind myself that Hashem is running all things. I would very much like for religious Jews of all persuasions to be more loving. That's my work. The demonstrations in Bar Ilan, the spitting, the rock–throwing give us a bad name.

S.F.: You love living in Israel. Do you feel this part of the process of redemption?

Dr. Adahan: I pray we are not headed for another Holocaust. I am not an optimist, but I trust that whatever Hashem needs for us to go through we will go through. This won't be a bed of roses. But everyone has to go through his own personal suffering in order to build true *emunah* (faith). In order to go to spiritual reality, one must detach from the world of illusions of separateness and personal control. I trust that God knows exactly how much we can bear. I just want to teach people to love, nothing else.

S.F.: You have so many turning to you for help. Do you feel pressured by this?

Dr. Adahan: I do not do traditional psychotherapy. I do not see myself as a therapist, more like a midwife. People come to me, and I tell them that they are going to have to work, going to have to help themselves, to do certain spiritual exercises in order to heal. I do not recommend most therapists because the traditional sitting and talking to someone does not usually relieve problems. The big problems of life have no easy solution, that is, being widowed, rejection from family members, loneliness, etc. I wish that more people were doing the non-dominant handwriting I do because that connects you to your source of latent wisdom.

S.F.: How did you first start helping others?

Dr. Adahan: I started when I first became *frum* and read *Tanya*, *Pirke Avot*, and *Mesilat Yesharim*. I went through them and wrote down all the important psychological principles. I thought I would help make people emotionally healthy through leading them to internalize these principles on their daily lives. This came after I had a doctorate in psychology and did not see much success in traditional therapy. Then I just started to teach it.

S.F.: And an increasing number of people turned to you because they heard others had been helped?

Dr. Adahan: People get well with the exercises in assertiveness, empowerment, love, etc. If you have a broken spirit, weak *emunah,* and *bitachon* (trust in God), I will give you the exercises you need. You are not going to strengthen *emunah* and *bitachon* simply by talking. And *emunah* and *bitachon* in oneself are directly related to one's *emunah* and *bitachon* in Hashem.

S.F.: But what about that person who has so internalized the criticism received in childhood that he has difficulty overcoming it?

Dr. Adahan: Well, this is what I have tried to do for the last thirty-five years. I have tried to accept and love myself. With people who have had very critical parents, it's going to take a few years.

S.F.: How is this process affected by the fact that you are so well-known, respected, and loved by many?

Dr. Adahan: It's a very lonely life. Fame is a joke. As someone who was so rejected—it's like *"even maasu habonim haytah l'rosh pinnah"* Ps. 118 v. 22 ("the stone the builders rejected has become the cornerstone")—who suffered so much scorn and rejection, when I look at the situation now, I know that even fame is a kind of *gezerah* (decree) from Hashem.

S.F.: I don't understand why you were so rejected as a child.

Dr. Adahan: I couldn't figure it out. As a child, I was nice, intelligent, and loving. I was pretty. Yet for most of my life, almost every human being I would try to connect with would scorn me.

S.F.: Do you have a sense of the difference between the "public name" you have and who you really are?

Dr. Adahan: Yes. People look at me and expect something special. I'm not. I think I had to go through it all so that I would not get a swelled head. Fame makes most people egotistical, but I have been so crushed. I am just grateful for any bit of kindness anybody shows me. It's a miracle. But I don't let anyone get too close.

S.F.: You do not have a group of followers who support you?

Dr. Adahan: I do not let anybody do that. I do not want anyone to worship me. I work on myself every day. And I am very ordinary. I have my own crises.

S.F.: Do you find that people who were loved even by one parent only have greater strength than those loved by neither?

Dr. Adahan: Yes. But the love could also come from a teacher, an aunt, or a grandparent. Love provides a sense of basic optimism and a feeling of confidence. But certainly if there is no one, it's crippling.

S.F.: One of the big problems for parents is not to do the harmful things to their children that were done to them.

Dr. Adahan: All my books have to do with overcoming destructive urges. I try to help parents to be more caring and accepting, and yet also teach their children to be responsible, disciplined, considerate. My children are different from me. They have taught me what unconditional love is, for they are not like anything I put in the order form for.

S.F.: Do you think it's possible to be a good, caring person, a responsible person, a person with meaning in one's life without having a belief in, a relationship to God?

Dr. Adahan: I don't know. I think God is Love. And if you are a loving person, that's certainly the essence. But certainly the *bittul* in doing God's will, and getting rid of the ego, is what Judaism is about.

S.F.: You have treated people both in Israel and in the United States. Is there some difference?

Dr. Adahan: Everywhere in this world there are addictions and frustrations.

S.F.: You teach people to appreciate the good things, the blessings of life, the spiritual victories.

Dr. Adahan: I am glad that I had to create a loving environment by myself, and figure it out all on my own. It's my victory, in a sense. People who come to talk to me sense that I have been through a lot. People will say, "I can't be nice to my kids because my husband does not love me." And I answer, "I was nice to my kids though I had a difficult marriage." There are excuses, people saying that they cannot be loving because they don't have this or that. And I say to them, "I didn't have anything either, but I became a loving person." I tell them the obligation is to be a loving human being no matter what you are going through.

   I have treated people with terminal cancers; women friends of mine who, having died of cancer, left their children folders containing their lists of spiritual victories. They felt they left something behind for the children, a real inheritance.

S.F.: There's a passage in your most recent book in which you speak about how writing helps people spiritually. Why do you think writing is so important?

Dr. Adahan: My son said yesterday when studying for his test, "I know, mother, if you do not write it down, it makes no impression." It really is true, physiologically. The act of writing things down makes us remember them in a better way. When I leaf through my miracle book at the end of the year and remember all the miracles Hashem had done, I know I would have forgotten many of them had I not written them down.

S.F.: You mentioned the other night the signs we get that show us when

God is with us, the many instances of miraculous help we receive in daily life. But what happens when things seem to work the other way?

Dr. Adahan: I always say to write down the positive: The bus driver who makes a special effort to stop for you, the nice people who help you. To focus on the positive is basic Judaism. The *"Shemoneh Esreh"* says there are miracles, morning, noon, and night. And there really are. I think they should be written down, for if they are not, then you cannot be grateful for a moment, and won't remember them. The more you write them down, the more you see them. The other day I dropped my glasses in the street on the way to a class—this was in a busy street. When I got up the stairs to the class, I saw that they weren't on me, so I ran back out. They were lying unbroken in the street. For me, at that moment, that little miracle was God's way of saying, "Miriam, I love you. I'm with you."

Rabbi Nachum Amsel

Rabbi Nachum Amsel is the author of one of the finest guides to Jewish living written in recent years, *The Jewish Encyclopedia of Moral and Ethical Issues*. He received rabbinic ordination and his doctorate in Jewish education from Yeshiva University. He has been the director of the 1–year program at Bar Ilan University, and taught at Michlalah College for women. He has also taught at the Shaal program, which teaches rabbis to be more effective teachers, and has lectured extensively throughout Israel and the United States.

I met with Rabbi Amsel in his home in the Ramot district of Jerusalem.

CℜℬↃ

S.F.: Could you please describe your present work?

Rabbi Amsel: I am currently dean [Agust 1996] of Michlelet Torah v'Regesh, a post–high school Torah program for women that combines Torah, high–quality *shiurim* with *regesh* (emotional–spiritual experience), and prepares students for the real world. We teach study leadership and study Torah text skills based on the methodology of Nechama Leibowitz. The students also have many experiences in Israel including forty days per year of trips.

S.F.: What is the educational background that led you to do this kind of work?

Rabbi Amsel: I went to Yeshiva University probably more years than any other student in its history, starting with high school, college, *semichah* (Rabbinical ordination), and finally a doctorate in Jewish education. I got a secular as well as a religious education through Yeshiva University. I also studied for two years in Israel and one year at Yeshiva Kerem b'Yavneh. I was the first student of the Gruss Collel of the Yeshiva University in Jerusalem. I have my *semichah* both from Rabbi Soloveitchik *z"l* and Rabbi Fin *z"l* the Av Beit Din of Haifa.

S.F.: Your book *The Jewish Encyclopedia of Moral and Ethical Issues* is a work in which you look at many of the central issues raised by modernity and provide Jewish answers deeply rooted in the tradition.

19

Could you explain how you came to write this work, and what you hoped to do in it?

Rabbi Amsel: One of the reasons I went into the field of Jewish education was because I wanted to give my students a better education than the one I had received. My teachers did not prepare me for the real world. Not only was I, but my colleagues were also taught Judaism in a way that it had been taught for many many years. Unfortunately, many people got turned off or have been turned off, as you probably know, because they see traditional Judaism as something that relates only to the past. Most students of afternoon Hebrew schools understand Judaism in a child-like way because we learn most of our Jewish concepts as children. As I became older and learned more, I realized how deep and sophisticated and adult Judaism is. And for every moral problem, Judaism has a particular viewpoint and direction to go.

Dedicating my life to work on values, morals, and ethics in the Jewish context, I saw that there was no text in English that dealt with these issues—nor in Hebrew. Though there are many articles, there is no comprehensive work that takes the form, "What does Judaism say about . . .?" Therefore, after teaching adults and students for many years, I decided to put what I had learned on paper.

S.F.: A number of the essays in your book speak about the subject of assimilation in the Jewish world today. In one of these essays you speak about countering assimilation through having special Jewish clothing and Jewish names that are unique. In another article, you speak about how ineffective *herem* (excommunication) and "isolating wrongdoers" are today, and how much we need to bring people back to Judaism through love. Could you further elaborate your views on how to counter assimilation?

Rabbi Amsel: I think we've passed the generation where people are non-observant out of conviction. People today are non-observant out of ignorance. They don't understand the beauty, the sophistication, the warmth—the whole sense of satisfaction that can come out of Judaism. As you know, in advertising if you have any kind of product and you don't know how to package it, it is not going to sell well. Our job is to show people to put Judaism in a package for the 1990s. Frankly, the future of the Jewish people depends on this. It does not depend upon the Jews of Borough Park. There is an estimate that we are los-

ing approximately a thousand Jews a day, 355,000 Jews a year to assimilation. This is a problem that most people are not dealing with on
a regular basis. We need formal education, informal education, and outreach at all different levels. We have to train individuals who are coming out of the yeshivot and the day schools. We have to train people
who have the talent and the charisma to go out to all corners of the
earth to meet with Jews who do not have skills and background. Not
to be Habad, and proselytize, but to teach what it means to be Jewish.
That's on one level. On another level, institutes and programs have to
be developed to be able to train these people. There are people who
are doing tremendous things, but not enough. Certainly in the Haredi
world this is not done. Imagine if the Rosh ha-Yeshiva would send
students out to the sticks in Nisan and Av when there are no classes. I
have a friend who once drove a truck of Jewish books around the
United States. People heard about it and came out of the woodwork.
There are many ways of making a difference, but it has to become a
priority. The money, time, and effort must be dedicated to this end.

S.F.: Counter-balancing assimilation, there is a process of Jewish learning going on that in depth and strength is unprecedented.

Rabbi Amsel: The polarization has intensified during the past 25 years.
There are more Jews eating *treif* today than ever before, and more eating *Glatt Kosher* than ever before. There are more Jews who do not
know how to read the Alef–Bet and more Jews learning Torah in a
deep sense, *Daf Yomi*, than ever before. There are probably more people
learning Torah now on a regular basis than at any other time in our
history. Yet the simple Jew who in Europe knew a lot today simply
does not exist. We have the Jews who know how to learn, and we have
the Jews who know nothing. It's exciting to see so many Jews learning. But for every one learning, there are ten who never step into a
synagogue.

S.F.: You are talking here about the Diaspora world. I had a sense in
spite of the wonderful chapters you wrote on Israel, that your book
really was more addressed to the Diaspora world than to the community in Israel.

Rabbi Amsel: Obviously, if the book is in English, it was designed for
the English-speaking community. Yet a lot of this is going on in Israel

as well, not only among the *olim*, whether it be Ethiopians or Russians, but among the general population. There is no sense of values in the state school system. There is no relation to the *shul* except perhaps at Rosh Hashanah and Yom Kippur. Unfortunately, we can see a generation developing Western values, American values. And basically, everyone in Israel is beginning to realize that, without Jewish values, the next generation has no reason to stay. If you have American values, you should go to America to get the real thing rather than the imitation.

S.F.: You have cited figures showing the level of observance here is much higher than in the Diaspora world.

Rabbi Amsel: Even if you have no Jewish education, you in Israel know that Purim is a special day. Tisha B'Av is a special day. Pesach. Shavuot. Succot. You have a feeling of being Jewish, Jewish nationhood. Is it enough? There's no question that the typical assimilated Jew in Israel, the Israeli, is more Jewish and feels more Jewish and prouder to be Jewish than the assimilated Jew in America who may not even know that he is Jewish.

S.F.: When I say it was more directed to the American–Jewish community than to the Israeli, I also think about your not having touched some of the most controversial moral issues in Israel. You wrote, for instance, a beautiful essay on peace without considering the morality of "land for peace" in the Jewish tradition. You do not write about the secular–religious conflict in Israel.

Rabbi Amsel: There are two reasons I did not touch on the land–peace issue. One, this is not a *halachic* book. It uses *halachah* as a demonstration of what the normative Jewish value is. Two, if there is so much controversy, it is hard to present a normative view. I purposely left out a chapter on Zionism. I didn't want to make a book where people see the political issues and focus on them. People would focus on that controversial chapter. And the purpose of the book, which is to enlighten people and give them a sensitivity, might be lost.

S.F.: Is it for similar reasons that the tensions between modern Orthodoxy and the Haredi world are not touched upon?

Rabbi Amsel: Again, there are different outlooks. At the beginning of the book, I cite Rambam and Rabbi Soloveitchik *z"l* who say that when it comes to *hashkafah* (worldview), there isn't any one right path in Jewish thought. I do not know if you want to call it morals. How do you look at secular education? There are diverse views, and a number of books on that subject. How do you look at the founding of the state of Israel? Is it something miraculous, or not? How do you look at the secular Jew? All these issues, which divide the centrist Jew from the right-wing observant, are purposely not touched upon. I wanted to write a book that would unite rather than divide people. I wanted to address things in which there is not an Orthodox, Reform, Conservative, or Haredi view, things such as honoring your parents, or senility, or peace. There are values that are Jewish. This is why I try to use traditional sources only as late as the Talmud, Maimonides, Ramban, and sometimes the *Shulchan Aruch* in order to give a normative view. I chose not to take nineteenth and twentieth century works, because there you already have controversy. I purposely did it this way.

S.F.: But you quote Rav Hirsch and other modern Jewish thinkers?

Rabbi Amsel: One of the problems is that I have taken so many *shiurim* and seminars, and have read so many books. I hate to take from people without giving them credit, especially because it is a mitzvah to give such credit. So whenever I remember, I cite the source. I quote Rabbi Soloveitchik *z"l*, who certainly has influenced me. I have also been tremendously influenced by Nechama Leibowitz, with whom I have learned over the past 8 years. I have heard *shiurim* from students of the Maharal that take a totally different tack. I am an eclectic. If it's *emet*—and really "truth"—then you see it again and again. In other words, if you have a concept that rings true, then it pops up in the strangest places again and again. I am not a strict Soloveitchik or Brisker disciple. If something rings true, then you find it in many places in the literature. Shlomo Zalman Auerbach influenced *halachah* which influenced *hashkafah* in many ways as well. So it is not just one thing. Obviously I am a student of the Rav, as he influenced me the most.

S.F.: What is your method as a teacher? Do you have a special approach to teaching?

Rabbi Amsel: One of the things I learned from Nechama Leibowitz, who is a tremendous teacher, is the difference between passive and active teaching. I have tried in my classes to use active teaching. Most teachers ask a question and two or three hands go up, while the rest of the students do not pay attention. The students do not listen to each other because the teacher is expected to repeat anything worthwhile. That, to me, is the wrong way to teach. Nechama Leibowitz had everyone, even adults, write down the answer. While I may not do that in every class in *hashkafah*, I make sure that I am not calling exclusively on those who raise their hands. I work to make students relate to other students. I try to induce the students to make their own discoveries because this is the only way to true internalization of knowledge. If you take down the wall between students and teachers, then the students have to seek and find out by themselves. Sometimes we don't have the luxury of doing this, when the group is large, but I try to make them as active as participants as possible.

S.F.: You try to reach each student?

Rabbi Amsel: Most students sense that no one cares about their viewpoint. Teenagers especially believe that no adult figure ever cares about what they think. They may talk among themselves, but they do not have adults who ask them what they believe, especially in relation to God. There are techniques I use which enable me to bring out their feelings without making them feel exposed. For instance, I may use videos in a group setting. Basically, this allows them to hear different ideas from different people, and then find those ideas that are really powerful in Judaism. This is the way that they internalize the values so that years later they may say "When I was sixteen, I did not understand what you were talking about, but I do now." To implant those values is the goal, so that they are internalized, if not now, then eventually.

S.F.: You wrote a previous work, *A Curriculum of Jewish Values*. Could you describe it?

Rabbi Amsel: "Curriculum" was not written for the wider public, but for the school or informal setting. It is thirty lessons for a 1–year course on many of the same issues, each with a video or trigger film. This is to help the students see the dilemma within the particular value, and get them to react both emotionally and intellectually.

years ago the Reform did not believe in the state of Israel, did not have
any day school, repudiated all ritual. Now the Reform movement encourages all the rituals, because they realize that without them there is
no future to Judaism. The Orthodox *shuls* that people attend just because their parents did are not going to last. So it's not the affiliation
that is going to keep someone Jewish. Out in the field, it is the people
who are identifying as Jews, who want to have their children identify
as Jews, who are learning what it is to be Jews. The greatest compli-
ment I get when I teach a session at CAJE is when people come up to
me and ask, "Are you Orthodox, Conservative, or Reform?" The fact
that I wear a *kepah* does not reveal my denomination. Certainly, I keep
the *halachah* and this makes me a Torah Jew. But the Reform is coming much closer to this today than ever before. This it because they
have seen that the idea that the "more you water it down, the more
you are going to attract people" has failed. The strongest movement
today, as you know, is the Orthodox *Baal Teshuvah* (Return to Jewish
Religious faith) movement. Very few people brought up Conservative
stay that way. So too with modern Orthodoxy. Fifty years from now
we are not going to see those divisions.

S.F.: I see something different happening, a greater strengthening of
groups that wish to be self-contained, groups that are not open in any
way to other Jews. I see too how often even Orthodox groups are in-
timidated by others they take to be more *frum*.

Rabbi Amsel: Let's understand something. In the Haredi world, there
are as many divisions as among all the other groups put together. The
Belz have a totally different outlook on many issues from the Lubavitch
or the Satmar. They fight with each other. Therefore, there is not a
monolithic Haredi group. In Israel we see that. In America, they are a
little more tolerant. And yet there is a struggle between the Haredi and
modern Orthodox for the soul of the Orthodox in Israel. Their political power has made them more assertive. And their having eight, nine,
ten children, as opposed to one or two for the general population, also
means that they have growing power. I think this going to change. The
children will have to go out into the real world to support themselves,
and will have to learn to dialogue with the non-Haredi world. You
cannot sell a diamond to someone who is not Jewish if you cannot talk
to him about some other things as well. They will have to move out
to the world. In fact, it's starting to happen. All the things that plague

others are starting to happen to Haredim, higher divorce rates, for instance. I am not saying it's good. But it does help them appreciate others who are not like them. You can't work side by side with someone for years, and interact with them without beginning to appreciate them as human beings. This is true for meeting the secular, and for relating to those in the army. I won't go into the whole issue of Haredi serving in the army. But when people meet, stereotypes break down. And this is what is going to happen. Does this mean that it will destroy the Haredi community? No. It won't break down, but there will be a certain sense of appreciation of others, less resistance to dialogue. And by the way, it works the other way too. Non–religious Israelis will interact with the Haredis, and the idea that they are so backward and not intelligent will break down.

S.F.: You mention the "breakdown" of the traditional family. Do you believe that *tikkun* (correction) for the social structure is the return to the traditional family?

Rabbi Amsel: This is a problem that is bigger than you and me, and whatever I want to happen is not necessarily going to happen. The reason why the Jewish family has fallen apart in America relates to the breakdown of values in the secular world, the "anything goes" morality in so many area of life. This began to occur as the family began to break down. The schools did not take the place of the family in teaching values. The breakdown is in the Christian and the secular world. Ideally, the family should make a comeback. There is no substitute for having a father and mother as role models. Unfortunately, this is not going to happen soon. The trend toward single–parent families continues. This phenomenon is a danger to traditional Judaism and I do not have any easy answers.

S.F.: Do you relate this breakdown of the family to the rise of egalitarianism, the changing role of woman in society?

Rabbi Amsel: When I was growing up, no girl had a Bat Mitzvah. Today it's much more common. There is no question that all segments of society have been made more sensitive to the needs of women. But needs are different from rights. The American Jewish community is concentrating on the rights of women; however, in traditional Judaism, we talk about needs and responsibility. One hundred years ago

people talked about the melting pot in America. We realize now that
it did not exactly work out, that today there is a return to the idea
that each group should maintain its own roots. Respecting differences
is the new way. Dennis Prager said something interesting. The Torah,
everybody knows, says, "You should love your neighbor as yourself."
Yet the verse following that famous one, which talks about *shatnetz*
(separating linen and wool), is one that no one pays attention to. According to Prager, Torah is telling us the way we love somebody is by
respecting the differences between us and them. We shouldn't try to
make them become like us. In the last few years, studies have begun to
show that there are substantial differences between men and women,
not only physically but mentally. Egalitarianism tries to reduce the
differences. Judaism recognizes the differences, different wants and
needs. Without putting anyone down, Judaism says that people have
different roles. A grandfather's role is different from a father's, and a
man has a different role from a woman. It may not be the popular view
today, but the view that these differences should be recognized is now
coming back to greater respectability.

S.F.: But in the area that gives the greatest prestige in the traditional
Jewish world, "learning," there is a great transformation taking place
today. Why should a woman's learning be "less significant" than a
man's?

Rabbi Amsel: First of all, you should know that, in terms of traditional Jewish learning, it was only the top five percent who did the
higher learning. That continued past the age of 13 in the European
world. Second, one hundred years ago the Beit Yaakov movement
started. Some years ago Rabbi Soloveitchik *z"l* went against the trend
of observant society when he gave a *shiur* at Stern College's *beit midrash*.
Today, women are certainly allowed to learn any Gemara that relates
to practical observance. I am not going to get into Gemara learning,
but someone much greater than I said "If a woman is not satisfied learning up to a high school level but wants to learn more, there is no prohibition. The prohibition is chiefly on a man teaching Gemara to a
woman." That's why we have a woman with a Ph.D. in Talmud teaching our optional Talmud class at Michlelet Torah v'Regesh. Women
today who are brought up in the centrist Orthodox community are
getting the same education as men. Realizing that high school is not

enough, and they are continuing after the year in Israel. Institutes for women such as Michlelet Torah v'Regesh, for example Nishmat and Matan, are sprouting up. There's a friend of mine, as good if not better than all the men I know teaching Chumash. Her name is Bryna Levy, a brilliant, sensitive, phenomenal teacher whom I would put up against anybody. No one questions a woman's ability to learn. The only question is how open society will be to this phenomenon. My daughter goes to a school, Midreshet Lindenbaum, where she is doing what women have not done before, learning Gemara 3 hours a day. This is the trend.

Rabbi Eliyahu Avichail

Rabbi Eliyahu Avichail is the founder and director of Amishav, the institution that works to return to Jewish religious life lost and dispersed Jewish communities. Rabbi Avichail has traveled to many of the most remote areas of the world in this particular effort in Jewish education. Rabbi Avichail has written numerous articles and books on this subject, most notably *The Tribes of Israel (The lost and the dispersed)*. A man of great personal courage and deep faith, Rabbi Avichail has devoted the past 15 years to educate Jewishly those with uncertain Jewish background.

I met with Rabbi Avichail, a hearty and warm person, in his home in the western Jerusalem district of Kiryat Yovel. Our conversation centered not only on his outreach work but on his vision of redemption in *Eretz Yisrael*.

S.F.: Can you please describe the work you do as head of the organization Amishav.

Rabbi Avichail: The work of Amishav can be divided more or less into four parts. We are concerned primarily with what in the end turn out to be converts to Judaism. We know according to the Babylonian and Jerusalem Talmuds and also perhaps from Tanach, that the remnants of the lost Ten Tribes live as non-Jews and have to be returned to the Jewish people through conversion. This is the work we are doing. We have recently converted 200 of those who are related to the Biblical tribe of Menashe. The second part is more clear, and the conversion less required than with the tribe of Menashe. I refer to the *Anosim* (hidden Jews). We participated in the conversion of the community of Belmonte, approximately 100 people. Third, we are concerned with communities that are seeking after Judaism. These are communities that for many years searched on their own, which by and large came to Judaism through Tannach. And we, with the agreement and recommendation of the Chief Rabbinate, have helped convert them. One community from Peru of around 150 people is called B'nei Moshe. Another from Mexico, called "On the Way to Jerusalem," numbers 100. All of them made *aliyah* to Israel. A fourth group we deal with is not a group at all, but isolated individuals who come to us seeking conversion. We care for them, but this is on one condition, that they will be *gerei tzedek* (converts to Judaism). That is, we check whether their motivation is true, and if it is, we help them.

Amishav publishes educational materials too, including books on these subjects. We have brought out books on those related to the Ten Tribes, both in Hebrew and English. One is called *The Tribes of Israel*. We also have published books on Judaism for the converts. This work, *Judaism*, has appeared in more than ten languages. Because we are interested especially that the subject of the Ten Tribes will be understood in the world as something authentic, and not as a bizarre curiosity, we work to have the material published in other media, newspapers, radio, and through lectures, one of the important aspects of the work. I lecture in English, French, and Hebrew, with slides and film. I have given more than 1,000 lectures through the years, and made many appearances on radio and television. There are hundreds of articles in the press. So it is possible to say that the subject today is more or less known.

Another aspect of our work is research. We do not see ourselves as academic researchers, but rather as collecting information on various peoples and their life customs. This is done through an investigation of the literature that has already appeared and is not necessarily well known, and through direct contacts with the people and tribes involved. We take interest, seek to clarify, question, and if we determine that there is a serious case for a certain group, then we work with them. In most recent years, we have come to believe that the *giyyur* (conversion) is the main process, and not the question of determining whether the group has some prior Jewish identity. Since we think the question of "motivation" is the central one, we may well decide to help a group even if we are not persuaded scientifically that it has some real prior Jewish connection. With all these groups, it is almost impossible to make clear definite, non-ambiguous claims about their Jewish connection. In the most recent English edition of the Ten Tribes work, I write on a number of groups that I had not written of previously. Foremost, I write on the groups from the Caucasus, those living there as Jews, and those who were forcibly converted to Islam. This group is very large, several millions. I speak of those who sought Judaism in the past, such as the Sanicondro community in Italy and the Bayudaya—we just recently received books on them—we now are investigating in Africa. We try to help in other areas in whatever way we can. Additionally, I am responsible for providing the financial means for these activities.

The documentation of these activities, through picture albums, articles, a library on these subjects, concerns me too. This material is intended to be a storehouse of information for coming generations.

S.F.: Can you tell me something about your personal background and how you became involved with this work?

Rabbi Avichail: I first of all come from an Ashkenazi family. My mother was born in the Ukraine, and came to Israel in the 1920s as a *chalutza*. The family was religious, Hasidic. My father came from Lithuania before the turn of the century. He had left to study either at Oxford or Cambridge, and became a teacher of Hebrew in England. When he came here, he worked in the Mandatory Government, in translation and library work. I never knew my father, *alav ha-shalom*, who died when I was only three and one half years old. He was not strictly religious, but for my mother's sake, he went to synagogue with the children. All seven of us were orphans at a very young age. Conditions were extremely difficult. Yet when people have strong motivation, they grow and develop. We see how children in Mea Shearim, who according to all rules and measures are very poor, become nonetheless great sages, serious and respectable people. Here the key factor is not the social condition but the inner motivation of the individual to learn and to develop. This was true of us, though we were in orphanages in very difficult conditions. When I was a small child, my mother said to me that she wanted me to be either a rabbi or a doctor. Baruch Hashem. For fifteen years now I have had a doctorate, and before this, *semichah* as a rabbi. My sisters became university professors.

After passing through a path of learning in yeshivot, I was a member of a settlement group in kibbutz. I was in the army as a commanding officer in the *Nahal* (Army Settlement Corps). I was among founders and its first class of company commanders. I was at Tirat Tsvi in training in 1948–49 and after that joined the *garin* in Kibbutz Saad. I went to the class of company commanders, served as the commander of the Nahal in Kibbutz Yavne, and then, in the regular army served as a one of the few "religious officers." In Kibbutz Saad, where I lived for five years. I met my wife, who came from France to the *ulpan*. Leaving the kibbutz, I made an agreement with my wife that we would marry and I would continue to learn. But she was not able to work. Slowly, I began to work. I learned for three years at Merkaz ha–Rav and after this

moved to a *kollel* in Even Shmuel. There I began working on the idea
of establishing something like Levirate cities. That is, we would establish a center in which we would learn Torah, and from there go out to
teach. But I did not want to make my livelihood as the Levis did, from
tzedakah, so I taught in the morning in the local school. In the evening,
we would learn together. In the middle of the week, each of us would
go out to some yishuv to teach, also on Shabbat. We were drawn to
this idea, but there were few of us. I tried to recruit more, but could
not. So I moved from Even Shmuel to Petah Tikva. Over time, I became a department head at Yeshivat Nahalim, and a teacher of Tanach
and Yahadut in a high school. For nine years, I was a teacher in the
Petah Tikvah region, until one year after the Six-Day War.

Moving to Jerusalem, I continued to teach in high schools Horev,
Himmelfarb, the Yeshiva for Youth, and Lifshitz. At the same time, I
received my doctorate. Then, approximately twenty years ago, I moved
to teach only at *michlalot* (colleges). I taught Tanach, *Tamei ha–mitzvot*,
and all kinds of subjects related to Judaism.

In order to dedicate myself to the subject of the Ten Lost Tribes,
I took early retirement a year and one half ago. I had begun to investigate the Ten Tribes in the 1960s. Prior to this, I through the years
wrote books on various subjects, with a strong emphasis on Jewish
philosophy and *Eretz Yisrael*. I wrote things on Ha–Rav Kook that I
loved. I edited and wrote a commentary to *Chazon Yisrael* and published *Key Stages in the Teaching of Rav Kook*. The book *Zemanim
Mikudashim* ("Holy Times") that has now had its fourth printing. I also
published the book on the Tribes of Israel and one on ideas of the Redemption called *L'Or ha–Shachar*. Now I am working on another book
on interpretative ideas regarding Mishnayot.

As a *Ram* in Yeshivat Nahalim in 1960, I met a Jew who seemed
to me then somewhat strange, but he spoke about the Ten Tribes. His
name was Zonnenschein and he had written a little book called *Ohr
Chadash M'Tzion*. After he spoke and read this material, I was persuaded
that this is a serious subject, so I by myself began to take an interest,
collect material. For years, I sought literary material in libraries but
found that its connection to reality was questionable. Much of it was
simply wild imaginings. Only after fifteen years of research did I understand that this is not the way. So I paved an entire new approach to
the matter. What was important was my determination that the Ten
Tribes live as non-Jews retaining certain signs of Jewishness rather than

as Jews. After this, I began to take interest in peoples in the East, and gave up purely theoretical investigations. I began to travel to visit and investigate various peoples. But I wanted to investigate not only the signs of their Jewishness, but what there is in their motivation to become Jewish fully. And I asked them whether there is a chance that they will return to Judaism.

For fifteen years, I worked on this alone, giving lectures. Then I gave a lecture in Yeshivat Merkaz Ha–Rav to great enthusiasm, especially from Rabbi Zvi Yehuda Kook and Rabbi Avraham Shapira. The next day the important people there including Rabbi Zvi Yehuda asked me, "Why are you not doing anything about this?" I said, "It's impossible to do alone. It's necessary to found an organization" And Rav Zvi Yehuda replied, "*Nu, nu*" ("well, well"). It's necessary to found an organization. So he sent a rabbi and slowly, slowly we founded Amishav, in 1975. The same day that the organization was established, I sent an investigator to Afghanistan to inquire about the Pathans. Since the 1980s, there has not been a year in which some exploratory journey was not made. In this regard, one of the most important things was to form personal connections.

Since then, we have made progress. The first tribe we have dealt with intensively is Menashe. So far, we have brought 200 to Israel. There are many road blocks with government offices, but I learned that he who is stubborn, and sticks to his way, succeeds. It is necessary to be persistent.

S.F.: I would like to ask an unpleasant question. Today there is a problem in Israel with a considerable number of *olim* who are not regarded to be Jewish. Is there much sense in bringing more and more people to Israel whose Jewishness is questionable?

Rabbi Avichail: One important thing I have learned through the years is that this question of the Ten Tribes is not a question of the coming of the Messiah. But it is we who have the important determining role in what happens, throughout the process of the Redemption. The students of the Vilna Gaon were pioneers in this idea, the necessity of addressing the Ten Tribes and bringing them to Israel. They did not believe it necessary to bring all of them, for this is impossible. I thought that this is our task, to bring small groups (not the whole people) and to prepare them to be teachers, then send them back to their people. What is important is that the *giyyur*, the conversion process, be authen-

tic, that they will be good Jews. The truth is, we did not want to bring
more than ten from each particular people. But what happens is that,
because of the nature of things, it is not always possible to halt the
process. The tribe of Menashe, which began to arrive here in 1980, numbers only 200 16 years later. So we are not talking of flooding the land.
And this too came only after taking counsel with various leaders, including the Lubavitch Rebbe. What is important is to bring numbers
that we can supervise and be certain that they are truly *gerei tzedek*, to
bring them to learn Torah in yeshivot and to live in religious settlements. If the *aliyah* from Russia would receive the kind of intensive
treatment that we give people, then this I believe would be only for
the good. Yet it is of course very difficult, primarily because these often are people who are not interested in learning more about their
Judaism. I repeat, the path is not an easy one. If there is success, it comes
because I am in personal connection with each one of the people who
come. We do not bring them and simply throw them into the water.
If there were people from Russia who wanted to receive our help, I
would do it willingly, although too many people are already paid to
do this. We do all our work voluntarily.

It is impossible to do everything. Often I am asked why I do not
deal with Jews in the United States who are assimilating. While I cannot do everything, this is not to say I forbid myself to do these things.
If I am in the United States, I give lectures on the need to make *aliyah*,
and on Judaism. I recently published two articles on the current political process in terms of traditional Jewish thought. I believe it is our
task to continue to teach Judaism to the people of Israel. But I have a
specific task. This is like a person who deals with a *massekhet* (talmudic
tractate) no one else does. He has a special reward. And I have to my
regret my own *massekhet*. I say to my own regret because I wish there
were someone else who would dedicate himself to this matter. I will
not be here forever, and I hope Messiah will come soon, but if not,
this subject requires a great deal of effort and concern.

S.F.: There are potentially millions of Jews to be brought to *Eretz
Yisrael*, and this when the land is contracting with our withdrawals from
areas of Judaea and Samaria. Are you disappointed by this? Do you
see it as a setback for your work?

Rabbi Avichail: Because I am involved in Jewish thought and Tanach,
20 years ago I began to speak about what is happening today. I said

there will come a time when Arafat will accept ostensibly UN reso-
lutions 242 and 338, and then all the world will press us to give up
Eretz Yisrael. But I said then that the deal will explode around the subject of Jerusalem.

The principal idea—the basis of my optimism—is just as there was
in the exodus from Egypt four purposes: God wanted to punish the
Egyptians; God wanted all nations to know and recognize Hashem; God
wanted an Israel to know Hashem; and God wanted all people to know
Israel as people of Hashem, so there will be the same four purposes in
the Final Redemption. There was not one time that my world was
destroyed. I am always optimistic. I look on everything as a person who
reads Tanach. History for me is like *Sifrei Tanach.* It does not disturb me.

I believe "*Lev Melachim B'Yad Hashem,*" ("The heart of kings is in
the hand of God"). The *Kadosh Baruch Hu* directs history. The despair
comes precisely to secular people who cannot read history through
Tanach. They work according to the rational mind. If I were a completely secular, rational person, perhaps I too would arrive at the conclusion that it is necessary to try the Oslo process. But as a person who
believes, I believe the process is nonsense and will not succeed. It is
forbidden for us to give up any part of the land of Israel. I have no
problem with that. But in the meantime, we are in a transition period,
a period very difficult yet interesting.

S.F.: I would like for a moment to return to the matter of the peoples
and tribes you have been dealing with. There are some that are very
large. The Pathans, who number around fifteen million, come to mind.
As Jews they would seem to solve any "demographic problem" we
might have. But what exactly is involved here, their lack of motivation and desire?

Rabbi Avichail: We have not tried to operate in a massive way, to address the situation of the Pathans and others who may truly be from
the lost tribes. We work intensively with the tribe of Menashe. Apparently this follows a divine decree, because there is a Mishnah on this.
If this is really them, then they are truly the first. I try also, as best I
can, to make contact with the Pathans. I sent awhile ago an emissary
to them. I want to go myself, hoping in the near future to get to Pakistan. Recently I heard that Pakistan might recognize Israel as a state. I
do not know for certain. But I hope so. We are speaking about fifteen
million people. What will we do with them?

S.F.: There are millions of people in the less economically developed regions of the world who want to get to the developed areas, which today includes Israel. In other words, many have wanted, and more will want, to get here without any connection to Judaism or a process of *teshuvah*.

Rabbi Avichail: Right, and that could be dangerous. There is in the meantime *mazal* that Israel does not let each one simply enter freely. Someone who comes from a poor country cannot enter without some special arrangement with the Interior Ministry. I am happy about that. But I also suffer from it because I cannot bring the people I would bring. That is good, and it is good that there is a Chief Rabbinate who stands watch. There are many peoples who would like to come here for material reasons only. And since we are speaking about *giyyur*, we really can only bring small numbers. If I could bring ten Pathans here and teach them Judaism and send them back to teach the millions there, and they would remain there until the coming of the Messiah, that would not be so bad.

S.F.: Is there in the sources a figure for the ideal number of Jews which should be living in the land of Israel?

Rabbi Avichail: There is an ideal number: 600,000. Six hundred and ten thousand is called a "population." Six hundred thousand is the foundation number of *Am Yisrael*. Just as we in Egypt were 600,000, and after 40 years when we entered the Land of Israel we were 600,000, in the last of days when we will return we will be 600,000. As to how many will be included in Am Yisrael, there is no way for us to know. But it is written, "*lonidach mimanee nidach*," each and every *neshamah* ("Jewish soul") that exists in the world today will return to *Eretz Yisrael*. We know that *Eretz Yisrael* will expand, but we do not know to where. It is not our task to consider such questions now. Our task is to act in accordance with the *halachah*, with great caution. It is forbidden for us to see things, God forbid, from a point of view that may be destructive. We have to be careful not to destroy, but rather to build things carefully. If we have a certain view of the world, which is in contradiction to the *halachah*, it is forbidden for us to act upon it. I may know that the situation will, God forbid, deteriorate, but it is forbidden for me to contribute to this. Shabbetai Zvi, who did things according to a certain view, brought great destruction. It's forbidden for us in every subject to act against the *halachah*.

S.F.: You have said on the radio that you are against Conservative and Reform conversion. Can you explain why?

Rabbi Avichail: The problem is that they do not worry that those who are converted live by mitzvot, since they themselves do not keep the mitzvot. A Conservative Rabbi in Mexico converts a group in a non–kosher mikvah. Afterwards, these people live without any semblance of Jewish practice. These are considered converts? So this is a disaster for the people of Israel. One thing is important to understand. It stands as a basic principle in all I do. A *ger tzadik* ("righteous convert") is a Jewish soul who is returning home, and we have to help this return because this is a Jewish soul. To convert someone who will not keep the mitzvot, who has no real motivation to live as a Jew, is a disaster. We as a people have to think of quality not quantity. Quantity is not important for us. For the Conservative and Reform, it is quantity that is important.

S.F.: Do people like the Pathans have "Jewish souls"?

Rabbi Avichail: A good share of them do. Even so, it is necessary to do personal individual *giyyur* to check the motivation of each and everyone. Even then, it is necessary to be very careful and restrained in action. The principle is to wait until the coming of the Messiah, but before then do something in relation to returning Jewish souls, small and symbolic.

There are among the Pathans here and there signs of Judaism. It seems to me that, with today's Islamic fundamentalism and openness to the modern world, these are diminishing. How much can they hold on to for the younger generations? But if we succeed, it will be by producing a true nucleus, teaching people that this is something good and important. For instance, we put out a pamphlet for the Pathans in Persian, in a language they understand about themselves. We sent it out and it was returned because, to my regret, we did not have addresses. This is a problem. Thus I am interested in traveling there. But one thing is clear. Even if one is the best Pathan in the world, the best human being in the world, I will not agree to his *giyyur* unless it is true *giyyur*.

S.F.: Who helps you? Do you have any partners in your work?

Rabbi Avichail: I have good partners: first of all, the *Kadosh Baruch Hu*. To do the things I do without help from above is impossible. I also have friends in Israel who help me. As for financial help, there are people outside of Israel, both Conservative and Reform. A newspaper, *Koolanu* ("All of us"), has appeared six times. When I saw that they would give a different spiritual direction to the work, I told the editors not to use my name. I said, if you want to build an organization, go ahead, but on your own name.

S.F.: The main subject of these interviews is *avodat Hashem*. What do you understand by the concept and how do you understand your work to be *avodat Hashem*?

Rabbi Avichail: You see, I am first and above all a Jew of very deep and great faith, which is for me an enormous source of strength and power. I am perhaps less punctillious in mitzvot than I am strong in faith. And I have a way of seeing the world, in which I believe every Jew has a special role to play. Not always does someone find what his task is in the world. But for me there have been enough signs—certain mysterious signs, Kabbalistic signs—that I have found my role. I found interesting things in regard to my personality and what I am obliged to do. I am very strongly dedicated to the things that I do, and I have God to thank for those qualities that make me fit for what I do: my work with people, with ideas, in teaching. All these qualities help me in everything I do. This is the special *avodat Hashem* of mine. I serve God with the special qualities with which God graced me. And I think it's a great privilege to be able to work on such a historic task, which is so important and interests people all over the world, Jews and non-Jews. They write to me, call me, turn to me. This is what the Vilna Gaon meant by our making the effort to bring the Redemption closer in all that we do.

Rabbi Shlomo Ha–Kohen Aviner

Rabbi Aviner is the spiritual leader of the Jewish community of Beit El in Judaea. He is also the director of the Ateret Kohanim Yeshiva in the old city of Jerusalem. A popular lecturer and radio teacher of Torah, he is also the author of a number of books including *The Dew of the Hermon*. Considered one of the spiritual leaders of the Jewish communities in Judaea and Samaria, he is widely known and respected in Israel as a person of great love for the people of Israel.

I spoke with him in the communal dining hall of Ateret Kohanim in Jerusalem.

CR ᘓ

S.F.: Rabbi, would you give me a brief description of your work now?

Rabbi Aviner: I do what every rabbi does, teach and help people.

S.F.: You teach here in in the Old City in Ateret Kohanim. Where else?

Rabbi Aviner: In the *yishuv* of Beit El where I live and in a number of other places.

S.F.: Could you tell me about your background?

Rabbi Aviner: I studied at Mercaz HaRav and afterwards, for many years, I would come to the lessons of Rav Zvi Yehuda *z"l*. I would come to ask his advice, and I for many years studied his books.

S.F.: In reading your book *The Dew of the Hermon,* I had the impression that a large share of your thought comes from the teachings of Rav Zvi Yehuda.

Rabbi Aviner: The main teachings are from him and from his father Rav Avraham Yitzhak Ha–Kohen Kook, of blessed memory.

S.F.: How do you see our present situation in Israel in relation to the process of Redemption as outlined by Rav Kook?

Rabbi Aviner: We see from one side that the people of Israel have risen

up to life again. All that happens is no accident. That the land of Israel
was destroyed and has been revived, is no accident. It is rather the realization of the vision of the Prophets. The people of Israel returning
to its land is no accident. Also, the establishment of a Jewish state is no
accident, so too Israel's return to Jerusalem. All this is no accident. And
the nations stand ready to destroy us, and have not been able. This is
no accident. That Israel has been built and is being developed and growing stronger, this is no accident. At the time of the founding of the
state, the God fearing, the religious, were troubled, worried that there
would not remain one Jew with a *kepah* on his head. And now there
are so many yeshivot, *ulpanot*, and institutions for the teaching of Torah. Along with this, there are many difficulties and problems. This is
a sign that we have not arrived at the complete Redemption. The road
before us is still very long. The *geulah* goes little by little. It is not
necessary that it all happen suddenly, in one day. We, after all, do not
decide for the Holy One, Blessed be He. If He wants, He does in one
day. And if He wants, He does through many years. If He wants, He
does by means of miracles. And if He wants, He does by natural means.
And if He wants, He does by miracle and by nature. It happens in
various ways and forms. There are periods of greater light, and those
of more darkness, better periods and worse. But on the whole and in
the main, the people of Israel have come back to live in their land, in
all matters and areas, *Baruch Hashem.*

S.F.: How do you see the relationship between the state of Israel, its
historic goals, and any particular government of Israel?

Rabbi Aviner: It is written in the Torah that it is a mitzvah to possess
the land, *Eretz Yisrael.* And this is done through the state. As the
Rambam explains, "not to leave this land to any of the nations aside
from *Am Yisrael.*" So of course when there is a Jewish state, this is a
great mitzvah as well as a great source of rescue. This is part of the
process of Redemption. But it does not mean that all that happens in
this country is good. There are things that are not all right. The educational system is not all right, as it is necessary to educate in accordance
with the Torah and this is not done. So too the system of justice, as
we have a hybrid system based on Turkish and British law, and not on
our own. Yet we are happy that we have a Jewish government, as
opposed to being ruled by others. But this does not mean that all the

government does is all right. When it does things that are right, we must support it, and when it does those things that are not right, we must protest and try to lead it to change. Still, we have to be happy that we have a Jewish government, not a British or Turkish one.

S.F.: If the existence of a Jewish state signals that the process of Redemption is underway, does this mean too that it is a religious obligation of every Jew to make *aliyah* now, with the ideal end being every Jew in the world living in Israel?

Rabbi Aviner: Two things are important. First, every Jew is obliged to live in the land of Israel. Redemption, or no Redemption does not change this. Every generation is obliged to make *aliyah* to *Eretz Yisrael*. As the Rambam says "Every Jew is obliged to make aliyah." Since it is a great mitzvah to make *aliyah*, one's partner cannot say, "I am not obliged to make *aliyah*." If this is said, then the other can say, "You are obliged to, and if you do not, I will write you a bill of divorce, or demand one of you." Then there is another aspect. All the generations that were not allowed to make *aliyah*. When the *goyim* did not enable us to make *aliyah*, many Jews did not have the desire. It was not in their head. But in the last 100 years, the two things began to straighten out. First, the barriers to immigration began to fall. Second, Jews began to wake up. So the mitzvah returns. All the generations have not been given an exemption from the mitzvah of *aliyah*. It is no accident that all the generations could not, and now they can. The fact that we can is a sign of the Redemption. The Rambam says that if one does not believe in the Messiah, then it as if he does not believe in Moshe Rabbenu. For there it is written, "We will gather the exiles." The Redemption is the re–gathering of the exiles in the land of Israel. Each one who makes *aliyah* helps bring forth the Redemption.

When the Admor of Kotzk from Pilof, the grandson of the Kotzk Rebbe, wanted to bring Jews to the Land, in order to have them work in agriculture, there was the question of whether this was a mitzvah or not, because the Land was not in our hands. Reb Yehoshuah answered, "You are right. The land is not in our hands. The mitzvah is to be in *Eretz Yisrael* when it is ours. But there is a *mitzvah gedolah* to be in *Eretz Yisrael*, which is greater than the mitzvah from the *halachah*. This mitzvah is a privilege, a special right. And it is great because through it will come the *geulah*." Now I see that there is being created a strong desire for *Eretz Yisrael*, both in the *Tzadikim* and the *Benoninim* (the intermediates). This is a sign that the light of the *geulah* is beginning to flicker. After 100 years we truly see that this is so.

In all the generations, Jews made *aliyah*. The Vilna Gaon made *aliyah* without his family. Afterwards he returned. But to make *aliyah* without one's family is dedication (*mesirut nefesh*). What a great danger, to expose oneself to sickness, to risk being killed by the goyim not to see again one's wife and children. But many came, established settlements, both religious and non–religious. Petach Tikvah was founded by extreme Haredim who made *aliyah* and were happy to be in the Land. But now, because *Eretz Yisrael* is being built, it is a time for *mitzvah ha–sha-ah*, the "mitzvah of this time."

S.F.: I had hoped to ask you if you see *aliyah* as the one way to contend with the problems of assimilation, which are so great now in the Jewish world.

Rabbi Aviner: In the State of New York, there is now a greater than 50 percent rate of intermarriage, and more than 70 percent of Jewish parents do not show great concern over whether or not their children will marry Jews. Every day, 500 Jews assimilate; in a year, 150,000; every 10 years, 1.5 million. Now there are 9 million Jews in *galut*; perhaps in another sixty years there will not remain even one. And this is on the condition that the pace of assimilation will not increase. But it is increasing. The situation there is catastrophic.

S.F.: But there is religious awakening among Jews in America.

Rabbi Aviner: That reminds me of the story of the sinking ship. On the upper levels, the people did not know, so they danced and danced, as the boat was sinking. In the book *Five Sermons*, Rabbi Soloveitchik z"l writes that he had been against the Mizrachi, those communities in America in which everything is directed toward *aliyah* to Israel. He says that his grandfather, Rabbi Haim from Brisk, was against this. But he said, "I changed my opinion." And don't think it was easy. He did not sleep for a long time, but simply saw that the Mizrachi were right. "My grandfather was right for his time and I am right for mine," he says. Now it is apparent that *Eretz Yisrael* means "rescue." It is impossible to rely on American Jewry. Anything and everything could happen. Now I do not speak from the side of "rescue" but from the side of Redemption, the building of the nation. Even if it were secure in the Exile, that is not our place, because our redemption can come only in the land of Israel.

S.F.: We continue to talk about the Redemption. Do you have a clear picture in your mind of what the Redemption in its final stage is?

Rabbi Aviner: Yes, I was afraid you wanted a clear picture just from me alone. In Ezekiel 36, it is written "I gathered you from the nations," and afterwards "I sprayed upon you the waters of purification," and "finally you were purified." First of all, come to the Land, build it, build the state. After this, do *teshuvah.* How much time will this take? No one can know.

S.F.: Does this Redemption mean a change in the nature of nature? in human nature?

Rabbi Aviner: The Rambam says that, in the days of the Messiah, there is no change in the nature of man. He does not say the non-Jews who were previously wolves will become like sheep. Rambam does say at the end of *Hilchot Malachim* that all will be involved in the study of Torah, all will be striving to know God. This is not a change; this is already part of the nature of man. To worship and serve God—that is natural. At this point in time, we are not natural because we do not worship and serve God as we should.

S.F.: Go back for a second to the relationship between Redemption and *aliyah.* There are those who claim that we must do everything possible to preserve more than one great Jewish center, not only because this has been the rule throughout Jewish history, but because this is the way to prevent a total destruction.

Rabbi Aviner: Our sages say, "Mercy Hashem did to us in scattering us among the nations, because the enemy comes on one camp, and the other is saved." All right. It is not however written in the Torah, "You settled in the land and possessed it, and also possessed America," or "You settled in the land and possessed it, and also possessed Russia or Rumania." No, in all the Torah, the emphasis is on us being in one place only. When there are dangers, we need *mesirut nefesh.* The Holy One Blessed Be He also knows there is a great problem in this, but nonetheless commands us to do it, to possess the land. We should not try to out–sophisticate God. If the Holy One Blessed Be He tells us to do it, we know it is good and there is no real danger. What is danger-ous for Jews is *galut*, life outside Israel. There is the story of Rav Hanina who sailed on a boat and came to a beautiful green island. And it was beautiful. So he got off and began to make his home there, but then it began to sink. This is *galut*. The Jews were in Spain for hundreds of years. The Jews in Germany also felt well there. It was not good to feel so at home there, because things came to a bitter end. Look at Herzl. He was for assimilation. This nonetheless did not save him. Dreyfuss wanted to assimilate and they would not let him. In *Medinat Yisrael* there is protection and, guarding it, an army.

So on the realistic level. First of all God commanded us to be here. How can we go against this? And secondly, if God commanded it then this in itself is the sign that is good.

Here we are guarded, and we are not afraid. Who knows how and in what way anti–Semitism can come, even in America? We must also remember assimilation itself is for Jews a danger of losing their souls and lives; this is the main element there. So there is no reason to fear. It is necessary to come here. If all will come, then there will be a tre-mendous increase in the "brain power" of the society.

S.F.: Nonetheless we see many now proclaiming that there is a greater danger than ever in Israel—and this from ourselves. How do you think we should act in Israel?

Rabbi Aviner: Two things—what Rav Zvi Yehuda would call "two Alephs," *amuna* ("Faith") and *ahava* ("love"). It is necessary to help instill faith in the people of Israel, faith in God, in *Eretz Yisrael*, and in the Torah. All the crises come because of our weakness in faith: a lack of strength, courage, and consciousness. There has to be unity. There can be differences of opinion, but this does not mean there must be hatred. Criticism of someone is permitted. In fact, it can be mitzvah, but not with hatred and not with contempt. This is the big difference. There is a weakness that comes from lack of understanding; for instance, in regard to the meaning of what *Eretz Yisrael* is. In ideological struggles, it is impossible to defeat an opponent with sticks and stones. Ideology involves a war of opinions. Even at the time of the founding of the state, it was possible to persuade only a small number (of the religious) that this was really necessary. And now to explain that we need a state that operates in accordance with Torah and Tanach involves even greater work.

S.F.: Isn't there a problem with the teaching methods of the religious in Israel, which somehow do not allow them to reach out to the secular Jews?

Rabbi Aviner: The religious community also has to reach itself. The secular community will, if it sees that there are those in the religious community with something to say, serious people with serious things to say as well as great qualities of character, develop a desire to hear them. It is not right to put yourself above others, thinking you will bring them back. Each one has first to lead himself in *teshuvah*.

S.F.: And is there something special about your program in the *yeshiva* which does this?

Rabbi Aviner: Our program is the regular program of *yeshiva*, primarily Gemara, also *halachah*, Jewish thought, *Musar*, Tanach.

S.F.: And the relation to *limudei chol*, secular learning?

Rabbi Aviner: In the yeshiva, there is no secular or academic learning. Everything is dedicated to holy studies. If one wants to learn secular studies, then this can be done before the yeshiva. It is impossible to have two wives at once. If one is a student of the university and he wants to learn here, it is possible. This is open. But it is difficult. Yeshiva requires someone who is wholly dedicated, day and night. There are exceptions, perhaps a married person with children, for purposes of *parnassah* ("livelihood") doing a more restricted course. We always encourage a student to have a good general education. But he can do this alone in the evenings. He can read at night and get this.

S.F.: Could you say something about the *hashkafah* of the yeshiva?

Rabbi Aviner: The hashkafah is of HaRav Kook's. But a definition is difficult. A book of translations, *Torat Eretz Yisrael*, from some of the things I wrote in Hebrew, does outline this.

S.F.: It must be very difficult to summarize the complex poetic personality of HaRav Kook. I think one element of his teaching was without doubt to find the good in each and every Jew, the sacred quality in each one of us. Do you feel that, in your work, and now I think especially of your radio talks on Channel Seven that reach a wide audience, you are realizing this goal?

Rabbi Aviner: I hear from a great variety of people responses to the radio *shiurim*, both religious and non–religious. It can be someone in the Army General Staff or someone who sells juice at a kiosk on the street in Tel Aviv. I have not done a survey. If, however, the heads of the radio continue to want to broadcast the *shiurim*, this is a sign. I also hear criticism. Sometimes I am accused of being not extreme enough.

S.F.: I have a question about something I may have misunderstood in your book. In your *perush* of Parashat Korach, you seem to imply that it is impossible for a Jew not to be "holy."

Rabbi Aviner: I do not write that a Jew cannot not be holy; I say that the *nefesh* (soul) of the Jew is holy. Of course I am no Korach who says "All the community is holy." But all are potentially holy but *ahava* ("love") is potential. This means that you love your son although he does things that are wrong. We don't say that every Jew is in fact holy; we say that every Jew has the potential for holiness. He is capable of being holy. He is obliged to be holy. But of course not everyone is holy. It's only Korach who says that, as if Aaron ha–Kohen, who all his life was devoted to Torah and holy things, were on the same level with someone simply ordinary. Of course this is not right.

S.F.: And how about the souls of non–Jews?

Rabbi Aviner: The non–Jew does not have a Jewish soul, but it is impossible to say that he does not have a soul. In *Sefer Ha–Tanya* it says that the Jew has one kind of soul and the non–Jew a different kind. When it is written that a man is created in the image of God, this refers to all people. It is not only Yaakov Avinu. In *Pirkei Avot* it is written, "Beloved is the person created in the image of God." But for the Jews, it is special: "very beloved," we are "children of *Ha–Makom*."

I was invited to a symposium of a kind I generally do not like to attend. But I went. Someone there said that there are two sides to Judaism: one universal, general, all–human, and a second, the nationalistic, chauvinistic. I answered, I can't help it that it was the same Rabbi Akiva who said both things. Two approaches, both of which complement each other and taken together are correct. Rabbi Israel Salanter used to say, "If you want to be a great person, do not make a small hole, build a great mountain." Rabbi Kook used to say that we are more than the Gentiles. This does not mean more than the great evil figures of history, rather, more than the great positive figures; Plato, for instance. Tiferet Yisrael on *Pirkei Avot* interprets this: of course *tselem elokim* is all the goyim, for after all, the righteous of the Gentiles have their place in the world to come. They are not beasts. And it is written that we are to be chosen from all the peoples, not from *behomot* ("beasts"). Don't you see how this non-Jew made this contribution and another that invention? And don't you remember how one non-Jew struggled to save the Gemara from the flames? There are degrees. As is written in the Kuzari, there is an image of God that is general, B'nei Noach, and there is image of God that is Jewish, Torah. With the *goyim*, *kedushat* ("holiness") of the individual, with us holiness of the people, a holy nation.

S.F.: How does this fit in with the notion of *or l'goyim*? Is it our task today to show the nations to find their way to one God or perhaps to a higher moral code? What is the role of the state of Israel, in this regard?

Rabbi Aviner: Moshe Rabbenu does not say, *or l'goyim*; Yeshayahu says it. There were many thinkers who thought our task is to be scattered among the nations, but often, where the Jews tried to spread the Torah, they instead wound up being burned to death. In fact, it is not written that we are to wander about among the *goyim*. It is more a matter of what we radiate to others. If this nation is a good honest nation faithful to God, if this is a country of justice, righteousness, and truth, then we can radiate this to others. For example, the British Labor Minister Macdonald visited a kibbutz in the 1930s and said to his wife, "All we are speaking about socialism they are doing." I don't of course mean in regard to socialism, but in regard to justice and goodness. This is the way we should be "doing" and setting an example for others.

S.F.: How do you understand the concept of *avodat Hashem* in the daily life of each individual and for the people?

Rabbi Aviner: There are degrees of *avodat Hashem*. An ordinary person in Israel is called upon to be righteous, as is written in *Mesilat Yesharim*. Part of his time he prays and does mitzvot. And most of his time he is involved in his own things. But he is obliged to do these things with purity, to make money honestly, to be with his family, in honesty. But there is a degree higher than this, Hasid. Every minute he is serving God. This is the ideal of his life. As a man who loves a woman and all the time thinks of her, so the person who is righteous all the time thinks of serving God. Every minute he thinks "What can I do for the Ruler of the World?" The absence of *Kavod Hashem* pains him, the absence of the honoring of God in the world. Of course he cannot correct everything. But not everyone can be a Hasid, says *Mesilat Yesharim*. It is impossible that all will be Hasidim, but also impossible for a society if it has no Hasidim. There are many levels in the service and worship of God.

Rabbi Joshua Berman

Joshua Berman is the author of *The Temple (Its Symbolism and Meaning Then and Now)*. He is director of admissions and lecturer in Bible at Nishmat, The Jerusalem Center for Advanced Jewish Study for Women. A graduate of Princeton University, he received his ordination from the Israeli Chief Rabbinate after studying at Har Etzion Yeshiva in Alon Shevut. A contributor to numerous publications on biblical subjects, he is also an active community worker in the town in which he and his young family make their home, Beit Shemesh.

I met with Rabbi Berman at the offices of Nishmat in the quiet, religious, hillside Jerusalem neighborhood of Bayit Vegan.

Cg 8O

S.F.: Could you tell me about the work you are involved in now, and relate it to your background?

Rabbi Berman: My background is in a sense neither here, nor there. I came from a home that was very Jewishly strong, yet I would not consider myself either a *frum* from birth, or a *baal teshuvah*. At home, the dishes were kosher, yet Shabbat was not wholly kept. Kiddush was made on Friday night. Most importantly I had the good fortune of having parents who believed very much in Jewish education. I was sent to a very fine day school, the SAR Academy in Riverdale. I had a tremendously inspiring rav in high school, Jack Beiler, who today is the Hebrew Studies Principal of the Hebrew Academy of Greater Washington. Everything that I have done in education is really due to his initial inspiration. Subsequently, I studied in Gush Etzion for a whole bunch of years, and there I received much of my formal training. My background is one in which I have needed to search to strengthen, and so I have had to do much discovering of things on my own; this, with the benefit of not having to start completely from scratch. At least I started with the basis of knowledge of someone who grew up in a traditional home, and in the day school world in America.

Today my job is working in admissions and publicity for the Torah teaching institution Nishmat. That takes up a great part of my time, but my soul, and I think this is where I really do my most important *avodat Hashem*, is in teaching Tanach. Tanach is what makes me tick. Just sitting and listening to the Prophets talk to me, trying to understand the patterns and structural literary aspects of Tanach are what move me most, religiously. This is at the heart of my *avodat Hashem*.

S.F.: You recently published your first book *The Temple: Its Symbolism and Meaning, Then and Now*. For me, this book opened up new paths of thought. Could you say something about the genesis of this work?

Rabbi Berman: There is an analogy in the Talmud about a midget on a giant's shoulders, and my answer begins with that. I was learning in Har Etzion, a *hesder yeshiva* that, as do all yeshivot, has its primary focus on Gemara and *halachah*, though it too has a keen interest in what's happening historically to the Jewish people and the land of Israel. Because there is a very strong understanding of the importance of studying Tanach, they have come up with many innovative ways of teaching it. Tanach has been, I believe, a relatively neglected area of study in *limudei kodesh* (Jewish religious studies in yeshivot) for hundreds of years. Since the Abarbanel, there really has not been a major commentary and exposition of the written Torah (*Torah sh'bichtav pashuto shel mikrah*) until the Malbim. That's a period of 700 years. If you were to quote a *pasuk* ("sentence") and ask a yeshiva student where it's from, he will not quote the Biblical chapter and verse, but rather tell you where it comes from in the Gemara. But when you have a whole milieu that places great interest in the Tanach, a theme that repeatedly comes up is the *Beit Ha–Mikdash*. I don't think there is another source in our holy writings that devotes proportionately so much to the *Beit Ha–Mikdash* as does Tanach. I studied the *Beit Ha–Mikdash* with Menachem Leibtag, well–known on the Internet for his *parasha* sheet. Working with him and within the whole environment of Yeshivat Har Etzion, I felt this is a topic that has not been given adequate attention, neither in English nor in Hebrew. Writing on the subject for a variety of forums, I believe I have found an opportunity to put something together that would be of value to the community at large. What we have done is just the beginning; there is much more to be done on this subject.

S.F.: You write of the Temple as meeting place between God and man, a meeting place in which there is rededication and renewal of the Covenant. Can you further elaborate? And what is comparable to this today, if anything?

Rabbi Berman: I treat most aspects of the *Beit Ha–Mikdash* on a symbolic level. What this means is having a sense of being able to come close to the *Kadosh Baruch Hu*, in recreation or re–simulation of the Revelation at Sinai. That is what is supposed to take place at the *Beit Ha–Mikdash*, which raises the question of how we do this in the age of *hurban*. How is this to be effected? On some level, we do this symbolically in the synagogue. Take the notion of minyan. All the *pasukim*, the verses from which the Gemara derives the notion of minyan are verses about *Knesset Yisrael*. But I think that the type of confrontation we have with the *Kadosh Baruch Hu* in the synagogue is really, in a sense, a kind of tease, in order to get us to set our sights on re–creating a true national convocation with the *Kadosh Baruch Hu*. It is as if we almost have to leave the synagogue if we are to return to the *Beit Ha–Mikdash*. The origin of the synagogues, according to the Gemara, is in Babylonia, where Ezekiel was told to build the *Mikdash Maat* ("The Small Sanctuary"). Today it is, in a sense, not possible to do that. This is the intent of *hurban*. The *Kadosh Baruch Hu* is saying, in effect, "I don't want to be together with you." While I consider myself a religious Zionist, who was driven to make *aliyah* by a sense of *Bereshit tsemachat geulatenu*, I feel that we have become a little bit carried away with one side of the coin. It may be the beginning of the Redemption, but to look at it in another way, it is *reshit hafoogat chorbatenu* ("the beginning of the withdrawal of the destruction"). The *Beit Ha–Mikdash* is still in *hurban*. Sometimes we become carried away with how much good the *Kadosh Baruch Hu* has given us in history. It's as if we are saying, "Here we are, it's the *geula*, Redemption. "No," I say. "It's *reshit*," the beginning. We still have a very long way to go. When we look at the Temple Mount, and see what is and isn't there, this should be a sign to us that the *Kadosh Baruch Hu* is saying "I am not with you fully. If I felt fully comfortable with you, I would allow you to build the *Beit Ha–Mikdash*. But you are not where you need to be in order for us to have a whole that symbolizes our union."

S.F.: You are speaking about a kind of collective *avodat Hashem*, something more than the individual *avodat Hashem* of each one of us separately. You also speak in the book about a kind of social and educational process necessary for this to happen. Can you explain this?

Rabbi Berman: We have 2,000 years of *galut* without having the kind of communications that we have today. We have had a community there, and a community here, so it was difficult to speak of collective *avodat Hashem*. That's certainly not the case in our day and age, where Jews are linked by modern communications. Most significantly, we are four and one half million Jews in this country. We elect governments and make policies, so there is definitely a collective identity. Those of us on the religious side of the fence have a tremendous responsibility to set a tone. But I have a lot of criticism of the emphases that our own religious communities have made. Sometimes we look out for our own vested interests—important as they may be—be they supporting yeshivot or preserving *Kedushat Eretz Yisrael*. These are holy and critical objectives, but I think that we sometimes relate to the general population in an us versus them attitude that is irresponsible. It's not realistic to speak today of making everyone *frum*. All of us, even if we are not *baalei teshuvah*, know many *baalei teshuvah*, and know that this process does not happen overnight. When it does happen overnight, it does not last very long. While process is slow, one of the very first steps is to remove any hatred for those not like oneself. If there is ignorance, then there needs to be a gradual process of education. Maybe I am a pessimist, but I don't see a tremendous return to Torah and mitzvot occurring in the next ten or twenty years. Still, we can begin this process. This is the responsibility of our generation. The Ramchal opens his *Mesillat Yesharim* by saying that a person has to know what his responsibility is, here and now. Not just the final goals are important. It is important to know what the final goal is, that everyone should be *shomer Torah* and *shomer mitzvot*. But what about today? I don't believe our obligation today is to say "We have to make people *frum*." I don't know if that is possible. Yet I do know that we can remove barriers from communities. I do know that we can spread Torah and education.

I'll give you a concrete example. I live in Beit Shemesh, where we organized a Rosh Hashanah service for the Russians. It wasn't a five hour affair like you and I sat in, but there was prayer for an hour and explanations. *Aliyot* were given to people for the first time in their lives, and there was a kiddush afterwards. For many, this was the first time that they had ever been in a *shul*, or seen the inside of a *Sefer Torah*. This is the kind of thing that, if we are doing in Beit Shemesh, others should be doing elsewhere. But I think that our community, the Orthodox community tends to keep within its own little space. We all give a lot of lip service to the idea of giving to and educating the community, but where are our energies truly being directed? Where is the ingenuity and creativity? I just don't believe that there is enough commitment in those areas to make a real effect.

S.F.: In your book, you talk about what has been done on a national level. You talk, for instance, about our not having any "formal guild of priests or Levites" who teach Torah from Zion, with Jerusalem as the learning capital of the Jewish people. You say we do not make pilgrimage festivals as we did in Temple times, but we do have Jews from all over the world gathering at Jerusalem's Western Wall on the pilgrimage festivals. You speak about Jerusalem standing as a symbol of unity for the Jewish people.

Rabbi Berman: My gut feeling is that the notion of our actually having something like a universal synagogue, where everybody comes together to *davven*, is not where our focus should be right now. We need to focus more on building community. You cannot really build a nation until you build communities. When the nation is fragmented in the way that it is today, there is much work that needs to be done on a local level for the people as a whole to come together. Now of course there's an eternal notion of *B'Rov Am Hadrat Melech*. We maintain that the *Kadosh Baruch Hu* is receptive to our prayer to a greater degree when there is a mass of Jews praying together at the *Kotel*, or *Har Ha–Bayit*. But as to having the kind of formal institution that we had when we had the Temple, the *Kadosh Baruch Hu* is saying that we are not ready for that yet.

S.F.: But what about the role in prayer in relation to other peoples? You speak in your book about how at the Temple non–Jews were allowed to enter and pray. What about our being "a light to the nations," in bringing in others to God?

Rabbi Berman: We rescue Ethiopian Jews though we know that they are going to be a drain on our economy and create all kinds of social challenges. We do this because it's a tremendous *Kiddush Hashem*. When we create a thriving economy and induce companies like Intel to build their plants here because they will get a higher level of worker, it's in my judgment, a *Kiddush Hashem*. Even winning Olympic medals may be a *Kiddush Hashem*. I don't think that has to be the primary aim of society, but any pursuit of excellence is in a sense *Kiddush Hashem*.

Obviously, the most important areas are in *middot*. There should in our society be a bridging of the gap between rich and poor. Unfortunately, the opposite is happening, although we have the capacity to be a light to the nations. Still, the miracle of creating the Jewish state, of ingathering so many exiles, is *Kiddush Hashem*, a process that's unparalleled anywhere else. So there's been accomplishments but there's a long way to go.

S.F.: You speak about the Temple as the meeting place between man and God, where the Covenant is dedicated, and about the expiatory role of the sacrifices. In terms of public worship is there something comparable to this today?

Rabbi Berman: There are a lot of statements in Gemara about the things that come in the place of *korbanot*. My own view, and I think this is the view of most *Gedolei Yisrael*, is that these are only temporary. We will one day return to a situation where a person can bring a *korban* when appropriate situation arises. *Korbanot* have tremendous symbolic meaning. There are many sources that see theurgic meaning in them as well. In other words, no matter what the symbolism might be, the *korban* works. But as I point out in the book, we have some mitzvot that are affected by the presence of the *Beit Ha-Mikdash*, while others are not. I think that most of the Mitzvot are dependent on the Beit Hamikdash. (Certain *korbanot* are not dependent on the *Beit Ha-Mikdash*; *Pesach* for instance.) But the general category of *Korbanot* is. Why is it that, when the *Beit Ha-Mikdash* was destroyed certain Mitzvot fall out and others don't. Certain Mitzvot which I have to do no matter what. Whether the *Beit Ha-Mikdash* is lacking or not I have to put on Tefillin every day. Even if I don't keep Shabbos or *kashrut* or anything else, I have to put on Tefillin every day. I have to keep the Mitzvah and the *Kadosh Baruch Hu* is pleased when I do. Why isn't it the same with *korban*?

There are certain mitzvot that we are not simply called on to obey, but that constitute, as it were, an intimate gesture to the *Kadosh Baruch Hu*. They are not just to obey but to address, to come to relate to. And these mitzvot do not have any meaning when the basis of the relationship is rotten. In somewhat the same way, think about the example of bringing flowers to one's wife. Is it a good thing or not? You should always make your wife happy. If you were to bring home flowers today, she should be very pleased. But what if you had a situation where there is tremendous tension between husband and wife, suspicions about infidelity? The wife suspects the husband is unfaithful and he shows up at the door with flowers. She'll fling them in his face. The gesture is misplaced. That's one way in which I look at the *Beit Ha–Mikdash* and the *korbanot*. The *Kadosh Baruch Hu* is not interested in the *mikdash* from us at this time. He would like to have a situation in which there is true Covenantal loyalty. Just as a woman would like to be in a situation where the husband brings her flowers out of love. But first the creation of the proper condition is necessary, the bedrock of the relationship itself. The Gemara lists acts that come in the place of the *korbanot* today. I don't think this means that we will never go back to the *korbanot*. But before we get to the flowers in the relationship, let's work on the substance. Substantive learning informs us of the will of the *Kadosh Baruch Hu*. Inviting people to one's Shabbos table, reaching out, and eliminating baseless hatred are ways to work on the substantive relationship. If we do the substantive things, we would be able to return to the *Beit Ha–Mikdash*.

S.F.: You don't believe both on a symbolic and substantive level that prayer has come in the place of the *avodah*, of the *korbanot*?

Rabbi Berman: Prayer, we know to a large extent, is only as good as the person who is saying it.

S.F.: But the person ideally is made better by prayer. The Baal Shem Tov teaches that, if you are not a different person after you have prayed than when you began you have not really prayed. Isn't prayer a principal means to come closer to God?

Rabbi Berman: Isaiah says, "I don't need your days and fasts and I don't need your tefillot." True, *Hakadosh Baruch Hu* is *mitzaveh le–tefillatam shel Yisrael* (God commands that the people of Israel pray). But I think to a large extent that depends on where Israel is standing. I don't sit up there by the *Kiseh Ha–Kavod* (Throne of Glory), but I think that if an individual or group is really doing horrible things, then *shul* doesn't help. Obviously there is a *halachic* obligation to *davven*. Even if a person's horrible, he should *davven* because it will influence him. But I have to believe that the *Kadosh Baruch Hu* relates to prayer on different levels, and some aspect relates to where the person is holding in their *avodat Hashem*. Rav Soloveitchik writes that a person really should be in the process of *davvening* the whole day. What is *davvening*? I am relating directly to the *Kadosh Baruch Hu* with every experience I have, whether I am a student or teacher. When we are talking, relating to each other, we are also relating to the *Kadosh Baruch Hu*.

S.F.: That's really the great question. How can we make everything we do *avodat Hashem*? As I am relating one to one to you, I should be serving God. Also, are we able to know our level of *avodat Hashem*? Can we possibly judge ourselves in this?

Rabbi Berman: There are times when I feel my existence more worthy. I set up a *shidduch*, feel good, then find out that it didn't work out. If I give a good *shiur*, that gives me strength.

S.F.: You love to teach Tanach. I suppose if one opens a new area in learning, this also gives a sense of true value.

Rabbi Berman: It's not just a *vort* (piece of Torah wisdom) here or there, but rather the whole approach that I find important. Rav Haim Brisker really revolutionized the teaching of Talmud Torah, but then he was a *gaon* (Torah great) who provided a methodology. A methodology is now needed for the study of Tanach.

S.F.: This may be tangential, but are you dealing with Biblical criticism here? A near neighbor of yours in Bayit Vegan, Rabbi Natan Lopes Cardoso, has a wonderful long article on this subject in his book *Between Speech and Silence*.

Rabbi Berman: What's referred to as the "higher Biblical criticism" is of little interest to me. Our foundational assumptions as believing Jews are different from those who follow that approach. But there are many literary qualities to the Tanach. I don't care about academic questions, such as where it came from and how many sources it had. Even in the academic world there is a different approach today which tries to look at the whole.

S.F.: In your book, you talk about Hashem prescribing the place and time of meeting. The Temple, which is symbolically likened to the Garden of Eden, is where we are to meet God. But how do we meet God in our everyday lives, in all we do?

Rabbi Berman: It's all-encompassing. Everything we are involved in is *avodat Hashem*, whether it's *kodesh* or *chol*. In all the small actions of life, we can find *avodat Hashem*. For instance, I think of it now in relation to an activity I am involved with, changing a diaper.

S.F.: And this requires a specific *kavvanah* (intention) in each particular action?

Rabbi Berman: The *kavvanah* are just the purification of our character. They are something in the background. I'll be very frank. At home, my wife has things she is involved in, and I, things I am involved in. For something like changing a diaper, I have to work myself up, free myself to help out. If that isn't *avodat Hashem*, then what is? It's at home that I am challenged more in terms of my *middot* than anywhere else. So for me the notion of *avodat Hashem* is all-encompassing. I only wish I could be as conscious of it every moment of the day as I should be.

S.F.: It can direct and inform us internally without our having to keep it directly in mind?

Rabbi Berman: I hope so.

Phil Chernofsky

Phil Chernofsky is the associate director of the Israel Center, the Orthodox Union's base in Jerusalem. Along with organizing such popular programs as Torathon (twenty-five hours of continuous Torah teaching), he teaches regularly at the center. But "Phil," as he is called both by students and friends, is best known for his remarkable weekly Torah *parasha* sheet, *Torah Tidbits*. This sheet not only gives a summary and outline of the readings, but is filled with *halachic* information. It is a must read for thousands, not only in Jerusalem but throughout the English–speaking Jewish world. Before making *aliyah*, Phil Chernofsky was a high school math and science teacher, and teacher of Torah.

I met with him one Friday in his office at the Israel center. While I enjoyed the interview, I had the sense that he would much rather be speaking about the intricacies of the Jewish calendar rather than about himself. Outgoing, good–natured, with a warm smile and word for everyone he meets, Phil Chernofsky is both a wonderful teacher of Torah and, for all who know him, a true *mensch*, a wonderfully warm and good Jew and human being.

Cʒ ʒ

S.F.: Could you please describe the work of the Israel Center and your part in it.

Phil Chernofsky: The Israel Center is to a large extent involved with informal adult Jewish education. This means that, if somebody has the time for a full yeshiva program, we recommend his studying elsewhere. The Center is for the person who is looking for a *shiur*, here and there, now and again. There are regulars and those who come several times a week, but most want to have the ability to say, "I couldn't make it last week, I won't be able to make it next week, and yet I may make it the week after." In other words, we want people to have the feeling that they are always welcome, even if for an isolated *shiur*, because from that too they will be able to get something. Basically we have two kinds of *shiurim*; the weekly (every Wednesday, Rabbi Eisen's *shiur* in Kuzari and Rambam's Guide; every Thursday, a *shiur* in *davvening*; every Monday night, a *shiur* on *Parashat Hashevuah*, etc.) and the one–time. One week, a guest may be giving a *shiur* on "Torah and Science," another week, there may be a special talk on medical ethics. I give some of the *shiurim* as well as programming the educational content of the center. I also prepare the weekly sheet of Torah commentary, *Torah Tidbits*, which has grown in a relatively short time to a circulation of 5,000, plus another 1,000 via e–mail, and a Website that has several hundred "hits" every week.

S.F.: You also have other special activities such as Torathon.

Phil Chernofsky: Most of our activities derive from our goal of strengthening the bond between the Jew and Torah, between the Jew and the Land of Israel, between the Jew and his fellow Jew. One of the ideas we came up with several years ago was to have a Torathon. But before I speak about that, I would like to briefly describe our activities on the night of Shavuot, when we have an all-night program, including the *shiurim* in English and a late-night walk to the Kotel. We learn for three-quarters of the night and then go to the Old City for one more *shiur* before early morning *davvening,* which is almost always in the very emotional, almost romantic setting of the Hurva. We sit outdoors and someone gives *shiur* on *Bikkurim* or the *Beit Ha-Mikdash,* or some other Shavuot-related topic. We also have a Hoshana Rabba evening, which years ago went all night but, once that proved to be impractical, has been replaced by a program including a *simchat beit Ha-shoeva* reception in the sukkah followed by several *shiurim* that go on into the middle of the night. As an offshoot of that, we came up with the idea of one complete 25-hour "day" of *shiurim* only. Hundreds of people come to the center through the course of the day, some for one class, others for five, others for ten, and some make it all the way through. This all stems from the same basic idea of the Israel Center, which is to present Torah in a comfortable, non-threatening setting. We have teachers who are very animated, capable of generating great excitement in the learning of Torah.

If I may digress with a nice bit of Torah that I saw in *Sefer Ha-Charedim,* a work on the 613 mitzvot: it says that, if someone teaches you something you had not known previously, then both of you have fulfilled the mitzvah of Torah study. The Torah says "And you should teach them to your children"; that there is a commandment to learn and teach Torah. If, however, you not only learn something from the Torah which has been taught, but get as excited about it as your teacher is, then in addition to the mitzvah of Torah study, there is the mitzvah of "Loving the Lord Your God." The *Sefer Ha-Charedim* says the commandment of loving God can be fulfilled in many ways, and one of them is to learn and teach Torah, and be excited about it. I believe this idea is to a large extent the description of Israel Center. Again, it's not school, but rather a place to which people come because they want to, and leave with a glow because they have been energized in a spiritual way. It is not dry knowledge alone, but rather what has affected the mind, the heart, the soul.

S.F.: I feel this very much in your own *shiurim*, and perhaps most especially in the very short *shiurim* you often give between the longer *shiurim* of others. It is as if you do not want to let a moment go by without there being a joy of Torah in it. Could you say something about how you came to this way of feeling?

Phil Chernofsky: I grew up in a religious home in Crown Heights in Brooklyn, at a time when there was great diversity of Jewish types there. I went to Crown Heights Yeshiva, to Yeshiva University High School in Brooklyn, and to Yeshiva University, where I studied in the rabbinate program and took graduate courses.

I have always taught, even before being formally authorized to do so. If I had to pick a time when I started teaching Torah, I would go back to when I was 11 or 12. I tutored a boy 1 year younger than I at a bungalow colony during the summer. I remember as a teenager having the opportunity to teach basics in Yiddishkeit in the framework of B'nei Akiva, I was a counselor for many years, and for many years a director in various *shuls*. Then for 9 years before I came on *aliyah*, I taught sixth, seventh, and eighth graders both secular and Jewish religious studies in the Yeshiva of Central Queens.

My teaching has always included not simply Jewish studies, but science and math as well. A special emphasis of mine has been on the concept that secular studies are not isolated from Torah studies, but should be part of our overall Torah learning. For example, when teaching biology, I was discussing the digestive system and told my students the esophagus is called the *veshet* and the windpipe the *kaneh*. This led to our speaking of *vashet* and *kaneh* in terms of *kashrut* since in ritual slaughter they have to be severed. It also led to an interesting Gemara, and the dispute in *Pesachim* as to which side we must recline at the Seder. It is well-known that reclining is done to the left, and Rashi teaches that this is because it is convenient for right-handed people. Leaning to the left, one's right hand is free. Rashbam, Rashi's grandson, gives a different reason, explaining that reclining to the left is a matter of health. As I explained in biology, there is the danger in leaning to the right that the food will go down the wrong tube, that the epiglottis, which is a flap of muscle covering the trachea when a person swallows, can be partially opened if one is not sitting to the left, or straight up. And since lefties do not have a different internal arrangement of organs, they also, for health reasons, should lean to the left.

As I was explaining this, one of the students asked, "What is this, a biology class or a Gemara class?" And I answered, "That's exactly my point." The very next morning in a different class, I was teaching a piece of Gemara about Rosh Chodesh. In order to better illustrate for the students how determining the time of Rosh Chodesh worked in the time of the Sanhedrin (and how it will work in time of a future Sanhedrin), I took a working model of the sun, moon, and earth from the science cabinet, then showed them how the moon revolves around the earth and how the moon and earth go round the sun, allowing us to determine when Rosh Chodesh is. A different student asked the same question about whether this was a science or a Gemara class. And I made the same point, that "This is a class for knowledge, and a Jew's quest for knowledge does not stop at the pages of his Gemara." This quest for knowledge is a quality I hope to bring to the Israel Center as well. I have given lectures here on number theory (not Jewish number theory), which shows numbers not as human invention but as human discovery. There are properties that numbers have which show a certain beauty and harmony of the world. This can lead one to feel "How glorious thy works, O Lord."

S.F.: From being a teacher of Torah in America, how did you come to being a teacher of Torah in *Eretz Yisrael*?

Phil Chernofsky: For a long time, maybe for as long as I can remember, I wanted to live in Israel. I can remember a discussion I had with my father many years ago, when he told me that even though he looked comfortable and set in his ways (and he had at the time several degrees and two professions, both accountant and lawyer), it really didn't mean so much so long as he was living outside of Israel. He always had his sights on *aliyah* and, *Baruch Hashem*, he and my mother and all my brothers are now here. We all came on *aliyah*. One brother decided immediately after marrying to come, and he has been here the longest. I went a different route, as I chose to work for awhile in the States as a teacher. It was not as some people do to earn money in order to make a more comfortable *aliyah*. Teachers in elementary and junior high schools do not make all that much money. But I felt that I needed to do that for awhile.

The year that my wife and I made the decision, I informed the school that I would not be back in the fall, and started looking for work in Israel through meeting with various *aliyah* emissaries. There was even a pilot trip to Israel, interviews with several schools, and my giving sample lessons. I also had a social meeting with a friend who was on the committee of the Orthodox Union. He told me about the Israel Center, which was then a fairly new operation run by one man, Shai Solomon, who is still our director. Shai was looking for another person, a full–time professional educator, so I submitted my name and interviewed with him and with the then–chairman of the Center. This secured me a job that coincided with our coming on *aliyah*. So I did not have to look for work as many new *olim* do, but had a job waiting for me. After arriving in mid–September 1981, by October I was officially working, though I came in even sooner than that. *Baruch Hashem*, I have been here ever since "and loving it," as Maxwell Smart used to say. The job has grown with me to its present form.

S.F.: And this is holy work, the work of Jewish education. Do you consider all your life and work to be *avodat Hashem*?

Phil Chernofsky: I think it would be arrogant to answer that the whole of my life is *avodat Hashem*, though I would like to think this so. In relation to what I have been telling you, teaching and learning with enjoyment are central to what I believe about *avodat Hashem*, especially if you stress "knowing Hashem in joy."

I often think in terms of analogies. When a parent asks a child to do something, different responses are possible. One child will refuse, another will do it but with a resentment, and a third type will genuinely seem to want to do with joy as his parents desire. We have this same set of responses in our relation to the demands of God. There are Jews who do not do what God asks them to do, Jews who do it reluctantly and resentfully, and Jews who do it in joy. As an example of the second type, I remember an incident where I asked a person who wore Hasidic garb and a *tallis* over his head to be quiet during *davvening*. I went over to him and said "I don't see how your interrupting the pray fits in with your external appearance." He snapped at me, "I don't believe in any of this stuff. I just do it because my father does it." Some Jews just go through the motions. But then, *Baruch Hashem*, there are many Jews who love God and Judaism, Torah and their fellows. And what they do is motivated by that love.

I am reluctant to talk about myself in this regard, but I can give you an example of my own attitude by talking a bit about the production of *Torah Tidbits*. There are few in this country who produce a

Torah parasha sheet in English. I began to try to fill that void with the additional idea in mind that this would help us get the Israel Center list of activities to a wider audience. If I can judge by the long hours, the sometimes sleepless nights, there is something more than just going through the motions that motivates me. I think what I am doing is part of my *avodat Hashem*. I am very much influenced by the Rambam in his description of the *Mosheach* in the last chapters of *Hilkot Malakhim*, where he says that the *Mosheach* has three main tasks: one, to bring the Jewish people closer to their Torah; two, to bring the Jewish people back to the land of Israel; and three, to build the *Beit Ha-Mikdash*. Now I believe with all my heart in all three of these tasks, although for the third task, and this is a technical point, we need the correct guidance of a prophet or of the Messianic king. So far as bringing Jews closer to Torah and bringing them back to the land of Israel, I have devoted all my life to these goals. One tiny example is my taking Shabbos early during the summer. Strict in adhering to the demand to repeat the reading of Shema at the proper time, I don't wait until I go to sleep, and don't even wait until after the blessing over food. In the middle of my meal, when the stars come out, I say the Shema. But I also teach about it, write about it, and probably thousands have read my piece about it. If that encourages more people to be meticulous in observance, then it is *avodat Hashem*. Last night I conducted a model Seder for beginners with little or no experience of the Seder. Two people who have attended Seders all their lives came in furtively, but walked out saying that, in 70 years of Seder–going, they had not learned as much as they had in this model Seder. The ability to teach Judaism in such a way that others practice it with enthusiasm is *avodat Hashem*.

S.F.: You deal by and large with an English–speaking public, a small minority of the greater Israeli society. Have you thought about doing more for those who are not in this English–speaking community?

Phil Chernofsky: In theory, such an educational program should be on every observant Jew's agenda. Practically speaking, however, I find myself more effective with English speakers. I do speak to groups in Hebrew on certain occasions. Recently, we heard a talk from a fellow who does *kiruv* work with the Israeli community. He said he made a conscious decision to speak English to them because he found that, when the average American does speak Hebrew, the Israeli listener is too distracted by the awkwardness of the language, the accent, and vocabulary. He found that, when he speaks in English, the listener is able to concentrate more on the content, and so be more receptive. As for the Israel Center, which occupies more than 100 percent of my time, it is directed to filling certain voids here. We have, for instance, become involved in the Russian *olim* community, whom we have taught in easy Hebrew. But our main focus is still on English speakers and, so long as there is so much to be done, I do not feel guilty about not dealing with other audiences.

S.F.: There is an idea that, while the bulk of the world's Jewry is moving toward greater assimilation, a minority is deepening its intense devotion to Judaism. What is your perspective on the assimilation question?

Phil Chernofsky: I lament the polarization that has led to a certain self–enclosedness within the Orthodox community. I feel that a truly committed Jew can and must have influence on other people. When you run into an attitude of "We have to take care of our own, and God forbid that my children should be exposed to a secular or even slightly less religious attitude," then there is the potential lost for moving the non–religious to greater religiousness. To use an analogy, if a person wants to wear a bigger and blacker *kepah* before the non–committed, then he may present religiousness as an impossible contradiction to that person's way of life. The wearing of a more normal *kepah* and more Western dress sometimes says to the non–committed, "You should not dismiss the concept of being religious, because it means not living in the modern world. There are people and there is a way of being both religious and living in the modern world." I am over–simplifying now, but I hope I am making the idea clear.

Another illustration of this came to me when I was doing a stint of army reserve duty, working in a room twelve hours with another person who was not religious. The first day he hardly spoke, though I tried to talk with him. In the middle of the second day, he allowed some conversation and slowly warmed to it. He confided in me that he felt very uncomfortable with a religious Jew in the army, because this contradicted his particular stereotype of religious Jews as shirkers of duty. He could say to himself, "I am not like them because I have a commitment to Israel and the army. And since they refuse to share the responsibility, I can refuse to have anything to do with what they hold dear. But when I see fellows like you who hold Shabbat precious, and

Israel precious too, I don't have excuses anymore for my non–religious attitude." It's like the bumper sticker that says "Every yeshiva student should join the army, and every Jewish soldier should join a yeshiva." When one says "I have my things and you have yours," there is a self–enclosed self–righteousness. But when one has a commitment to what is not narrowly one's own, one can have a positive influence on others.

S.F.: You have given a prescription for *kiruv* work. But I was also wondering about your sense of how *Am Yisrael* is doing at this time. I ask this when I have in mind the *parasha* sheet you wrote a couple of weeks ago on the question of celebrating Purim and Pesach when there have been tragic events happening at the same time.

Phil Chernofsky: I believe, based on sources, that God has a certain plan by which, at a certain time, whenever it is, we will enter the Messianic era. The two possibilities are that the Jewish people will be ready for the *Mosheach*, or they won't be ready. A third possibility, that they will be ready much sooner than that time, will move God, so to speak, to bring the *Mosheach* sooner than the anticipated time. It's like pouring hot water into a vessel, a glass. If the glass is cold, then it will break. In order to prevent this, you've got to warm up the glass at least. And it is better to make it hotter so that the contrast is not so greatly felt. Now that specifically addresses one aspect of it. But the task we have is to prepare the Jewish people in a positive way, so that the *Mosheach* and the *Beit Ha–Mikdash*, and the time of the reinstitution of the Sanhedrin, and the whole next phase of our national existence will be a natural one. This, so that God will say, "There is no reason to wait anymore," which means placing the emphasis on Torah education and observance of mitzvot. But I also mean Torah practice, which is associated with the proper personality traits. Judaism, Torah Judaism, has a high regard for the mitzvot that are between man and his fellow human being. These are strict regulations in regard to not embarrassing people when in the process of reproaching them, and hopefully bringing them closer to the Torah community. Many elements are acting rightly in this, while some or not. Standing and screaming and throwing rocks on cars on Shabbat seems to me not the right way to accomplish this goal.

Among the many organizations that adopt a more positive approach to non–committed Jews is the Israel Center. We have a warm atmosphere where they are free to come and learn something. For example, I taught a class a number of years ago on the laws of milk and meat, called "The Cheeseburger and the Jew." In one class, I asked a girl from Beit Yaakov why, after years of studying such laws, she felt she needed such a class. Her answer was that she had many questions she had not been able to ask there, and here she could ask the questions without being yelled at. In the same session, there were college girls, one barely Jewish who, the previous night, had asked for a glass of milk at a meat restaurant and had been refused. They came to the class in order to understand. A Lutheran minister also attended. So we had all kinds of people, including those who work to teach the seven Noahide mitzvot to non–Jews. Our goal is to teach Torah, but in the background, or maybe the foreground, is our effort to improve the general condition of Jews and move humankind toward Messianic times.

S.F.: We have had many terrorist incidents recently. What do you believe we can do about them, in religious terms?

Phil Chernofsky: What the average Jews in the street can do to combat terror, and it might sound corny and old–fashioned though I believe it's true, is to have more true awe of Hashem. The more true awe we have and the more we come close to Torah, the less God will allow these things to happen to us. This does not mean that any specific terrorist act is a result of some action on our part.

S.F.: If this is the prescription, then why was it precisely the most *frum* communities that most suffered in the Shoah? I am not asking this on a sociological level, but rather a theological one.

Phil Chernofsky: Basically, when a bad thing happens, we generally cannot attribute it to any specific cause, unless the Torah has specifically stated this. The Torah tells us that leprosy was the specific punishment for the slander of *leshon hara*. Yet I think it is irresponsible to say that a bus of schoolchildren that is plowed into by a train, resulting in many dead and injured, is as some religious people maintain due to the fact that movie theatres are open in Petach Tikvah on the evening of Shabbat. I find myself somewhere in the middle, between the two attitudes, that all is coincidence, and all evil is definitely traceable to specific wrongs done by human beings. I do believe that it is often possible to take events as reminders that God is not 100 percent pleased with us. Otherwise, there would be no reason for these things to happen. Above all, the calculations of God are totally unfathomable. We do not know God's accounting of things. An 11-month-old baby who dies of infant death syndrome is not guilty of anything, because a baby clearly cannot have responsibility for his actions. We do not know God's calculation. Perhaps a soul required another 11 months in this world to wipe a slate clean, before moving on to another dimension of existence. I also do not believe it's a matter of punishment of the parents, for the Torah teaches that children are not killed for the sins of their parents. So there is another kind of calculation involved here that we do not understand. Similarly, an adult might die without being culpable, guilty of no crime. Yet his dying fits in somehow with God's plans. This, for me, is sufficient explanation. It does not mean that I am not going to cry, nor that I am not going to wonder, but I do think I have an insight on this. I base it on the verse "The hidden things are for the Lord our God. And those revealed to us are for our children" as a heritage forever. This, when the identification as something as hidden or revealed changed all the time, from person to person.

Another idea is that the Mosheach will come as a result of a continual deterioration of the human situation, without any hope of improvement. To return to our glass analogy, when one glass breaks, a new glass is to replace it. And this glass with its new material will handle the hot water of the evil times. I am hoping that we human beings, we Jews, can by our good deeds take significant strides in the hastening of the coming of *Mosheach*. Since we do not know how God keeps score, the only thing we can do is improve our behavior, act righteously. This means individually that I must be the best Jew and the best human being that I can possibly be. I am not an angel and this cannot happen overnight, but one must make a continual effort at improvement. Sometimes there's an improvement in one area, and backsliding in another.

I have said before that the individual has an obligation to family and community. As a lifelong educator, I reject the notion that parents can turn over their children's education to a school, pay the tuition bills, and wash their hands of it. I believe that there's a constant challenge set before parents to raise their children in a proper way. This is true even when the children become adults and have children of their own. A process of education still continues. We have an interesting illustration of this at the Seder table. If a child has his father and his father has his own father at the Seder table, then the small child asks the "*Mah nishtanah?*" of his father, and the father turns around and asks it of the grandfather. Even if it causes the little children in the house to giggle, it's part of the statement of a continual, non–ending responsibility of parents toward their children.

S.F.: I understand what you are saying about individual responsibility, even toward bringing about Messianic times. I would like however to know your assessment of where you believe the Jewish people are historically in relation to the process of redemption.

Phil Chernofsky: I believe that we quite some time ago entered the beginning stages of the Redemption, what is called "*atchalta d'geulah*" or, to use another phrase, "*iktava d'Mosheach*," "the footsteps of the Messiah." I personally believe that the state of Israel, not just the land of Israel, is the beginning of the flowering of our redemption. I also know that this is controversial in religious circles. But I believe that the state of Israel, is a step in the right direction and will hasten the ultimate coming of the *Mosheach*. I know that there are Jews who feel the opposite. I don't believe I will convince them, nor will they convince me. I am hoping that, if my approach is correct, then their refusal not to see it will not be held against us, nor against them. I am equally sure that, if in some way I don't have it exactly as it should be, then I will not maintain a false position out of stubbornness. I believe very strongly that the establishment of the state of Israel was guided in a positive way by the hand of God. I believe that, for all Israel's problems, it has very significant positive elements.

And I believe it is important to distinguish between the individual Jew and Judaism in judging behavior. If a religious guy is caught for fraud or some other kind of anti–social behavior, though he *davvens* three times a day and keeps meticulously kosher, this is a poor excuse for indicting Judaism as a whole. So too the individual actions of Jews in Israel may at times not reflect positively on the state of Israel, but this is no reason for wholesale condemnation of it.

I get angry when I see someone not standing for the siren on Holocaust Day or the Memorial Day for fallen soldiers. I believe standing in respect for those Jews who died because they were Jewish is perfectly proper and right. The Nazis did not ask people "Do you wear *tzitzit*? Do you keep Shabbat?" In fact, there were those who denied their Jewishness and nonetheless were murdered. It is necessary for each and every Jew to have respect for the sanctity of the life of those who our enemies have murdered.

Attempts to use extreme examples of individuals' poor behavior in order to delegitimize whole communities are wrong. I mean, don't take it out on Torah and don't take it out on God because a particular person rubbed you the wrong way. Both the Haredi and the religious Orthodox communities must show mutual respect and understanding toward each other.

S.F.: But in regard to the religious and non–religious, aren't we talking about two closed communities, unable to see the way of the other?

Phil Chernofsky: I believe that the religious person, the Torah–educated and trained person, should, by virtue of the education he received, have a better attitude toward the non–religious and anti–religious. I know you are supposed to hate an "evil one," but I am not talking about that. There are sources that tell us to hate the evil and not the evil-doer. It is similar to the principle of child psychology, which says that you are not supposed to say to your child, "You are bad," but rather, "You did a bad thing." If you tell him he's a bad child, then he very likely will become one. Meanwhile, the secularist, the one with a bad attitude and lack of education toward things religious, often acts out of lack of understanding. If he drives on Shabbat and offends religious sensibilities, it may be because he does not truly understand what Shabbat is. The proper response is not to curse and throw rocks, but rather, through classes and home hospitality, to give an appreciation of the Shabbat.

S.F.: In this field of teaching Judaism to "all comers," what is special about your approach?

Phil Chernofsky: For years, I taught math, elementary algebra, geometry, and intermediate algebra. Now, while I know I am not the greatest mathematician in the world, I believe I do have a capacity for taking sophisticated concepts and making them understandable. Perhaps I even have a way of generating interest and excitement about these concepts. What's true in my approach to teaching science is even more true in my approach to Judaism. One doesn't have to be a *talmid chacham* (which I do not consider myself to be) in order to teach others and ignite in them that internal flame of desire to learn. I can give a poignant example. Recently, I ran into a fellow whom I did not recognize and who introduced himself as my former pupil. Married with children, having learned for 12 years at Mir, he said with tears in his eyes, "You were the first person who taught me to love learning Torah." I was not the first to teach him Torah, but the first who taught him Torah learning could be an experience he could love. I have come across many newcomers to Torah and veteran learners who need this kind of loving Torah. Another example: I have a pair of letters in my files, remarkably similar in content, from two teenage girls who thank me for showing them the beauties of Judaism. One of the girls grew up in a non–religious environment and the other in a Hasidic *shteibl*.

In the introductory *berachah* to *Keriyat Shema*, we ask God not only to allow us to learn Torah. We say "Let my eyes light up and sparkle in Your Torah." In other words, let me not just go through the motions, but let my heart cling to the mitzvot so that I fully enjoy what I am doing. If I in my own life am able to do this, and give some of that over to my children, who are my first priorities as students, then have a little left over for the students I have, whether in the formal setting of schools or in the informal setting of the Israel Center, then that's what my life work is. And I pray to God that I will be successful in this and not, God forbid, misdirect anyone, but only help toward bigger and better things in Torah.

Rabbi Chaim Eisen

Rabbi Chaim Eisen is a teacher of Jewish thought at Yeshivat HaKotel and the OU–NCSY Israel Center in Jerusalem. He is also a lecturer within the Educational Unit of the Israel Defense Forces. Rabbi Eisen served as editor of *Jewish Thought: A Journal of Torah Scholarship* for its first 3 years. He has published numerous articles in a variety of publications on Jewish thought.

Our interview took place in the 'Israel Center' on Strauss Street. After his weekly class in Pirke Avot, Rabbi Eisen then used the transcript of our conversation as a basis for what I believe to be a remarkably profound statement about the way Torah is the basis for all we do in true *avodat Hashem*. He is a teacher whose warmth and consideration make him the personal embodiment of the Torah that he teaches.

C03 80

S.F.: Rabbi, could you describe your present teaching and writing activities?

Rabbi Eisen: I began teaching at Yeshivat Hakotel about sixteen years ago, and, except for a brief leave of absence, I have been teaching there since. Presently, I direct and teach the Advanced Seminar in Jewish Thought, a program offered by Yeshivat Hakotel for students with the acumen and commitment to engage in an extra course of study in addition to the traditional yeshiva curriculum. Its syllabus comprises in-depth classes in Rabbi Yehudah Ha–Levi's *Sefer Ha–Kozari*, Rambam's *Moreh Ha–Nevochim*, and Ramban's *Perushei Ha–Torah*. Together with a weekly seminar on the philosophies of Torah and science and their interrelationship, all these classes focus on the foundations of classic Jewish thought from the period of the *rishonim* (early rabbinical authorities), while stressing basic methodology and critical analysis of the subject matter. Simultaneously, as a prerequisite of such incisive thinking, important concepts in philosophy—epistemology, in particular—are developed. Additional *shiurim* in *musar* (ethics) and a weekly class in *Pirkei Avot* (Ethics of the Fathers) complement the more philosophical sessions by emphasizing the realization of devotional and religious ideals in practice. Through such composite study, students are encouraged and expected to glean the raw materials for beginning to cultivate an individual Jewish philosophy, built upon the seminal pillars of classic Jewish thought, and to translate it into a practical, all–encompassing commitment in their lives.

87

Besides these *shiurim*, I deliver a variety of open lectures and seminars at Yeshivat Hakotel on timely topics, both relating to the holidays and addressing various contemporary issues. (In the latter category, students vote each year on subjects of special interest to them.) In part because of these *shiurim*, both current and former students frequently engage me in private consultations on philosophy–related and personal problems. I dedicate much time and effort to these conversations, both inside and outside the yeshiva, as one of my highest priorities.

I have also been teaching at the OU–NCSY Israel Center for about fifteen years. My *shiurim* there include weekly classes in *Pirkei Avot*, *Sefer Ha–Kozari*, and *Moreh Ha–Nevochim*, as well as occasional special lectures. In addition, as a reservist in the IDF Rabbinate's *Yechidat Ha-Martzim* (Torah Lecture Corps), I engage in much the same work with diverse groups of soldiers whom I might otherwise rarely meet. In this role, I address military units of varied (largely nonreligious) backgrounds from around the country. I often serve as rabbi–in–residence at air force bases for Shabbat, where I deliver up to ten different talks over the course of the day to interested soldiers. Apart from these responsibilities, I am involved in writing several books, including elaborations on some of the material I published when I served as the first editor of the OU journal *Jewish Thought*, for the first three years of its existence.

S.F.: Could you say something about your educational background?

Rabbi Eisen: As a youngster, I attended Yeshiva of Flatbush High School, leaving after my junior year upon acceptance by Columbia University. I initially came to Israel on an academic leave of absence, after two years of study at Columbia, and studied at Yeshivat Hakotel for two years. For the following year, I returned to Columbia University, continuing my studies of the natural sciences and general philosophy, and completed my degree in biophysics. Immediately thereafter, I returned permanently to Israel, resumed my studies at Yeshivat Hakotel—including rabbinical studies in the *kolel rabbanut*—and began teaching there.

S.F.: So you have a scientific education, which you do not now use in an active, practical way?

Rabbi Eisen: I do not like to regard anything as impractical or irrelevant. Of course, on a direct level, my seminar on the philosophies of

Torah and science and their interrelationship is predicated largely on my background in science and philosophy. But on a broader and deeper level, all knowledge can and must contribute to a more holistic Jewish philosophy. General knowledge can have significant implications for Torah knowledge. Thus, while the Midrash discounts the possibility of Torah existing "among the nations," it affirms that, "if a person tells you that *wisdom* exists among the nations, believe it" (*Eichah Rabbah 2:13*)—because indeed it does. To cite just two major examples, both Rabbi Yehudah Ha-Levi (in *Sefer Ha-Kozari 2:64*) and Rambam (in *Mishneh Torah, Hilchot Sanhedrin 2:1*) stress the requirement that the preeminent sages, who were eligible for membership in the Sanhedrin (the chief rabbinical court), be not only well-versed in all aspects of Torah learning but also knowledgeable in all branches of general scholarship. And, more broadly, the Vilna Gaon—whom his closest students, among them Rabbi Yisrael of Shklov in the introduction to *Pe'at Ha-Shulchan*, described as having personally mastered all extant faculties of knowledge, "knowing them all completely"—warns *all* students of Torah, "To whatever extent a person lacks knowledge of the other wisdoms, one will correspondingly lack Torah wisdom one hundred-fold, for the Torah and wisdom are coupled together" (quoted by his student, Rabbi Baruch of Shklov, in the introduction to his book, *Euclid*).

S.F.: Not to be critical or skeptical, but do you think that really applies in the case of most *gedolim*? Do you think it applies in the Jewish world today? Who, aside from Rabbi Soloveitchik or, in another way, Rabbi Kook, really meets this standard? Do you have examples of other role models who have that kind of comprehension of other worlds—or are even seeking it?

Rabbi Eisen: I definitely think that examples abound throughout Jewish history and even today, which emulate the approach of the Vilna Gaon in varying degrees. However, I would prefer to focus on ideas and ideals—rather than personalities, which are, at best, particularized, imperfect approximations of them. Conceptually, the increasing tendency toward specialization and compartmentalization at the expense of a holistic sense of the total picture is a major problem in the world at large, not just the Jewish world. (It was Robert Heinlein who protested that, compared with the grandeur of human potential, "specialization is for insects.") But especially in Torah scholarship, we can keenly appreciate the Vilna Gaon's recognition of the vital need for such holism in order truly to grapple with Torah—the most intense means through which we can interconnect with God—in all its dimensions. After all, God revealed Himself to us principally through two media: not only Torah, through Revelation, but also the world, through Creation. Any author's works are better understood when another work by the same author is also studied. Likewise, to whatever extent one is steeped in an understanding of the world, one will better appreciate the message of Torah, and vice versa. Moreover, God gave us the Torah to guide us in the challenges of living *in this world*. Thus, to whatever extent we learn better to deal with this world, we are better equipped to relate to Him and to the Torah. Ultimately, our involvement with *both* media enhances our connection with Him.

S.F.: It is often claimed that all knowledge is contained within the Torah. However, we know that the great part of scientific and intellectual work is done without any reference whatever being made to the terms and conditions of Torah. How do you understand this?

Rabbi Eisen: The issue you are raising is certainly important. Let's further sharpen the question before attempting to respond. In principle, we could say that the Torah contains not only all knowledge but the totality of all existence. After all, the Midrash describes God as "gazing in the Torah and creating the world" (*Bereshit Rabbah 1:1*). The Talmud and Midrash repeatedly stress that Torah is the blueprint of the universe, which predates Creation and transcends the world. To that extent, Torah encompasses everything—and any "peripheral investigations" should be considered superfluous. But this final conclusion clearly appears incongruous with the *midrash* mentioned earlier, which advised that "wisdom exists among the nations," even though Torah does not—implying that "Torah" and "wisdom" are distinct and that those "peripheral investigations" may well be indispensable.

　　To clarify what Torah signifies, then, we should consider the Midrash's portrayal of the primeval Torah, which predates Creation, more carefully: "When the Holy One Blessed be He created His world, He took counsel with the Torah and created the world. . . And in what was the Torah inscribed? *Upon white fire in black fire*" (*Tanchuma Bereshit:1*) The metaphor of fire is significant; God Himself is similarly described in the Torah: "For God your Lord is [like] a *consuming fire*" (*Devarim 4:24* and *9:3*). In *Moreh Ha-Nevochim* (*1:30*), Rambam relates the symbolism to fire's destructive capacity. Terrestrial fire cannot be grasped, and the mere attempt to grasp it would *consume* the tools with which we physically grasp (our hands). Only from a distance can we be safely warmed. In likening God to a consuming fire, the Torah emphasizes that He cannot be grasped *intellectually*—the mere attempt to comprehend Him would *consume* the tools with which we *intellectually* grasp (our minds). Similarly, while our Torah, which is *tangibly* inscribed upon white parchment in black ink, was given to *this* world, the primeval Torah, "inscribed upon white *fire* in black *fire*," is *beyond* human grasp.

Indeed, the Midrash assumes such a distinction between this primeval, transcendent Torah (upon which the world's existence is predicated) and our terrestrial Torah (which, as the basis for our lives in this world, explicitly presupposes the world's existence):

> '*No man knows [wisdom's] value*' [*Iyyov 28:13*]—Said R. Elazar: The sections of Torah were not given in order, for, had they been given in order, anyone who would read them would be able to resurrect the dead and do miracles (*alt. v.*: immediately would be able to create a world). Therefore, the order of Torah was concealed. But it is revealed before the Holy One Blessed be He; as it is said, 'And who like Me can read and recount it and set it in order for Me' [*Yeshayahu 44:7*] (*Midrash Tehillim 3:2*).

In its references to "order," were the Midrash alluding merely to questions of chronology, reading the unmodified version would obviously not enable "anyone . . . to resurrect the dead and do miracles," much less "immediately . . . be able to create a world." Evidently, the unmodified version relates to an ontologically different domain—the realm of the divine—in which the realities of this world, which normally exclude acts of resurrection, miracles, and creation, do not apply. This level of Torah, emphasizes the Midrash, is inaccessible to humanity, which inherently functions on a distinct, earthly level.

Expounding the same verse from *Iyyov*, the Gemara apparently regards this dichotomy as so obvious that it comments rhetorically:

> Regarding the Torah, it is written, '[It is] *hidden* from the eyes of all living and concealed from the birds of the heavens' [*Iyyov 28:21*]. [Are we to assume that 'hidden'] implies that [Torah] was ever known? But it is written, '*No man knows [wisdom's] value*' [*Iyyov 28:13*]! (*Shevuot 5a*).

Maharal comments on this passage that even "Moshe did not receive all of the Torah . . . It is impossible to say that Moshe received the entire Torah . . . Instead, he received of the Torah *what it is possible to receive*" (*Derech Ha-Chayyim* on *Avot 1:1*). Moshe's receipt of Torah is the maximum possible specifically within the limitations of human ken.

Thus, the Talmud affirms, "Fifty gates of understanding were created in the world, and *all were given to Moshe save one*" (*Rosh Hashanah 21b, Nedarim 38a*). Since the number fifty symbolizes the absolute—as in the counting of the *omer* (fifty days) and the *yovel* (fiftieth year)—the distinction between fifty gates and forty-nine is the distinction between the absolute and the maximum level attainable in this world. *Tosafot Yom Tov* cites this statement to verify "that all of the Torah was not delivered over to [Moshe] . . . but *only what was suitable for him to receive* he received from Sinai" (commentary on *Avot 1:1*).

Still more explicitly, the Midrash emphasizes the inherently limited nature of Moshe's receipt of the Torah:

> And did Moshe learn the whole Torah? It is written regarding the Torah, 'Its measure is longer than the earth and broader than the sea' [*Iyyov 11:9*]! And in forty days Moshe learned it? Rather, it was *principles* that the Holy One Blessed be He taught Moshe (*Shemot Rabbah 41:6; Tanchuma Tissa:16*).

Maharal identifies these "principles": "These are the rules through which Torah is expounded, for each rule teaches countless [derivative conclusions]" (commentary, *loc. cit.*). But these conclusions are necessarily to be derived by man—a terrestrial dimension that clearly has no place in the transcendent Torah of heaven.

It is only in this light that we can begin to appreciate what the revelation of Torah at Sinai means to us and to the world. And it is only in this light that we can begin to grasp the real message of an *agadah* that many of us first learned in nursery school:

> *Malachei hasharet* (the ministering angels) said before the Holy One Blessed be He, '[The Torah is] . . . a hidden treasure, cached for You 974 generations before the world was created. You wish to give it to flesh and blood? "What is man that You remember him and a human that You take account of him?" [*Tehillim 8:5*]. "God our Master! How glorious is Your Name in all the world, You Who *place Your majesty [the Torah] upon heaven!*" [Ibid 8:2].
>
> Said the Holy One Blessed be He to Moshe, 'Answer them!' . . .

He said before Him, 'Master of the universe! In the Torah that You are giving me, what is written? "I am God your Lord Who brought you forth from the land of Mitzrayim" [*Shemot 20:2*].' He said to them, 'You descended to Mitzrayim? You were subjugated to Paroh? Why should Torah be yours?' (*Shabbat 88b*).

Five additional challenges are leveled by Moshe (*loc. cit.*), citing commandments revealed by God at Sinai and emphasizing their irrelevance to the heavenly arena. While *malachei hasharet* ultimately concede, the premise of the debate seems elusive. Given the content of the Torah, what motivated them to posit initially that it should be placed in heaven? Had they no familiarity with the treasure they wished to possess so exclusively?

With our recognition of two distinct levels of Torah, the Gemara's message is evident. Obviously, in characterizing the Torah as "a *hidden* treasure" that preceded Creation, *malachei hasharet* were not referring to a Torah of inapplicable terrestrial commandments. Their Torah "is inscribed not in the present, but in the primeval, order" (*Shenei Luchot Ha–Berit* [Rabbi Yeshayahu Horowitz], "*Masechet Shavuot*," p. 112a). They contend that Torah should be placed in heaven, because they perceive Torah as a transcendent secret, inappropriate to earthly man. It should therefore be kept hidden in a transcendent realm: heaven. Moshe's decisive response is that there is, in addition to the *hidden* treasure, a *revealed* level of Torah that is relevant specifically to people and mandates the descent of Torah to this world. While the transcendent Torah of white and black fire remains essentially in heaven, the terrestrial Torah of parchment and ink is consigned to man and revealed to the world at Sinai.

Thus, what took place at Sinai had no bearing on, or *direct* contact with, the absolute, transcendent Torah of heaven. On the contrary, the Midrash portrays the giving of the Torah at Sinai as "a time for that which was placed beyond the heavens [the transcendent Torah] to be placed beneath the heavens" (*Kohelet Rabbah 3:1*). The Torah that predates Creation is the fiery Torah of the *malachim*, inaccessible to human grasp. In contrast, the Talmud asserts that our "Torah speaks in the language of *people*" (*Berachot 31b*, etc.). Indeed, the Midrash emphasizes that the Torah revealed at Sinai was specifically in accordance with people's subjective ability to receive it: "With all of Yisrael, each and every one [heard] according to his capacity" (*Shemot Rabbah 5:9*). For Torah to descend to this world, it must be concretized corporeally, transcribed into tangible ink on parchment and tangible concepts that lie specifically within human ken. The Torah of heaven is the blueprint for this world, outlining the transcendent foundation of everything. Ours is the users' manual; given the world's existence, it teaches us how to live our lives properly here. If I am belaboring this point, it is because this fundamental distinction is so often misconstrued or misrepresented.

How, then—if at all—is our terrestrial Torah related to the transcendent Torah of fire, the all–encompassing blueprint of everything? Ramban explains that the implication of two distinct levels of Torah is not necessarily two different texts:

> We are in possession of a true tradition that the entire Torah is names of the Holy One Blessed be He [*cf. Zohar*: "The Torah, is all the Holy Name, for there is not one word in the Torah that is not included in the Holy Name" (II, 87a, etc.)], the words subdividing into names on a different level . . . Therefore, a *sefer Torah* in which [the scribe] erred in the insertion or deletion of a single letter is unfit . . . even though [the error] seems neither to add nor to detract [from the meaning] . . . And it appears that the Torah that was inscribed in black fire upon white fire was in the manner that we have mentioned: that the writing was continuous, without separation into words, and it was possible to interpret it in the manner of the names or in the manner of our reading regarding the *torah* [instruction] and the *mitzvah* [commandment]. And it was given to Moshe Rabbeinu [in writing] in the manner of partition [in order to] read the *mitzvah* (*Perushei Ha–Torah*, Introduction).

Rabbi Meir ben Gabbai amplifies Ramban's description of the Torah as names of God, and he concludes, "This is the primeval Torah that predated the world" (*Avodat Ha–Kodesh*, "*Chelek Ha–Yichud*," Chapter 21). But, while in principle it is also *our* Torah, it is clearly *not* the Torah as we perceive it.

By analogy, imagine a child beginning to learn the Alef–Bet, who is given a cryptic work of abstruse scholarship to use as a primer. The child may successfully use the book to practice letter recognition. But even if the child is told that the primer alludes to profound mysteries, any attempt to discern them in the Alef-Bet letters will be misguided and futile. Given the child's level, we may truthfully say that they are not part of *the child's* book. Likewise, while the users' manual of a car is necessarily a reflection of the car's blueprints, the manual teaches the layman nothing about the technicalities of automotive design. Similarly, the level at which Torah is revealed to this world is specifically on physical parchment in material ink: palpable media presenting palpable instruction to earthly man on how to live in this world. This is a limitation of our worldly existence, not our Torah. Although it is essentially the same book, the heavenly, fiery Torah of Names—through which God created this world—cannot be grasped from within this world, even in principle.

S.F.: But in terms of the understanding we do have and can attain, how should we understand the world as it develops generation to generation? How are we to relate to the specific historical–scientific knowledge that seems to accumulate? Is the thinking Jew's understanding of the world today to be identical with, or different from, that of *gedolim* in previous generations?

Rabbi Eisen: Naturally, the answer hinges on what we mean by one's "understanding of the world." Once again, we should recall the Midrash's distinction between general "wisdom," which "exists among the nations," and "Torah," which does not. In a fundamental sense, "understanding of the world" is understanding one's individual role and responsibility in the world—and, more broadly, connecting with the underlying and transcendent meaning of the world in general. Since these we emphatically place within the domain of immutable Torah values, such "understanding" certainly should not diverge substantively from that of previous generations.

However, within the domain of general "wisdom," no one has a monopoly. Indeed, the Gemara concludes a presentation of scientific disputes between "scholars of Yisrael" and "scholars of the nations" with Rabbi Yehudah Ha-Nasi's assessment that "their words appear more reasonable than our words" (*Pesachim 94b*). An alternative version of the passage—quoted by Rambam (in *Moreh Ha-Nevochim 2:8*), Rabbi Avraham ben Rambam (in his "*Ma'amar al Odot Derashot Chazal*"), and Rabbi Yitzchak Arama (in *Akedat Yitzchak*, "*Bo*," Chapter 37)—concludes even more explicitly: "The scholars of the nations of the world *vanquished* the scholars of Yisrael."

This is no reason for consternation or shame. On the contrary, we should certainly be awed anew by the greatness of the Sages, who, without curbing their insatiable commitment to Torah study, still strove so valiantly to master the developing sciences of their times. Even more to the point, we should learn much from the Sages' explicit refusal to arrogate any pretensions of infallibility in these matters. The Gemara depicts them in their uncompromising quest for knowledge, publicly and unhesitatingly conceding error, even when it entailed yielding to heathens.

In light of this *gemara*, Rambam states, "Do not expect of me to reconcile everything [the Sages] mentioned in matters of astronomy with the subject as found. For the academic faculties were in those times [of the Sages] deficient, and they did not speak about [those subjects] based upon a tradition from the Prophets, rather, by virtue of their own standing as experts in those generations in those subjects or by virtue of what they heard from experts in those generations" (*Moreh Ha-Nevochim 3:14*). Thus, concludes his son, "We are not obliged—in deference to the greatness of the Sages of the Talmud and their understanding of the meaning of the Torah and its subtleties, in the explanation of its principles and particulars—to defend [the Sages] and establish their opinions in all their statements concerning medicine, physics, and astronomy" (Rabbi Avraham ben Rambam, "*Ma'amar al Odot Derashot Chazal*").

I must stress that this conclusion in no way undermines the authority of the Sages in legislating Jewish law, even when it appears to derive from questionable scientific premises (as Rambam states explicitly in *Mishneh Torah*, for reasons that are beyond the scope of the present discussion). As stated previously, that belongs to the realm of "Torah," grounded in a tradition we consider divine. Nevertheless, in the realm of "wisdom," I think that the implications to your question in particular and our pursuit of knowledge in general are clear. As Rambam states, "Accept the truth from whomever said it" (*Shemonah Perakim*, Introduction). In context, he is referring to Aristotle and later, non–Jewish, neo–Aristotelian thinkers, whom Rambam quotes anonymously, lest "mention of that man's name impel one who lacks taste to think that [the] statement is worthless and contains evil, because he does not understand it." Rambam and countless other Jewish thinkers through the generations expressly disdain such a prejudicial attitude regarding general wisdom.

S.F.: But what happens when wisdom contradicts Torah? There are challenges, other worlds in thought. How much is a Jew obliged to know these worlds to contend with them? You studied at Columbia

University and met people who live in totally different intellectual universes. Also, how much time can you, in your own learning, afford to give to these challenges and other ways of learning?

Rabbi Eisen: First, let me state categorically that wisdom *never* really contradicts Torah. Since both spring from the same Source—God, Who gave us both Torah and the world—there can be no true conflict between them. As Rabbi Yehudah Ha-Levi exclaims, "God forbid that any matter of Torah contradict the testimony of direct observation or that which has been proven by logic!" (*Ha-Kozari 1:67*). And "God forbid that we believe in that which is impossible or that which the intellect rejects and regards as impossible!" (Ibid 1:89). A conflict between the Torah we study and the world we observe would necessitate regarding the Torah as divorced from our sense of reality—a totally unacceptable conclusion for Judaism.

Contradictions are possible, perhaps even inevitable, only when wisdom or Torah—or both—are misconstrued. For example, when logic is spuriously applied to intrinsically nonrational issues or when scientific models are manipulated as the putative basis of moral values (or their negation), wisdom has overstepped its bounds. Similarly—as affirmed by such recent authorities as Rabbi S.R. Hirsch, Rabbi A.Y. Kook, Rabbi J.H. Hertz, and Rabbi E.E. Dessler—when our terrestrial Torah is purported to be readable as a blueprint for (or refutation of) current scientific hypotheses, Torah has been perverted. Unfortunately, such misunderstandings and misrepresentations are rampant nowadays. Therein lies the real challenge.

For precisely this reason—to confront this challenge—I have dedicated a weekly seminar at Yeshivat Hakotel to the philosophies of Torah and science and their interrelationship, to define rigorously the domain, purpose, and "truth" value of each. Yet I would be the first to concede that even a seminar of this sort is guilty of innumerable oversimplifications (many of which I explicitly identify as such). After all, a thorough resolution of all apparent conflicts between wisdom and Torah is necessarily predicated upon thorough mastery of both. Obviously, complete fulfillment of this prerequisite is practically impossible in the limited time we each have at our disposal in life. This realization is not intended to justify despair. It simply highlights the extent to which an individual's pursuit of wisdom, both quantitatively and qualitatively, is an extremely subjective issue, especially considering the

unique role and mission each of us has been given. Certainly, college
(let alone an Ivy League education) is not desirable for everyone. But
that does not negate the possibility that this course may be justified
(perhaps even mandated) for some. Recall the instruction and example
of the Vilna Gaon (noted earlier) as a case in point.

More broadly, we should consider the Talmud's message to us:

> Said Rabbi Shimon ben Pazzi, quoting Rabbi Yehoshua ben Levi,
> in the name of bar Kappara: Regarding anyone who knows to cal-
> culate astronomical events and does not calculate [them], Scripture
> states, 'Upon the work of God they do not gaze, nor do they see
> His handiwork' [*Yeshayahu 5:12*].
>
> Said Rabbi Shemuel bar Nachmani, quoting Rabbi Yochanan:
> Whence [do we learn] that it is a mitzvah for a person to calculate
> astronomical events? For it is said, 'You shall safeguard and do [these
> laws], because this is your wisdom and understanding in the eyes
> of the nations' [*Devarim 4:6*]. Which wisdom and understanding is
> 'in the eyes of the nations' [i.e., in their reckoning as well]? Say
> then that this [refers to] calculating astronomical events (*Shabbat
> 75a*).

The context clearly indicates that the Gemara includes in this mandate
not only astronomy, which Rambam (in his epistle to the scholars of
Marseilles) describes as paradigmatic "wisdom," but natural science in
general. This conclusion is corroborated in citations of this passage by
Rabbi Bachyai ibn Pakudah (see *Chovot Ha-Levavot 2:2*), Rabbi Bachyai
ben Asher (see his commentary on *Avot 3:18*), Maharal (see *Netivot
Olam, "Netiv Ha-Torah,"* Chapter 14), and the Vilna Gaon (see *Kol Tor
5:2*), among many others. Furthermore, by juxtaposing two statements
on the subject, the Gemara is apparently emphasizing two distinct
points regarding science, and I can keenly identify with both from
personal experience.

First, I vividly sensed the splendor of God's handiwork in my
studies of the natural sciences. My major in biophysics enabled me (in
fact, required me) to study all the sciences quite intensively. I gleaned
from physics—and its quest to apprehend the grandeur of the universe
in terms of an incalculably vast yet fundamentally simple, all–encompassing structure—an awesome sense of "*mah gadelu ma'asecha, Ha-
Shem*" ("how *great* are Your deeds, God") (*Tehillim 92:6*). And, at the
opposite end of the scale, as biology opened my eyes to the incredible
complexity of life—such as living cells meticulously ordered down to

even the submolecular level—I learned a new appreciation of "*mah rabbu ma'asecha, Ha-Shem*" ("how *manifold* are Your deeds, God") (*Ibid 104:24*). Both levels definitely enhanced my sense of love and awe of God.

This, of course, is not a novel conclusion. Rabbi Bachyai ibn Pakudah bases the obligation "to examine the creations" (*Chovot Ha-Levavot 2:2*) upon, among others, the prophet's exhortation, to "lift up your eyes on high and behold Who created these" (*Yeshayahu 40:26*), and the psalmist's song, "when I see Your heavens, Your handiwork, the moon and stars, which You established," etc. (*Tehillim 8:4*). Rambam prescribes that "a person contemplate [God's] wondrous and great deeds and creations and apprehend through them His wisdom, which is incalculable and limitless" as "the way to [attain] love and awe of Him" (*Mishneh Torah, Hilchot Yesodei Ha-Torah 2:2* and *4:12* and *Hilchot Teshuvah 10:6*). He reiterates this mandate repeatedly in both his responsa and *Moreh Ha-Nevochim*. And later, major rabbinical authorities throughout the generations—including Rabbi Menachem ben Shlomo Ha-Meiri, Rabbi Bachyai ben Asher, Rema, Maharal, Rabbi Yom Tov Lipmann Heller, Rabbi Yaakov Emden, the Vilna Gaon and his students, and Rabbi S.R. Hirsch—have continually, emphatically upheld the need to study natural science *as a religious obligation*.

In addition, the Gemara stressed the significance of science as "wisdom and understanding in the eyes of the nations." In this light, Rabbi Hillel of Shklov testifies that his mentor, the Vilna Gaon, "engaged considerably in investigations of the properties of nature through worldly research, for the sake of apprehension of the wisdom of the Torah *and for the sake of sanctification of God's Name in the eyes of the nations.*" The Vilna Gaon's legacy in this regard—to his students and to us—is crucial:

> He also commanded his students to learn as much as possible of the seven wisdoms of worldly research, also in order to elevate the wisdom of Yisrael, based upon the wisdom of the Torah, in the eyes of the nations—based upon that which is written, 'because this is your wisdom and understanding in the eyes of the nations' (*Devarim 4:6*) . . . He said to us many times: What are our apprehenders of Torah doing on behalf of sanctification of the Name—as did the ancients from among the great men of Yisrael, many of whom sanctified the Heavenly Name through their vast knowledge in investigations of the mysteries of nature from the

wonders of the Creator . . . the men of the Sanhedrin, Mishnaic
sages, Talmudic sages, etc., and, in the later generations, our master the Rambam, [Rabbi Yom Tov Lipmann Heller] the author of
the *Tosafot Yom Tov*, and others, who did much to sanctify the
Heavenly Name in the eyes of the nations through their scholarship in worldly research? (*Kol Tor 5:2*).

Again, I must reiterate how keenly I have felt the Gaon's plea and protest, especially in the Torah world today.

For all these reasons—to meet these challenges—I still endeavor to
remain abreast of ongoing scientific research and development. Obviously, subdividing limited time resources, while maintaining the un-
equivocal supremacy of Torah study, is a complex and highly individual
problem. Still, in principle, pursuit of wisdom is not a diversion from
Torah but a necessary complement to it, in forging an all–encompassing whole in the service of God. Recall the Vilna Gaon's warning (mentioned previously): "To whatever extent a person lacks knowledge of
the other wisdoms, one will correspondingly lack Torah wisdom one
hundredfold, *for the Torah and wisdom are coupled together.*"

Nevertheless, to avoid a dangerous imbalance, the other side of
this coin must be noted. While extolling the usefulness of studying
nature, Rabbi Yehudah Ha–Levi warns that such study is "at once the
root of belief and the root of apostasy" (*Ha–Kozari 1:77*), since—depend-
ing on what we derive from it—it can lead to either. If we could rely
on wisdom and its proponents to remain always within the legitimate
bounds of wisdom, we might embrace their conclusions unreservedly.
Since that is manifestly not the case, a careful winnowing process is
necessary; at times, microsurgery may be a more apt metaphor.
Rambam's *Moreh Ha–Nevochim* is a dramatic case in point. Although
he incorporates much of Aristotelian thought into his philosophy,
Rambam unhesitatingly rejects certain components that he regards as
unproven and irreconcilable with foundational creeds of Judaism (see,
for example, *Moreh 2:25*). Clearly, knowing how and where to draw
the line is no mean feat; microsurgery is not for amateurs. Not incidentally, Rambam warns that his book is intended neither "for the
masses nor for those who are beginning to study nor to teach one who
has studied only Torah knowledge" (*Moreh*, Preface).

In conclusion, if you ask whether Judaism has the obligation and
the wherewithal to contend with the challenges you enumerated, then
the answer is, emphatically, yes. If you ask about the obligation of any

individual Jew, then the answer is far more equivocal. As an illustrative example, the Gemara states, just before the passage quoted earlier, " 'You shall not learn to do [like the abominations of those nations]' (*Devarim 18:9*)—But you [may] learn to understand and to instruct" (*Shabbat 75a*). Based upon this passage, Rambam (in *Mishneh Torah, Hilchot Sanhedrin 2:1* and *Hilchot Avodat Kochavim 3:2*) rules that familiarity with such "abominations" as divination, sorcery, witchcraft, and idolatry is obligatory for members of the Sanhedrin, who may be expected to pass judgment regarding such forbidden practices. In his epistle to the scholars of Marseilles, he testifies that he "read everything in matters of idolatry" to the extent that "it seems to me that I have not left any book in the world on this subject that had been translated from other languages into Arabic until I read it and understood its matters and grasped its opinion." But it would be foolhardy to recommend such a course of study to people who might be less adept at differentiating between learning "to do" and learning solely "to understand and to instruct." Each of us must reckon with our individual aptitudes and limitations, to which our unique missions in life are perfectly, divinely tailored. Through all these missions, collectively, Judaism accomplishes its mission "*letaken olam*" ("to perfect the world").

S.F.: Is part of that mission to construct for the world a philosophy that will give it a comprehension of itself? Western tradition has to a certain extent been a series of successive efforts to present a whole and complete picture of the world. Is this what you are trying to do in your work? Do you believe that there is such a Jewish total picture of the world, which can speak to those critical minds, Jewish and non–Jewish, in their striving to understand the world?

Rabbi Eisen: In principle, such a unifying effort is not only compatible with Judaism but, ultimately, a crucial reflection of the monotheism that Judaism bequeathed to the world. Affirmation of God's Oneness is a recognition that everything derives from, and is traceable to, a single, divine Source. Since everything is connected to that Source, everything is relevant to Judaism, and Judaism is relevant to everything. This is in marked contrast with the motto of the so–called Enlightenment: "Be a Jew in your home, and a human being when you go outside." That dichotomy should revolt us. No such division could ever be acceptable to Judaism. A Jew is a Jew every moment and in every pursuit.

This truth is first and foremost *halachic*. It is a tragedy that even many of Judaism's adherents have come to regard it as a religion in a purely ritual sense. Rabbi S.R. Hirsch (in *The Nineteen Letters*, "Eighteenth Letter," and many later works) eloquently decries this misperception, in which "a part of a work . . . referring to worship and holy days" (i.e., the *Orach Chayyim* component of the *Shulchan Aruch*) is mistaken for the totality of Jewish law. Notably neglected is the *Choshen Mishpat* section, encompassing the gamut of civil law and business ethics. That people can bemoan the phenomenon of so-called "dishonest religious Jews"—as if someone dishonest could possibly be regarded as "religious" (God forbid!)—is a sad testimony to this perversion of Judaism. In reality, Torah has a standard of justice and righteousness for every situation, a message of goodness and uprightness that can be applied to every aspect of life. On this practical level, our mission is to infuse the meaning and values of Judaism into every nook and cranny of existence. No "no man's land" should remain bereft of the light of Torah, in either our individual or communal lives.

This is the first vital step in realizing the goal we affirm at least three times daily in the "*Aleinu*" prayer: "*letaken olam bemalchut Shaddai*" ("to perfect the world through the reign of the Almighty"). We all should feel obliged to contribute to this end through whatever worldly activities we pursue, fulfilling the Mishnaic mandate that "all your deeds be for the sake of heaven" (*Avot 2:12*). Only in the wake of such a *practical* commitment can we advance the objective of an all-encompassing world view *conceptually*.

The corresponding *intellectual* endeavor entails first striving to distill from the diverse faculties of Torah study, both *halachic* and *agadic*, the underlying themes and structures, which provide the basis of a Jewish approach and attitude toward the myriad, apparently divergent aspects of life. Through applying such a Torah understanding to the various branches of general wisdom, one should cultivate a sense of the role and "truth value" each branch has to offer. All these must ultimately be subordinated to an increasingly comprehensive, holistic Torah perspective. Clearly, this is an ongoing, subjective mission, whose conclusions should be subject to continuous refinement in life. Twice every day, we aim to encompass ever more when we affirm God's Oneness in reciting "*Shema Yisrael*." I would describe this process as the lifelong struggle of each of us to construct one's own Jewish philosophy: the system through which one confronts, orders, and relates to the givens of reality in general and Torah in particular.

S.F.: How do you understand this process of knowing and learning in terms of *avodat Ha-Shem*? Do you consider your own work a form of *avodat Ha-Shem*?

Rabbi Eisen: I would prefer to focus on the broader question instead of the more personal one, which is too "easy." After all, to at least some extent, asking someone in my line of work if he considers his activities a form of *avodat Ha-Shem* anticipates an affirmative response. I must stress, however, that that response is not only because my work is teaching Torah in a yeshiva. Rather, whatever one's *avodah* is, in the sense of vocation, is necessarily a central aspect of one's *avodah*, in the sense of the service of God.

I recall an observation I once heard from one of my teachers: that a hotel manager with the proper attitude continuously engages in an unending chain of mitzvot. After all, such a person is always involved in *hachnasat orechim* (welcoming guests)! Of course, the manager must charge money for these efforts, because otherwise the hotel would go bankrupt and the opportunity for *hachnasat orechim* would be lost. But, as long as one relates to the money as only the means to perform the mitzvah, one is fulfilling the Mishnah's mandate that "all your deeds be for the sake of heaven" (*Avot 2:12*). (Conversely, there may also be hotel managers who relate to the money as the goal and the "mitzvah" as but the means to make money; they would obviously miss this opportunity.)

More generally, every legitimate career, which necessarily responds to some societal need and betters the quality of life, contributes to the mission emphasized before: "*letaken olam bemalchut Shaddai*" ("to perfect the world through the reign of the Almighty"). The scientist, the shopkeeper, the surgeon, and the street cleaner (to name just a few) each advance this goal in different ways, all of which are vital. It is all a question of attitude and commitment.

Consider, for example, the Torah's extraordinary praise of Chanoch, "Chanoch walked with God" (*Bereshit 5:22, 24*). An enigmatic *midrash* comments cryptically that he was a cobbler, "sewing shoes and unifying [God's] Name" (*Yalkut Re'uveni, "Bereshit"; Midrash Talpiyyot, "Chanoch"*). Rabbi Yisrael Salanter demanded: What could be laudable about such conduct? After all, the Tosefta and Gemara require day laborers to make various "shortcuts" in even mandatory prayers and blessings, to avoid effectively robbing their employers, who are paying for a full day's work (see *Tosefta Berachot 2:7–8* and *5:25*, and *Berachot 16a* and *46a*). Certainly, then, the Midrash would not praise Chanoch for "praying on the job," when a client was waiting and paying for his services! The response: Chanoch's "unifications" were not exercises in the obscure or abstract. On the contrary, he was unifying the reign of God with the earthly realm *of shoes* through focusing, with every stitch, on rendering his services as faithfully as possible by making the best pair of shoes he could (see *Michtav Me-Eliyyahu, I, 34–5*). *That* perspective is what the Torah calls "walking with God." Rabbi Ovadyah Seforno comments simply, "He walked in [God's] ways, bestowing good upon others through *tzedakah* and reproof" (commentary on *Bereshit 5:22*).

All of us should similarly strive to "unify God's Name": not by withdrawing into a realm of transcendence but by infusing every "stitch" of our worldly endeavors with a sense of and a dedication to Godliness—and, through it, perfection of His world. This is the all-encompassing nature of true *avodah*, that "all your deeds be for the sake of heaven." There is no "time out" from that mission. Even relaxation is ultimately a means to rejuvenation for renewed efforts. This is a commitment that involves everything.

S.F.: How does this relate to the role of the Torah and Torah study?

Rabbi Eisen: Recalling our earlier discussion of the extent to which we can know everything through Torah, we should consider the message of the penultimate *mishnah* of *Avot*:

> Delve into the Torah [literally, 'turn it over'] again and again, for everything is in it; and through it you will see, and grow old and worn through it, and do not depart from it, for you have no better way than it (*Avot 5:22*).

Although, as we saw, it is misguided to attempt to read Torah as a blueprint that transcends Creation, we are certainly obliged to read it as a users' manual that provides us with direction and instruction in *every aspect* of our lives in this world. Perhaps for this reason, Rashi comments that "*everything* is in it" in the sense "that *everything that you desire* you will find in it" (commentary *loc. cit.*) There are transcendent matters, outside the domain of that which one ought to desire in this world. But everything relevant to one's life in this world, which one *rightfully* desires, can be found through the Torah's guidance. In this light, the opening words of this *mishnah*. "*Hafoch bah vahafoch bah*," may be taken (homiletically) as a summons not only to "turn over" the Torah through incessant study but to "turn over" *oneself*—and be transformed—*through* the Torah.

Ultimately, this transformation must be all–encompassing. The concluding *baraita* of *Avot* expresses this final goal in cosmic, albeit cryptic, terms:

> Whatever the Holy One Blessed be He created in His world He created solely for His Honor; as it is said, 'All that is called by My Name and which I created for My Honor: I formed it; I made it' [*Yeshayahu 43:7*]. And it says, 'God will reign forever and ever' [*Shemot 15:17*] (*Avot 6:11*).

We are instantly struck by the apparent absurdity of the statement, which seems to explain God's motive for Creation, so to speak, as an egotistical preoccupation with self–glorification (God forbid!). After all, I surely would not fulfill any craving for honor by programming my computer to sing my praises, nor would my ego be boosted by listening to the program's execution. What possible satisfaction could accrue to God from the praises of a world He created?

Clearly, that is the point of the second verse quoted: "God will reign forever and ever"—unconditionally. He neither needs nor receives anything from the world He created. As we affirm daily in the familiar "*Adon Olam*" hymn, God is "the Eternal Lord, Who reigned before any creature was created . . . And, after everything ceases to be, He alone will reign awesomely." His dominion is in no way contingent on our actions. Therefore, Elihu rhetorically asks Iyyov, with words we paraphrase in the *Ne'ilah* service on Yom Kippur (see also *Moreh Ha–Nevochim 3:13*): "If you have sinned, how have you acted upon Him; and if your transgressions are multiplied, what have you done for Him? If you have been righteous, what have you given Him; or what will He take from your hand?" (*Iyyov 35:6–7*). So the *baraita* prods us to challenge it and ourselves: What is "His Honor"?

God transcends and encompasses everything; "His Honor" alludes to all that is Godly. In particular, from our perspective, God represents absolute Truth, absolute Justice, absolute Goodness and Righteousness—all that has abiding spiritual value. "His Honor" includes the glorifica-

tion of all of these. We could thus render the *baraita* as: "Whatever
the Holy One Blessed be He created in *the physical universe* He created
solely for *the honor of spirituality*." In other words, a *physical* universe
can never be self–justifying. Its existence can be justified only as the
means to some worthy *spiritual* end, realized through Torah. Just as
the world was created through the transcendent Torah of heaven, the
world could not continue to exist without our terrestrial Torah and
all it represents.

Therefore, regarding the Torah given to this world from Sinai, the
Midrash asserts, "Were it not for the Torah, the world would have
already reverted to formless void" (*Devarim Rabbah 8:5; Pesachim 68b,
Nedarim 32a*), and "once [Yisrael] said [at Sinai], 'We shall do and heed'
(*Shemot 24:7*), the world became firmly established" (*Midrash Tehillim
75:1*). Likewise, the Talmud and Midrash conclude, "The Holy One
Blessed be He made a condition with the work of Creation, stipulat-
ing, 'If Yisrael accepts the Torah, you [continue to] exist, and, if not,
I shall return you to formless void' " (*Shabbat 88a; Avodah Zarah 3a
and 5a; Tanchuma Bereshit:1*).

The implication here is certainly not that the continued existence
of the world depends on divine caprice but that the existence of the
world from its inception could be justified only as raw materials to be
elevated through Torah. A world left bereft of Torah would remain
substance without form: a hollow container with no abiding contents
to structure and uplift it. Similarly, the Sages characterize the first
millennia of this world's history (after Creation but before the millennia of Torah) as "two millennia of formless void" (*Sanhedrin 97a;
Avodah Zarah 9a*)—even though, superficially, the world was as struc-
tured as it is today. As Rashi notes, "since Torah was not yet given,
the world was *as if* formless" (commentary on *Sanhedrin, loc. cit.*). Structure versus formlessness is gauged not in terms of physical technicalities but in terms of an internal meaning that binds all the components
together in an organic whole. Without Torah, the world would have
never really left the state of formlessness.

In this light, let us recast your question about the role of Torah
and Torah study: Now that the Torah has been infused into this world,
what does it give us? We are familiar enough with the catechisms. Each
morning, we list Torah study among "the precepts for which no limit
is prescribed," extolling it as "surpassing all [the *mitzvot*]" (*Mishnah
Pei'ah 1:1* and the *baraita* quoted in *Shabbat 127a*, recited after "*Birchot*

Ha–Torah"), and we beseech God to "enlighten our eyes in Your Torah" (*Shacharit* service, "*Birkat Ahavah*"). Every evening, we declare that words of Torah "are our life and the length of our days, and we shall articulate them day and night" (*Arvit* service, "*Birkat Ahavah*"). And, at least three times daily, we pray that God "grant us our share in Your Torah" (concluding supplication of the "*Amidah*," based on *Avot 5:20*). Rambam summarizes that "no mitzvah among all the mitzvot . . . outweighs Torah study; rather, Torah study surpasses all the mitzvot" (*Mishneh Torah, Hilchot Talmud Torah 3:3*). But what is Torah study, which we claim to esteem so highly?

A crucial key lies in appreciating that our admiration of Torah study definitely does not reflect a preoccupation with sterile academics. On the contrary, Rambam (*loc. cit.*) explains the supremacy of Torah study by quoting the Gemara's conclusion to a debate on the relative greatness of *talmud* (study) and deed: "*Talmud* is greater, *because talmud* leads to deed" (*Kiddushin 40b*). The merit of *talmud* is not "*if*," "*when*," or "*insofar as*," it leads to deed; true *talmud* that does not lead to deed is a contradiction in terms. Likewise, the Mishnah teaches, "Study is not the essence, but deed" (*Avot 1:17*). Since not all "study" relates to practical *halachah*, "deed" cannot refer simply to direct *halachic* ramifications. Rather, the study itself is expected to alter the student fundamentally. As a changed person, *all* his deeds will inevitably be affected.

Therefore, warns the Midrash, "You [may] find a person reviewing *midrash*, *halachot*, and *agadot*, and if he possesses no fear of sin, he possesses nothing" (*Shemot Rabbah 30:14* and *40:1*). In Talmudic idiom, Torah is not simply learned but "acquired" ("*nikneit*"). Thus, the sixth chapter of *Avot*, whose theme is study of Torah, is "the Chapter of Acquisition of Torah" ("*Perek Kinyan Torah*"), not the chapter of Torah learning or study. Acquisition connotes an internalization process that transforms the acquirer.

This perspective may seem odd, given the frequent *mis*translation of "*talmud Torah lishmah*" ("Torah study for its own sake") as "knowledge for knowledge's sake" or "study for the sake of study." Yet, were "*talmud*" the antecedent of "*lishmah*" (i.e., "for *its* own sake" meaning "for the sake of *study*"), grammar would dictate use of the masculine "*lishmo*" to reflect the gender of *talmud*. The feminine "*lishmah*" indicates that the antecedent is the (feminine) Torah: "study of Torah *for the sake of Torah*." More generally, the Sages comment on Rabbi Yosei's

dictum: " 'All your deeds should be *for the sake of heaven'* (*Avot 2:12*)—
[This means] *for the sake of Torah*; as it is said, 'In all your ways, consider Him, and He will direct your paths' (*Mishlei 3:6*)" (*Avot De-Rabbi
Natan 17:7*). Rendering "*lishmah*" as "for the sake of Torah" is crucial
to understanding the true role of Torah study in our lives. But obviously further clarification is necessary: What does studying Torah "for
the sake of Torah" mean?

Any attempt to define "for the sake of Torah" must of course begin
by defining "Torah." We can easily discern that "*torah*"—from the same
root as "*hora'ah*" ("instruction")—means "teaching." But what, fundamentally, does the Torah teach? Our ready answer, as Maharal remarks,
is "that the Torah teaches and shows you the way of life" (*Tiferet Yisrael*,
Chapter 9, page 32). Rabbi Menachem Nachum of Chernobyl observes,
"The essential intention of engagement in the Torah is to lead to deed,
which is fulfillment of the mitzvot. Therefore, 'Torah' is so called: the
language of instruction on the 'way upon which they must go and the
deed that they must do' [*Shemot 18:20*], in fulfillment of the mitzvot"
(*Yismach Lev 13*). Within that context, however, the Gemara provides
a more specific reply:

> Expounded Rabbi Simlai: The Torah's beginning is loving–kind-
> ness, and its end is loving–kindness. Its beginning is loving–kind-
> ness; as it is written, 'God the Lord made coats of skin for Adam
> and his wife and clothed them' (*Bereshit 3:21*). And its end is lov-
> ing–kindness; as it is written, '[God] buried [Moshe] in the valley,
> [*Devarim 34:6*]" (*Sotah 14a*).

Clearly, the Gemara's message, beyond the individual examples cited,
is that the core of Torah is loving–kindness, which permeates it from
beginning to end. The Midrash adds that not only the Torah's beginning and end but also "its middle is loving–kindness" (*Tanchuma Va-
Yishlach:10; Kohelet Rabbah 7:2 [2]*).

Yet Rabbi Simlai's charitable assessment seems reductionistic. Is
the Torah simply a corpus of loving–kindness? What of all the laws it
mandates—not to mention the punishments it exacts? Maharal (see
Netivot Olam, "Netiv Gemilut Chasadim," Chapter 1, p. 150) interprets
"the Torah's beginning . . . and its end" as its primary intention and final goal, both oriented toward the world's ultimate goodness. His explanation of Rabbi Simlai's portrayal of Torah then hinges on equating such goodness with loving–kindness. This premise illuminates what

loving–kindness is. Since its essence is *giving*, what greater act of loving–kindness—of giving—could there be than giving us the Torah, all of which is intended "to remove evil and instate goodness" (Ibid) in the world?

Maharal's commentary surely strikes at the heart of the Gemara's lesson, appreciating how the message of loving–kindness permeates the totality of the Torah's content. However, Maharal does not explicitly address the specific examples Rabbi Simlai cites to bolster his thesis. What has God's preoccupation, so to speak with clothing the naked and burying the dead to do with the identity of the Torah?

The answer to this apparent riddle may lie in another passage that depicts God clothing the naked and burying the dead—and that immediately precedes Rabbi Simlai's exposition in the Gemara:

> Said Rabbi Chama ben Rabbi Chanina: What is [the meaning of] that which is written, 'Go after God your Lord' [*Devarim 13:5*]? Is it then possible for a person to go after God's Presence? Is it not already said, "For God your Lord is a consuming fire' [Ibid 4:24]? Rather, 'go after' the attributes of the Holy One Blessed be He: Just as He clothes the naked . . . you, too, clothe the naked. The Holy One Blessed be He visited the sick . . . you, too, visit the sick. The Holy One Blessed be He consoled mourners . . . you, too, console mourners. The Holy One Blessed be He buried the dead . . . you, too, bury the dead (*Sotah 14a*).

It is ludicrous to imagine that Rabbi Chama related to either the mandate to "go after God" or the analogy of God to "a consuming fire" in physical terms. However, while he obviously posited an allegorical understanding of the mandate to follow God, he recognized the same implication in the analogy of God to fire. As we noted earlier, likening God to "a consuming fire" suggests that any attempt to grasp the divine *intellectually* would be as ill–fated as an attempt to grasp fire *physically*. Is it possible, then, for a person to follow God in any meaningful intellectual quest to comprehend Him and thus attain spiritual self–realization? Rabbi Chama's reply: We can never comprehend what God *is*, but we can apprehend, through the Torah, how He *manifests* Himself in this world, as the basis of our quest for spirituality and our relationship with Him.

More generally, in describing the entire Torah as permeated with loving–kindness based upon divine example, the Gemara reveals to us the underlying purpose of the Torah in our lives. The supreme goal of all of Torah—and of all divine service—is the concept of *imitatio dei*: to emulate God as He manifests Himself to us in this world *and thereby to become Godly ourselves.* Recall the verse cited by *Avot De-Rabbi Natan* (quoted earlier) to vindicate its equating "for the sake of heaven" with "for the sake of Torah": "In all your ways, consider Him, and He will direct your paths" (*Mishlei 3:6*). More than any alternative, those "ways" and "paths" are of loving-kindness, of unbridled, Godly giving to everything around us in the entire world. This is the essence of what the Torah gives us, because this is the essence of what Torah is, from beginning to end.

Armed with the Gemara's definition of "Torah," we are equipped to explore its definition of "Torah for its own sake." We consider a perplexing comment on a familiar verse from Mishlei:

> Said Rabbi Elazar: What is [the meaning of] that which is written, 'She opened her mouth in wisdom, and a Torah of loving-kindness was upon her tongue' [*Mishlei 31:26*]? Is there then a Torah of loving-kindness and a Torah that is not of loving-kindness? However, Torah for its own sake is a Torah of loving-kindness; [Torah] that is not for its own sake is a Torah that is not of loving-kindness. There are those who say: Torah [in order] to teach it is a Torah of loving-kindness; [Torah] that is not [in order] to teach it is a Torah that is not of loving-kindness (*Sukkah 49b*).

The Gemara's very premise appears inscrutable. First, the question seems gratuitous: What problem lay in assuming at the outset that there exist "a Torah of loving-kindness and a Torah that is not of loving-kindness"? Second, the answers seem pointless: What difficulty have they resolved? But third and most vexing, what significance can there be to Torah "that is not for its own sake"? Such Torah, we are warned elsewhere, is "a potion of death":

> We are taught, Rabbi Benaah used to say: [Regarding] anyone who engages in Torah for its own sake, his Torah becomes for him a potion of life; as it is said, 'It is a tree of life to those who take hold of it' [*Mishlei 3:18*] . . . And [regarding] anyone who engages in Torah that is not for its own sake, his Torah becomes for him a potion of death (*Taanit 7a*).

True Torah—the basis of our connection to God, Who is the Source of all life—is necessarily "a tree of *life* to those who take hold of it."

Without this connection, Torah inevitably withers into "a potion of
death." What redeeming value could Rabbi Elazar possibly ascribe to
such a Torah?

Upon further reflection, that is exactly Rabbi Elazar's message.
Why, he asks, would *Mishlei* refer to "a Torah of loving-kindness"?
Since, as we have seen, Torah is loving-kindness by definition, the
expression is as redundant as a reference to a three-sided triangle! Could
there then be any Torah other than one of loving-kindness? Isn't any
alternative a contradiction in terms?

That is precisely the point of the Gemara's responses. Lest we be
fooled by an apparent "Torah" that is not of loving-kindness, the
Gemara warns us that such a counterfeit, however convincing, *is not
truly Torah*. "Anyone who says he has *only* Torah [without fulfilling it
(Rashi)] . . . has not *even* Torah" (*Yevamot 109b*). Worse than a contradiction, such "Torah" is a caricature. Like "Torah that is not for its
own sake," it is a fraud. After all, could authentic Torah, "a tree of
life," be transformed into "a potion of *death*"? Only a "Torah" severed
from giving, and thus from the Supreme Giver, could reek of death.
Even the flaw of learning Torah "not [in order] to teach it" may be
sufficient grounds for such disqualification. The qualities of "[being] one
who learns in order to teach and [being] one who learns in order to
do" are simultaneously both prerequisite to the acquisition of Torah
(*Avot 6:6*) and characteristic of those who have already acquired it, true
Torah scholars (*Derech Eretz Zota 3:4*). Torah is inexorably enmeshed
in giving. "Torah for its own sake" is necessarily "a Torah of loving-
kindness."

In this light, we appreciate some important equations. On the one
hand, the Midrash lauds "anyone who engages in Torah" as equivalent
to "one who does loving-kindness with the Lord" (*Yalkut Shimoni
Tehillim:767*). Moreover, the Talmud concludes, "Anyone who engages
in Torah and loving-kindness merits dwelling in the shade of God's
Presence" (*Yerushalmi Taanit 4:2 [18b]; Yerushalmi Megillah 3:6 [25b]*).
On the other hand, the Midrash cautions, "Anyone who denies loving-kindness is as one who denies the essence [of belief in God]" (*Kohelet
Rabbah 7:1 [4]; Midrash Shemuel 23:8*). Similarly, the Talmud warns, "Said
Rabbi Huna: Anyone who engages in Torah alone [without loving-
kindness] resembles one who has no God" (*Avodah Zarah 17b*). Even
more emphatically, the Midrash states, "It would have been better for
one who learns not [in order] to do not to have been created" (*Sifra* on

Vayikra 26:3; Vayikra Rabbah 35:7). Correspondingly, regarding those whose conduct is not refined by their Torah study, the Talmud quotes Rava's saying: "It would have been better for anyone who acts not '*lishmah*' not to have been created" (*Berachot 17a*).

Torah study "for its own sake" is not simply a good idea. It emerges as the basis of life itself, toward which we are each obliged to dedicate our efforts uncompromisingly. Insofar as humanity's most exalted goal is to become Godly dispensers of loving–kindness, Torah "for its own sake" provides the means to reach it. Since this is the pinnacle of potential human achievement, which inheres in each of us, such acquisition of Torah is the ultimate self-actualization.

It is in this sense that we can begin to understand the role of "Torah study, [which] surpasses all the mitzvot" (*Mishneh Torah, Hilchot Talmud Torah 3:3*). The Midrash comments, "Because the Torah teaches a person how he should do the will of the Omnipresent One, the reward of study is great" (*Bemidbar Rabbah 14:9*). Certainly, "Study is not the essence, but deed" (*Avot 1:17*). Fundamentally, "the object of wisdom is repentance and good deeds" (*Berachot 17a*) and, without such a commitment to practice, "wisdom does not endure" (*Avot 3:9,17*). But imagine a talented young student who, stirred by earnest altruism, decides to drop out of school to solicit contributions door to door to feed the world's hungry. While we should genuinely encourage such idealism, we still ought to discourage the plan. After all, by investing in a good education, the student's eventual capacity to alleviate global hunger and poverty will be vastly augmented. With so much potential seething within, why sell oneself—and all the world—so short? In our collective, ongoing mission to perfect ourselves and the entire world, "*talmud* is greater, *because talmud* leads to deed" (*Kiddushin 40b*). That is the Torah's definitive role.

S.F.: Moving to the realm of operative conclusions, how does this relate to your perception of the situation of the Jewish people now and the question of what it should be doing now to serve God in practice in historical terms?

Rabbi Eisen: Once we realize what the Torah is and what is entailed by the mission with which it charges us, the operative conclusions are inevitable. A Torah of loving–kindness necessarily impacts upon every aspect of our lives and colors our relationship with everyone and everything with which we share the world. The key word is: *responsi-*

bility. The Midrash expresses this as a warning: "When the Holy One Blessed be He created the first man . . . He said to him, 'See how becoming and praiseworthy My creations are! And all that I created, I created for you. Pay attention that you not become corrupt and destroy My world!' " (*Kohelet Rabbah 7:13*). Likewise, from God's decision to create man singly, the Mishnah derives that "each and every one is *obligated* to say, '*For me* the world was created' " (*Mishnah Sanhedrin 4:5*). This is not a prerogative but a mandate: Each and every one of us must bear responsibility for the world created on our behalf. Life is a gift *with* "strings attached."

The implications are many. One cannot be sensitive to a Torah of loving–kindness and indifferent to such causes as feeding the world's hungry, curing dreaded diseases, advancing universal peace and brotherhood, protecting endangered natural habitats, and healing past ravages of war, poverty, oppression, and environmental depredation. Properly conceived, consideration for all of these is not only compatible with concern for specifically Jewish issues. Ultimately, regard for both sets of causes stems from the same all–encompassing commitment to study the Torah "for its own sake" and realize its mission in the world created for "each and every one."

For all of us, the first step toward perfecting the world is perfecting ourselves. On one level, such self–help stems from the recognition that we, too, should be among the beneficiaries of our own loving–kindness. Thus, the Midrash applies the verse "A man of kindness bestows good upon his own soul" (*Mishlei 11:17*) to Hillel, who, upon departing from his students–would go (by his description) "to do a mitzvah . . . to wash in the bathhouse . . . to bestow loving–kindness upon this wayfarer [his soul] in the home [his body]" (*Vayikra Rabbah 34:3*). The same Hillel cautions us similarly in the Mishnah: "If I am not for myself, who will be for me?" (*Avot 1:14*). On a deeper level, only through such a commitment to self–love can we comprehend, much less fulfill, the Torah's essential mandate to "love your fellow *as [you love] yourself*" (*Vayikra 19:18*). One who lacks self–love will be incapable of bestowing love upon others and altogether unable to commit to refining oneself and the world. Finally, I reiterate the example of the altruistic student whom we should encourage to invest in a good education, not as a distraction from idealistic pursuits but as the best means to their lasting fulfillment. One cannot succeed in a giant leap without attending to all the small steps that are its prerequisites. By extension, *self*-actualization through studying Torah "for its own sake" trains and transforms us, to become Godly dispensers of loving–kindness for the benefit of the entire world.

Echoing this twin focus, Rabbi Yehudah Ha–Levi presents, on the one hand, his portrayal of the archetypal servant of God: "He does not separate from the world . . . and does not disdain life . . . On the contrary, he loves the world and longevity. . . ." (*Ha–Kozari 3:1*). In short, he is *worldly*; his gaze is directed *outward*. On the other hand, this realism stems from realistic *self*-appraisal and *inner* growth. Adjacently, Rabbi Yehudah Ha–Levi describes the archetypal pietist (with obvious allusion to Plato's *Republic*): "The pietist is the man who rules over his state [his inner self], who gives all its citizens [his faculties] their daily sustenance and provides all their needs in proper measure, and he treats them all justly, neither cheating nor overindulging any of them" (Ibid 3:3). "And he is the man who is fit to rule, for, were he at the head of a state, he would treat it justly, just as he dealt justly with his body and spirit" (Ibid 3:5). The capacity eventually to perfect the world hinges first on learning to perfect oneself, one's household, and one's community, one step at a time.

In conclusion, I'd like to respond in this light to your question about the situation of the Jewish people now. We should remember the preceding message when reaching out to all our brothers and sisters who, by dint of ignorance, feel estranged from their historic mission as Jews. Only "words that come from the heart enter the [listener's] heart" (Rabbi Moshe ibn Ezra, *Shirat Yisrael*, page 156). Clearly, if we have not yet dedicated our efforts to self–refinement, within, then we will have little or nothing to offer those still outside. A caricature of Judaism cannot be expected to encourage thoughtful commitment. Still, people sense instinctively that life has some deeper significance; in their lives, they cry out, often unconsciously, for a sense of meaning and purpose. As a reservist lecturer in the IDF Rabbinate, I am continually struck by the genuine thirst we all share for spirituality—especially by thoughtful young people's attentiveness to and interest in words of Torah, properly presented. A great rabbi of the last generation would reportedly reply to protests of atheism from his disputants, "Tell me about the 'God' in whom you *don't* believe; I'm sure I don't believe in him either."

Furthermore, we must all appreciate that advancing the mission of Torah is a process of self–realization, not self–abnegation. Moshe summarizes, "Now, Yisrael, what does God your Lord ask of you: but to be in awe of God your Lord, to go in all His ways, and to love Him, and to serve God your Lord with all your heart and all your soul; to keep the commandments of God and His statutes, which I am commanding you today . . ." (*Devarim 10:12–13*). And we wonder: Is that a small request? What more could God possibly ask? But this list of divine expectations concludes with two more small, crucial words: ". . . *letov lach* [for your own good]" (Ibid). And that, of course, is precisely the point. *What does God your Lord ask of you*—demands Moshe—*other than that which is for your own good?* Comments Ramban (and many others), "He asks nothing of you that is for His need; instead . . . all is 'for your own good' " (commentary *loc. cit.*). As Rabbi Yehudah Ha-Levi states, "All the [divine] service of the pietist is through happiness [i.e., self-fulfillment and satisfaction], not through self-negation, as we explained above" (*Ha-Kozari 3:5*). As the users' manual enables the customer to get the most out of one's purchase, the Torah enables us to get the most out of life.

To the not yet committed Jew—whose life may be dedicated to worthy, altruistic ideals—our salutation should never be "you are bad"; rather, "you (like all of us) can be even better." Don't sell yourself short! A life dedicated to lofty goals is certainly vested with meaning on various levels. We submit that Torah can infuse even more. Humanistic values alone may address life on a societal plane. But, while human beings are innately social, they are not *only* social beings. Torah addresses the totality of life, in all its aspects, potentially infusing meaning into everything we do, everywhere. It summons us relentlessly to be all we can be, always.

In that light, Torah provides us all with the ultimate challenge: to uplift ourselves as means to uplifting all of humanity. "I, God, have called you in righteousness and shall hold your hand; and I shall safeguard you and give you for a covenant of the people, for a light of the nations . . . I have given you as a light of the nations, that My salvation may be to the end of the earth . . . And nations will go by your light, and kings by the gleam of your shining" (*Yeshayahu 42:6, 49:6,* and *60:3*). By rising to the challenge, we have the capacity to raise—and redeem—the entire world.

Mimi Feigelson

Mimi Feigelson is one of the most popular and respected teachers in the "English learning" scene in Jerusalem. She teaches adult education in Yakar and in Pardes Institutes. She also teaches at the Maaleh film school, and in a number of other formats. She is recognized as an expert in the reading of Hasidic texts, primarily of her beloved Master, the Mei ha–Shiloah, the Ishbitzer. Her early training and introduction to these texts, and to the living Torah of Hasidism came through being a student of Rabbi Shlomo Carlebach z"l. American born, and having made *aliyah* with her parents at an early age, she speaks like a native both in Hebrew as well as in English. This contributes to her power to connect diverse worlds in Israel. Her teaching is imbued with a deep faith in Hashem and the teaching is given over with a true *simcha* of mitzvah.

CҀ ৪〇

S.F.: Could you describe your present teaching duties?

Mimi Feigelson: I spend most of my time learning and studying. Most of my teaching I do at Yakar, which is an institute for Jewish learning, a Beit Midrash, though I call it a *shteibl* for the twentieth century. Its main goal is to create a relationship between the outside world and the inside world. In other words, there is not a page of Gemara or a page of Rishon or an Acharon which is not completely alive, and which is not in direct dialogue with what's happening now. Learning it is living it, helping us try to understand what kind of reality we are living in. It helps us know how to make some sense of reality and function in the world we are living in. At Yakar, I coordinate both the woman's Beit Midrash and teach Hasidut in different sectors. There is a learning community three mornings a week focusing on "Self, Other, and Community." Also, I teach both the Anglo–Saxon English speaking group, and the Israeli group. Interestingly enough, I speak the language of the Israelis, and I am learning the language of the Americans. The Americans once in a while say something that I don't understand: a phrase, someone's name, a reference. That's the price of growing up in Israel. But we're learning. And there's a Hasidic Beit Midrash. Once a week, I also teach in Pardes on Hasidut. It's only my second year, but it's really great. The students are fabulous. I am also teaching at Maaleh, which is a religious film college. This year they decided that they wanted a Beit Midrash in the school, so one day a week I am there. I also teach Hasidut there. And that's a very different set–up from what I have

119

taught before. The students are younger, very Israeli, very sure of themselves. A lot of them are not used to thinking for themselves and understanding their voice is a valid voice. For instance I had a student a month ago to whom I said "I don't care to hear what Rambam has to say about Yirat Hashem; I want to know what you think about it." Not knowing what to do she spent the rest of the class in complete silence. Sometimes I find there is a moment of silence because I am thinking about what they said. They are a little bit uncomfortable with that silence. So I say to them, "I am thinking about what you are saying. I understand that you are not used to people who are actually interested in what you are saying." Last week there was such a moment of silence and one of the women said "We are with you."

Otherwise I have been doing quite a few things in religious high schools. I think they are looking for women who are spiritual and learned, and yet not afraid of using the word God when they talk. So I think that puts me in good place, so like before the Yamim Noraim (High Holy Days) I went into the high school I once studied at. I knew before Yamim Noraim the way it used to be here. I grew up here. Before Yamim Noraim someone would come in all dressed in black and tell us that we are horrible sinners, and we are all going to burn unless we do *teshuvah*. Year after year they made the same mistake of putting 400 kids in a gymnasium with this rabbi in black telling us we were sinners. Thank God that the ulpana staff has realized that's not what it's all about. Because at Yamim Noraim they spend so much time they have asked me to do something in *shul davvening*, on *telfillah*, *kavvanah*, and meditation. If they are going to spend all these hours in *shul*, it's necessary to bring something meaningful to those girls. So I will do that kind of stuff as well. I have the same kind of set-up in Pelech. They want a different kind of voice, a Hasidic voice, a more spiritual voice. They have even asked me if I would do a couple of classes on *zemirot* for Shabbat. And what is Shabbat all about? How does one create a Shabbat? Last week I did an evening for fourth grade girls and their mothers in Efrat. They did a month of learning on "compassion" and "*ahavta reacha ka-mocha*" ("Loving your neighbors as yourself"). I did an hour of songs, stories, and some teachings for 50 girls and their mothers. So I wear different hats, and they are all very different. This year especially I am trying on all these different hats.

S.F.: It sounds wonderful.

Mimi Feigelson: It's great.

S.F.: What is your background? And how especially did you begin learning Hasidut?

Mimi Feigelson: When I was 7 years old, I got a Dr. Seuss book in which kids fill in all these details about themselves: the way they look, their favorite hobby, what they want to be. When I look back at what I wrote it says "teacher." There is an expression in Hebrew, "ha tovim letayis," ("the best go to the Air Force"). I guess I was brought up with the feeling that I wanted to make difference in the world, through teaching. In life, a lot of what we feel is that "it's a no choice situation." The *Kadosh Baruch Hu* does not ask us whether we want to come here or not. We are here. So now what do we do? A lot of what I do is not a question of what I chose to do, but rather what I need to be doing, or what I should be doing. It's the same with teaching. If I asked myself whether I could do it or not, I would not be able to do it. Who am I to get up and teach? Who am I to play a role and say I have an opinion? But I know that I have no choice but to do it. And I know too that what my teachers gave me, they gave me not to hold on to, but to pass on. This has always been my blessing in life, to be a teacher.

Since the age of sixteen, I have always had a rebbe in my life. I don't think I ever questioned or thought there would be anything else other than teaching. As for Hasidut, I think at some level in my heart I was always drawn to it. For years my dream was to be a history professor. Once I met Reb Shlomo, that dream shifted. I was sixteen, very involved in Gesher, which is the movement for bringing the religious and non–religious closer. One of my *madrichim* in Gesher was Yehoshua Witt, was his right–hand man, his *talmid muvhak*. He took me to the *Moshav*, to meet Reb Shlomo a couple of times. The truth is that, at the age of sixteen, I was very Israeli, and I didn't use English at all. I was definitely on the way to being very *frum*. I returned to Modiin more than once. On the one hand, I knew that there was a lot of spiritual truth there. On the other hand, I didn't understand what was going on, literally didn't understand what was going on. Reb Shlomo would speak and I would begin to put together pieces of sentences, but I could never hold on to it. And in terms of my Yiddishkeit, I was the only person who walked around the *moshav* wearing a "Don't touch me" sign. So the first time I saw him, I tried to hide myself in the back corner of the *Shul* as he was walking by because, God forbid, he might touch me. Between those two things, there was no other world I could hold on to.

Then I spent another seven years traveling around in Haredi land. I finished high school in Rehovot, did 2 years of national service, then went to the Hebrew University for my B.A. in special education and history. I thought special education was what people needed to go out into the world. If you want to be a responsible mother, you have to know something of psychology, something about the philosophy of education. Also, I had a dream at the time that I was going to have a foster family, have all these children. So the way I could model myself best was to be in special education. At about the age of 22 I realized that, if the language I was born to was English, if I had the *zekhut* of being born near the Major Deegan passing Yankee Stadium—and they almost named me Ruth after Babe Ruth—then this was my *yerusha* ("inheritance"). Who can say that a ball hit out of the stadium didn't become a baby? I realized, maybe there was gift in it, not something to resent. Because when people used to ask me when my parents came on *aliyah*, I would say "eight years too late" because I was eight when I came. In fact, I grew up knowing we were moving to Israel. My parents decided when I was 2 years old. I practiced my Israeli accent as a 5–year–old. Then it happened, and I realized that I was never going to be Haredi.

S.F.: How did you realize that?

Mimi Feigelson: It was just that I felt I wasn't *b'simcha* in my *avodat Hashem*. I think that was the bottom line. I didn't think I was coming closer to God, and I was just miserable then that there had to be a different place of the truth for me. I realized I was never going to be Haredi no matter how much I tried. You know to this day, there's a part of me that holds on to it.

Then, I realized that being born in the States was also a gift. The fact is I do all this teaching in English. When things finally came together, I realized that English wasn't *muktsah* American culture, and being born in America and having an American passport weren't the worst things in the world, which I grew up thinking. I remember my grandfather would stay with us 6 months a year, 3 months around Rosh Hashanah, and 3 months around Pesach. I remember us having a conservation about which one of my passports I'd give up if I had to. I told him it would be my American, and he would not talk to me for days. The truth is, when I walk into a class and speak English, the American students think I am one of them because I have an American accent. It takes a while until they find out that I am not, but during that while they have found out already that I am okay. It works, by the way, for the Israelis as well. In Hebrew, I speak like a true Israeli. I actually end up having the best of both worlds. And when I teach in English if I do not know a word, my students help me.

So I went back to Reb Shlomo. When I did, it was, first of all, not as if I were the new kid on the block, because I had been there 9 years before and had maintained some kind of relationship with Yehoshua. In those days, if you asked me what time it was, I would have thought that you had asked me a personal question. So when he would ask me to come and visit, it would never dawn on me to do it. Still I was a face, with a name and a context and past. So I immediately moved to the center of the circle. But I understood that what I was getting from Reb Shlomo wasn't sufficient. It wasn't sufficient for me to sit, learning with him for 3 hours and really feel that God loves me. Once Reb Shlomo moved on to the States, or to his next stop, then what? I knew I had to gain my own access to these sources.

S.F.: It wasn't enough to sit and learn through Reb Shlomo?

Mimi Feigelson: I knew I had to have my own personal relationship with these rebbes. Reb Shlomo gave me the knowledge of the back door. Who uses the back door? Only family. Until then, I felt that you have to use the front door and that's it, or you remain on the outside. One of my strongest childhood memories is Rosh Hashanah–Yom Kippur *davvening in* Yeshivat Ha-Darom. It's a *yeshiva Tikhonit*, but all the rabbis, the *ramim*, are Haredim. They always bring a *shaliach tsibbur* (Prayer leader) Haredi for the *Yamim Noraim*. I remember sitting upstairs pouring my guts out. I also knew that the *shaliach tsibbur* was pouring his heart out. It was the most amazing intense *davvening*. I always used to feel that, when *Ne'ilah* came, that was it. It was over. The gates shut and that was it. And the *shaliach tsibbur*—I can hear him today pouring out his heart over the *Asara Horgei ha-Malchut*, Rabbi Akiva. As for the "glory," you could hear by his voice the beauty of the *Kohen*. When those gates closed, that was it; it was over for me.

And what did Reb Shlomo teach us? He used to teach, in the name of Rabbi Meir Parmishlan, "The gates are locked, but you know what? They are locked behind you. And you are locked in." And that's what Reb Shlomo gave me, a sense of a living Torah. That I know when Reb Shlomo said "Rabbah" when he said "Abbaye" and when he said "Rabbi Yochanan ben Zakkai" and "Reb Levi Yitzhak" and the "Seer of Lublin," they were really alive for him. When I came to Reb Shlomo, I did not even know who the Ishbitzer was. Today there is not a moment of my life when I am not having a conversation with him. This year I did a Hasidic evening for the Film School. I went with a friend of mine, and because I am a woman, and there would be singing, we decided to have someone else with me. Yossi and I were sitting and waiting because they were late. I had with me a notebook with all the teaching I had from Reb Shlomo. So I said to Yossi, I have *mazal* coming to me tonight, "It is gimmel b'Cheshvan." And there I see in the notebook the entry from gimmel from Cheshvan 10 years earlier. On the side, I see written "Ishbitzer?"—with a question mark. I said "Yossi, tonight 10 years ago I learned who the Ishbitzer was. This is my tenth birthday." So what did Reb Shlomo give me? He gave me my way in.

My justification for watching television is that I always learn my most profound things about my relationship with God through watching television. I remember once watching a movie with Mary Tyler Moore in which she is a nun doing community service in some clinic. One day she is in the clinic when an autistic girl holding a doll walks in with her mommy. Something in her behavior made the doctor realize that her autism was not the beginning and the end of that child's story. So he took the doll out of the girl's hand and the little girl started to cry. Then Mary Tyler Moore, the nun, was holding the doll and the doctor was holding the girl. He said to her, "All you have to do is ask for the doll." And the viewer saw the hands of a clock on the wall moving hour after hour after hour. And the little girl was screaming hysterically, the doctor holding her in his arms, caressing and supporting her. All he said was "All you have to do is ask." This goes on for about 7 hours, until finally she stopped crying and asked for the doll. That's how I felt. I was autistic in terms of my relationship with God. There He was, holding and caressing me all those years as I was crying, completely autistic. And Reb Shlomo in some way enabled me to crack it open. All of a sudden I could have a relationship with God. This doesn't mean that life is easy. This doesn't mean that life is great.

What it means is that we are a family.

S.F.: So how did you began that process of learning and acquiring by yourself?

Mimi Feigelson: Two things happened. I turned to him and asked, for what he teaches, where are the sources? And there were times he would tell me and I would look it up. I knew I understood what he taught. I knew I understood the words of Reb Nachman I spent hours and hours and hours learning. In the beginning it was by myself. I would sit and read over my notes from Reb Shlomo. Then I would go and look at the *Mei Shiloah*, or at Rebbe Nachman. I would sit in front of the books sometimes and cry. I didn't understand where they were coming from. So that's how I started. Then I started learning with Yehoshua once a week, and also decided that I was going to change my major at the university. Instead of continuing to do my masters degree in history, I was going to move to the Jewish Philosophy Department to learn Hasidut. I knew that would force me to sit and learn. So I started doing a degree in Hasidut. I would say, to their merit, that as despicable as the university can be, it was very flexible with me. I spent a lot of time learning by myself and a lot of time learning in *chevruta*. There were years that I had a *chevruta* (learning companion) every day. There was one year when a lot of people wanted to learn with me, and this is a *beracha* in its own right. So I said that the condition is "You have to come to my house." Every day someone else came and learned, Or Meir and Tanyah. That's the only way it happens. That is to sit and to learn. If you sit and learn and don't understand, then you cry. Sometimes the tears will make the letters move a little bit.

S.F.: I don't know if you relate to this issue, that of a woman learning, especially in the hasidic world.

Mimi Feigelson: How can I not relate to it? I asked Rabbi Rosen a couple of weeks ago, "What does it mean that all our rebbes are not in the world?" We live in the Hasidic world and we don't live in the Hasidic world. I don't live in the Hasidic world of 5757, of 1997, but I live in Kotsk, in Ishbitz, in Berditchev, in Radzhyn, in Lublin. I don't live here. Is my rebbe the current Gerer Rebbe or the Sifat Emet? Is my rebbe Rabbi Yaacov Leiner who lives in Brooklyn or the Mei Shiloach? Is Rabbi Levi Yitzhak not my rebbe? He is my rebbe. So I said to Rabbi

Rosen, it's not a question of whether when I get up there, I am going to burn in hell or not. I am surely going to burn in hell. The only question is when I get up there, and all the rebbes are standing there, who's going to be first one to light the match? And that's what it is. But could I do it differently? I couldn't. Maybe it's the biggest *tikkun* in the world. I think that in some way it is, as painful as it might be for them up there right now. The Hasidic court wasn't the place for a woman. If I was a woman then I wouldn't have the access to them I have today. I wouldn't have had then the kind of conversations with the Mei Shiloah I have today.

S.F.: It would seem to me that the fact that you are capable of having the conversations means that you should have them. But I am no authority. I just wonder if it is a burden for you.

Mimi Feigelson: Just on the light side. Someone asked my *chevruta* if I live alone. And he said "No, she lives with twenty–five men who have been dead for 200 years." It's completely true. And it could not be any other way. They would not open their souls to me in the way they did if they did not want as there. When I went to Berditzhev and was *davvening* at Rebbe Levi Yitzhak's grave, and it was *Erev Shabbos*, I lit candles that they should still be burning when Shabbos came in. When I closed my eyes, I could see him in front of me. So if he didn't want me there, I wouldn't be there. I wouldn't be able to do it. To be honest, there is nothing more intimate than a relationship with *chevruta*. What this means is that there has to be complete clarity as to why you are learning together. The cause of *shem shemayim* has to be before your eyes 100 percent all the time. And people need to be very respectful about people's space, because of that.

S.F.: At this point and at your level, this is not a problem.

Mimi Feigelson: I would like to believe so. But *chevruta* is a kind of partnership. It has to be clear. Now there are some people who won't do it. There are some men who won't learn with women and I have to respect it. It's my loss; it's their loss. Yet, as I have said, I have been very fortunate throughout the years to have wonderful *chevruta mamash*. Two years ago I had a *chevruta* with Yoni Gordis. We learned together based on a learning program that Rabbi Shlomo created. Yoni and I spent 5 days together learning from 8:30 to 4:00. At 8:30 we learned Zohar on the *parashat*. From 9:00 to 12:30, we learned *halachah*, then took an hour's break. Then we learned Gemara and after that Hasidut. We hardly spent any time together outside of what we learned. But it was clear that our prime quality time that year was spent with each other. No one got from me what he got from me, and no one got from him what I got from him. Although we are close friends, dear friends, our focus really was on the learning. So that's why I believe that it is possible, that it can really be done with *kedushah*. So long as the *Shechinah* is there. If I didn't believe so, I wouldn't do it.

S.F.: How do you understand the concept of *avodat Hashem*?

Mimi Feigelson: Today, the last day of classes, when I was teaching the *meor Aynayim* on the *parashat*, it was important for me that they understand what we were dealing with this whole semester. If they think that the purpose was to gain knowledge of what the *Meor HaAynayim* thinks on this or that *pasuk*, then I have failed. What I did was bring them a piece from the Piasetzna Rebbe on "Vayetze." And he brings the *Pasuk* when Yaakov wakes up from his dream and says "*Achen yesh Elokim b'makom hazeh, v'anochi lo yadati.*" Rashi brings there I did not know that "*loyadati*" is "*yashanti*" ("I slept"). But he also brings that Yaakov possibly reached Haran and said that it's possible that there is a place where my forefathers *davvened* where I did not *davven*, and therefore he came back. So when he went to sleep that night, did he not know that there is God in this place? Of course he knew. So what is this "*lo yadati*"? So he goes into this explanation of what *Yaakov Avenu* is saying: "And what is he saying? He is saying 'I did not know *anochi*' and what is "*anochi*"? It is your core. It's your *shoresh neshamah*, (root of the soul), the core of your being." He says there is information that we know with our mind. Just as we see things with our eyes, and hear things with our ears, we know things with our mind. But that means that we know things that are fully external to us. It also means that we could sit and learn a whole day, and know it through our mind. But then he tells an anecdote about something, and that happened to him all the time. He said, "Sometimes you learn something and you hear something. And everything else that you know and learn that day is all part of it." And you do everything you can do, spiritual gymnastics, to connect everything to that one thought. Why? Because that's where you are alive. He says that's what *anochi* is. And 'anochi' from

Eseret Ha–Dibrot in *Massekhet Shabbat* says, "Out of my soul I wrote and I gave." So it's a question of *mesirut nefesh*.

"If you ask me what *avodat Hashem* is in a year, I do not know what my answer will be. But if you ask me today about what it is, it is about *mesirut nefesh*, about willingly giving your soul over to God. And whatever it is you are doing, it is not on the outside. It says *"v'lo zachar et Yoseph Va'yish kachehu."* ("Someone is standing in front of us and they don't even exist for us.") Why is it that there are people whom we can still continue to talk to although they are not here. Because it is not dependent on our eyes and ears. It's dependent on our soul. That's what *avodat Hashem* is all about. Whether we know one piece more or less of *Meor HaAynayim*, that's not what its all about. I told a student a few weeks ago that "What the Rambam is talking about is not what I am asking you about now. I am asking you about what *Yirat Hashem* is for you." But that's what *avodat Hashem* is about, *mesirut nefesh* and *kedushat ha–chayim*. It's about bringing Hashem into our life with every step that we take. It's knowing that we are not separate from him; we are one with Him. And I *mamash* 'feel' it very strongly. We give our life and it's over. It's not one time, and it's over. But every moment there is an opportunity for *mesirut nefesh*. It occurs when we are with people, being able to give ourselves over. I said to my students at the beginning of the year, "There are no exams. There are no papers. I ask of you only one thing. You are sitting here for an hour and one half, so I want you to be present for an hour and one half, otherwise it's *gezel*."

I think I told you the story about my Sukkah this year. I love Sukkot. I love going and buying the *arba minnim*. I love the building of the Sukkah, the whole agony and ecstasy experience. I go down to Mea Shearim and buy my etrog and lulav—and I know that this involves my eyes and my mind and my heart. But it's hard, as a woman, since most places are not so accessible, especially when women know what they are talking about. Each year I sit and go over the *halachot*. It has to be real. But when I was picking my *hadassim*, some guy handed me a note that said, "Women do not have a *chiyyuv* for Sukkot and they should not be in the Sukkah at all." So when I put up my Sukkah, it was really hard for me. And I said I should not be doing this by myself. The worst was the *schach* (Sukkot booth covering). It just kept on slipping. But I said 'You know, this is it. It's just like the *chuppah* above your head. It's one thing you cannot get your act together with.'

So I said, "*Ribbono shel olam.*" As much as I love my Sukkah, next year I am not doing it by myself. I said, "Either I am doing it with my husband or I am not doing it at all." Well, that was Wednesday night. On Thursday night there was a wedding. On Friday, the last 2 hours before Shabbat, I was putting up my Sukkah decorations and was completely high from it. So I said "*Kudsha Berech Hu,*" I cannot live without it. This year there was no Shabbat Chol HaMoed, so the first night I went to my rabbi. I come back on Shabbat evening. My Sukkah was beautiful. When I walked in, I felt as if was there was nothing in my life that I was missing. That's it. There's nothing I want or need. That's it. You are where you are.

S.F.: Another question that I expect you to answer in 5 minutes you are answering with your whole life. How would you describe what you have learned from the Ishbitzer?

Mimi Feigelson: I can't imagine my life without the Ishbitzer. I can't imagine my relation to God without the Ishbitzer. I feel he has given me the most ways how to understand how God wants me to live my life in this world, and how on the one hand, he demands from me complete obedience to Torah and mitzvot, and how on the other hand, this *anochi,* that the Piasetzna is talking about and Rav Kook talks about in *Bakashat Ani Atzmi.* He never lets me off the hook on either. He demands that we be completely alive all the time, that we can't create life if we are not alive. For me this was a call to be alive. And I heard it at the time when I really needed to hear it. What is central to the Ishbitzer is knowing that you have to do something, knowing that life has to be responded to, knowing you will push yourself to the limits to know that life has to be responded to, knowing you will push yourself to the limits to know what God wants you to do in a situation, and knowing that you will have to surrender because you will never know. On the one hand it demands of me to assume complete responsibility, as to who I am, and what I am, and how I live my life, my relationship with myself, with my world, with my friends. And yet on the other hand, I know it has nothing to do with me. It means that the Master of the World put me here for a reason, and I have no idea what it is. I am meant to be doing His will, and I have to believe that in some way I am. Otherwise, I would not be here. So you see, he never lets you off the hook for a minute. When he says everything has meaning, that's a great deal of comfort for me and responsibility. Yet it's enabled me to be at home in God's world. It's enabled me to know what I am a *bat melekh*.

S.F.: And how do you relate this personal vision to the situation of *Am Yisrael*? To your picture of Israel as a whole? Historically? Religiously?

Mimi Feigelson: When the Maggid of Mezeritch left the world, each one of his students took a different piece of him. And I believe all the pieces come together. Rav Nachman says that the clouds of glory were in merit of Aharon the Kohen, and that the breath that came out of people's mouths when they were speaking to each other words of shalom would create the Clouds of Glory. That's my vision. Now where does that breath come from? That breath comes from being able to talk from your core, your soul; your ability to share. So I feel that if I can just remind people that there is an *anochi* inside them, and that's what needs to be shared in the world, then I believe the greater picture will happen. There are two kinds of reprovers. One comes and says "That is not it." The second just comes and by being in your presence, makes you better. Reb Shlomo would say "There are two kinds of doctors. With one, you walk in and he says, "Well, your condition is not so great," and he makes you feel as if you are going to die soon. The other says, "Your throat is not so good now, but your heart is good, and your this and your that are good." He makes you feel better already. Reb Shlomo taught his *talmidim* to be the second kind of doctor.

I often think that life is about its details. When I teach and I see how people respond and I hear their questions, I know I will not come out of the class the same way I walked in it. Someone came to Yakar last week and asked me what life is all about. I said, "When I cook for Shabbos and I go shopping, I try to pick out the nicest vegetables. And I sing the whole time. They think I am crazy, singing and picking out tomatoes. When I am cooking, I sing the whole time. And yet sometimes I sit down and it just does not happen. It can be the people I love the most and it still doesn't happen. And sometimes its like magic." Some people walk in and teach and do their thing, and that's it. I cannot be like that. Last week I walked in and my students said "We are with you" and for me that's what it's all about. When I began, I was a schoolteacher with students in an obligatory lesson. And it took me weeks to bring them to that. That's when I think *tikkun olam* happens.

When we have all finished learning and we all come out of class, and we are all a little bit different, then the world is a little bit different.

S.F.: But in regard to the large questions about the historical situation of Israel and the Jewish people?

Mimi Feigelson: I *davven* a lot. In other words, when I think about what is going to be with Israel, and what is going to be with the Jewish people, what the shape of the nation is going to be, and what Torah is going to look like 100 years from now, I don't know. I know it will be different.

S.F.: In regard to Torah, there is a new secular interest in learning Torah, at least among a certain elite. There is also the growth of a kind of "magic and superstition" with people looking for all kinds of instant solutions for their problems.

Mimi Feigelson: What this means is that we have a great deal of responsibility. Those of us who are deep in the world of Torah as well as part of what is happening in the world today have a great responsibility to be out there, to walk in the streets and be open to conversation. Those of us who have other gifts—I think it's criminal for people not to be using them. If we really believe Torah is Torat Chaim then there really has to be a way to address all these issues. Last year in the learning community, we dealt with the issue of *tzedakah*. We have this idea of the poor of our own city taking priority over those of another city. But when we talk about a Global Village, when I sit in my living room and I see starvation in Rwanda, isn't that part of our "city" too? It's true that geographically it's a few hours' flight from here. But when it enters my living room aren't those children looking at me in the eyes? And what kind of responsibility do I want to assume about that?

I was talking with my students about Hebron. I said to them that the truth has many faces, "both these and those are living words of God. And the *halachah* to Beit Hillel" means that there is one action that will happen, but that does not mean that there is not more than one truth. We need to acknowledge this. If they want to say Hebron is liberated land that belonged to us for generations and we redeemed it, I say fine, but at least I acknowledge that there are people who are living there who see you as a conqueror. What does that mean that they experience being "conquered"? And what does it mean that they see us as "conqueror"? I just want them to acknowledge it. I just want them to look at the fact that that is how they are being looked at. And it doesn't mean the bottom line won't be, where you are standing right now. Similarly they might say it's conquered land and we should give it back, but then they have to acknowledge—we are now talking about the Jewish side—that there are people who are living there because they believe it is liberated, and they are willing to sacrifice and risk the security of their families to be there. So no matter where we go, we have to be able to see the other side.

S.F.: What do you dream about?

Mimi Feigelson: I sometimes dream about what I learn. I had this one dream in which I woke up in the morning having just gone through doing a *diyyuk* in the Rambam based on three handwritten manuscripts. If I could learn when I am awake as I learn like when I am asleep, I would be in business.

S.F.: How do you relate to the current situation of Israel? The peace process? *Eretz Yisrael?*

Mimi Feigelson: You know the Piasetzna Rebbe was also a *mohel*. I read a document today about a doctor who survived the Shoah. The Piazenta Rebbe called him in, and wanted him to go with him to do a *brit*. This was at a very hard time in the Ghetto. Also the Piasetzna was weak and because of his condition wanted to make sure that there was a doctor with him. So he made this doctor get another 8 men. The document describes how they were in mortal danger as the woman's house was at the end of the Ghetto. It was snowing too, very hard to get there. When they walked in, she started screaming, and crying hysterically. She said that she considered not circumcizing her baby because she thought that maybe she could give him to someone non-Jewish. But that same day, the Germans took her husband to a labor camp, so she thought that maybe if she circumcized her baby, that he would be in her husband's merit, and protect him. When we talk about deciding about peace and about *Eretz Yisrael* that's the way I feel.

Often I walk around with the sense that it is all *chesed chinam* (gratuitous loving–kindness). But I pay for it: When I don't know what to do when there is a situation with no way out, whatever it is—trying to crack a *suggiah* (talmudic problem) and just not getting it. When I finally get it, it's *chesed chinam*. I also know that the only way I got to *chesed chinam* was by hours of sitting there and feeling like a complete idiot. So I think the two of them go together. There's always a way to *hakarat hatov* (gratitude for goodness received). It's clear to me that those of us who merit to wake up in the morning in Yerushalayim every day must feel great gratitude. Generations dreamed to be here. We are living the dream of generations and so I dream about being able to continue to fulfill the dreams of generations, and to justify it.

.

Rabbi Emanuel Feldman

Rabbi Emanuel Feldman was the virtual creator of the thriving Orthodox community of Atlanta, Georgia, which he built up over a period of 35 years. The editor–in–chief of *Tradition*, a scholarly quarterly of Orthodox Jewish thought, he has written four books and over 100 articles. He has taught at Emory University Law School and Bar Ilan University. His work *On Judaism: Conversations on Being Jewish in Today's World* is a particularly fine introduction to Jewish religious life.

I met with Rabbi Feldman at the Institute for Talmudic Study in Jerusalem's Bayit Vegan district. Informal, kind, and efficient, he did his best to make me feel at ease. For a person of such eminence, he lacks pretension, which I greatly appreciated.

CB EO

S.F.: Could you please tell me what the turning points of your work life have been?

Rabbi Feldman: I don't know if I can answer that with any focus at all. I can't point to any one turning point. My father, Zichrono le-Bracha, was a rabbi. And growing up in a rabbi's home it was naturally expected (not necessarily that I would follow in his footsteps) but engage in some form of teaching for *Am Yisrael*. My father, who was a rabbi in Baltimore for many years, never actually pushed me or any of my brothers into the rabbinate though all of us became rabbis. I can't think of any particular turning point. When I got *semichah* and was looking for a pulpit, I found a little *shul* in Atlanta that was willing to take me, a young rabbi who had no experience, so I stayed with them for thirty-nine years. We grew up together.

S.F.: The story of the remarkable growth of that community through the years is within the modern Orthodox world a kind of legend. What is the secret of the success through all the years of work?

Rabbi Feldman: If I knew the secret, I would bottle it and can it, and give it out to people. I always say I knew I was getting older in the rabbinate when I turned about 35, having been in the rabbinate 10 or 11 years, and started getting calls from young rabbis from little towns in the area. "We hear so many people are coming to *shul*. What's the secret?" they asked. I said, "I don't know the secret. It's just happening."

They thought I was being humble. But the truth is, there is no secret. It happened. It was *yad Hashem* (the hand of God) that helped the community grow. And I was just at the wheel. We worked hard. We taught classes. But a lot of rabbis taught. We dealt with individuals on a one-to-one basis. We tried not to be judgmental of people, accepting them for what they are. Maybe my own background was helpful in that. Even though I was brought up in an Orthodox rabbi's home, when I went to high school, I went to a public high school. There was no yeshiva high school in those days. It was only for my last year in high school that my father sent me away to Haim Berlin Yeshiva High School in New York, and then I went to Ner Yisrael. But part of my elementary school and most of my high school years were in general secular schools. Maybe that gave me a better understanding of where people were coming from, even though I was always *frum*, all my life. The congregation itself is a *baal teshuvah* congregation. Most of them were not raised in Orthodox homes. One by one, little by little, they all moved into the orbit of Yiddishkeit.

S.F.: And how has the congregation developed in relation to the broader Atlanta community through the years? How has the broader community changed through the years?

Rabbi Feldman: When I came to Atlanta in 1952, there were about 25,000 Jews, divided among four synagogues: a large Reform temple that had about 1,000 families; a large Conservative temple that had about 1,500 families; a smaller Orthodox synagogue of about 600 families which at that time was already beginning to move away from Orthodoxy, and our little *shul*, which had forty families. There was also a Sephardish *kehillah* that was not 100 percent Orthodox. There were also three major Jewish country clubs, which wielded more power than the synagogues. On Tuesday, one of the clubs had bingo night, and you knew you could not call a meeting in the community because the people were playing bingo. But Atlanta Jews are very fine, nice, kind, gentle people. They were very nice to me when I came. They did not give me a hard time, as is done to the rabbi in many communities. That went for the general Jewish community as well as for my little *shul*. My little *shul* called itself Orthodox, but most of the congregants did not really know what Orthodox was. They would have been content if I had simply done what the other synagogues in town were doing. For example, they wanted me to wear a robe on Shabbos the way the Conservative and Reform did. They wanted me to bless the congregation *"Yevarechachah"* as the other Rabbis were doing. They said Rabbi 'X' does it this way, and I said, well, Rabbi 'X' is not Orthodox. There were a lot of interesting little pushes toward not being Orthodox. But I knew what I wanted, and I did everything slowly, with a smile. We learned together too. Some people became *baalei teshuvah* because I was able to beat them on the tennis court. I was able to bring a lot of people back through athletics. The synagogue itself gradually grew over the years. We don't know how it grew or why, but it did, *Baruch Hashem*. We offered something that was authentic. People responded to it. No gimmicks. I didn't allow gimmicks in my *shul*, no Boy Scout Shabbos, Sisterhood Shabbos, etc. The kinds of gimmicks other shuls used to bring people I did not permit. I think some people were turned off by this approach, but I also think some quality people were attracted by it. A young man said to me once, "You have one gimmick; its called 'authenticity.'"

S.F.: And despite the great mobility in America, the community has grown around a core of families who have stayed?

Rabbi Feldman: A community that was once forty families is now close to 600 families. Where once one person used the *mikveh,* now we have hundreds using it. People stayed. Not only did they stay, but their children began coming back. We sent off many children, youngsters, to yeshivot in America as well as, later on, to seminars and yeshivot in Israel. We probably have more young people studying in yeshivas in Israel per capita than any synagogue in the United States. And many of them have been happy to come back to Atlanta because now there is something there. There is a *kollel* in the city and there are good yeshivas, good day schools. There are all the material things you need. There are kosher restaurants, good weather, and very, very nice people. Even though many transplants from all over America have moved into Atlanta, the city has been able to maintain its Southern charm, its fineness and decency.

S.F.: And on the other side of Atlantic, when did your Israel connection begin?

Rabbi Feldman: Our connection with Israel began, ironically, because my parents moved to Israel when they retired. And my wife's parents moved to Israel about twenty-five, thirty years ago. I have a brother who's a Rosh Yeshiva and has been living here for 35 years. I had two or three sabbaticals during those nearly 40 years in Atlanta, and each time I spent the year in Israel. I taught at Bar Ilan for a year, at Ohr Sameach for a year. After I retired, I did not want to take a full-time teaching job. But I work here at Ariel on the project of translating Rashi. I still do writing too, having just written *On Judaism*. There are four books, and I am working on another now, even as we speak. I am kept busy, *Baruch Hashem*. I spend about nine, ten months a year in Israel.

S.F.: What are the subjects of your other books?

Rabbi Feldman: The first book I published dealt with the Six—Day War, a spectacular, miraculous victory. I lived here during that year, 1966–67 and wrote a daily journal of what was going on that whole month of June, when the war broke out. It's published as *The Twenty-Eighth of Iyar*, which is Yom Yerushalayim. Another book I wrote, called *The Biblical Echo*, is a collection of different essays, lectures, and ideas I had given over the years on various themes. Another was very technical, made out of my doctoral dissertation, *Law As Theology*, which dealt with *tumah* and *taharah*. The fourth book, *On Judaism*, is designed for people who are returning to Judaism in today's world.

S.F.: It's interesting that in *On Judaism*, which is a book of dialogues between a young married man who wants to learn more about Judaism and a rabbi, you do not deal with a wholly ignorant outsider. In effect, you take the advice given in an article I recently read by the sociologists Charles Leibman, Steven Cohen, and Jack Wertheirmer. They argue that more resources should be given not to the most marginal Jews, but rather to those who do have a fair degree of Jewish involvement.

Rabbi Feldman: I read that article and believe they are right. We have to give our energy to those who are interested. The person in the book is a mythical composite of a lot of people I came across: intelligent, well-educated, unfortunately Jewishly-deprived, but a person who wants to learn, wants to know.

S.F.: And in speaking to him you speak of *avodat Hashem*: "The ideal service of God is the kind that fulfills His will not because He rewards and punishes—although He surely does—but through a fusion of awe and love: the recognition of His overpowering greatness as contrasted to our vulnerability; the desire to be in His proximity through the means of doing His will; the avoidance of sin so that we not be torn away from His Presence; and the recognition that He loves us and wishes to be close to us." You also speak of *avodat Hashem* as the service of heart, and the way in which, through our moving closer to God, God moves closer to us. Can I ask you how you understand this *avodah* of the individual in relation to the *avodah* of *Clal Yisrael*? And how do you understand the *avodah* of the community in serving God, especially for communities outside Israel when they have the opportunity to come to Israel?

Rabbi Feldman: *Clal Yisrael* is really comprised of individuals. If you and I and eight other people come together, we are *Clal Yisrael*. We are a minyan that represents *Clal Yisrael*, past, present, and future. I don't particularly make a distinction between the individual Jew and *Clal Yisrael*. There is a difference, but in terms of *avodat Hashem*, each individual Jew has a responsibility to do the best *avodat Hashem* he is capable of.

S.F.: I was thinking in terms of such traditional themes as Jews as "Light to the Nations," the Jewish mission to help the world come to understand and believe in One God who rules over all, who has a moral vision for mankind. How does the Jew living in America relate to this theme? Can he relate to it as the Jew living in Israel can?

Rabbi Feldman: Let me make sure that I understand your question. Are you asking how a person can, wherever he is, do proper *avodat Hashem*?

S.F.: I am asking in a way whether there is a level of *avodat Hashem* that the person living in Israel can attain, which one living without cannot?

Rabbi Feldman: There are degrees of *avodat Hashem*. Sometimes a person living in an isolated town in South Georgia, who sacrifices a tremendous amount to *davven*, to keep kosher, to educate his children—sometimes a person living in such a place is doing higher *avodat Hashem* than a person living in the middle of Yerushalayim who takes everything for granted. He may go to minyan every day and yet take everything for granted. Everything is a habit. I just happened to be in South Carolina for a lecture once. After the lecture, a lady came over and said that she wanted to see me privately. Finally we sat down and talked, and during the course of the conversation, she told me that she and her husband were the only Jews in a community of 200 who were observant of anything. So she had no *shul* to go to, but they had to stay in that town for business, economic reasons. Still, she sent her children off to yeshiva to learn. Then she asked questions about a *mikveh*, and from her questions, it was evident that she was using a mikveh. I asked "Where do you have a mikveh?" She said, "I don't. I use the Atlantic Ocean." I said, "That's fine, but what do you do in the winter?" She said, "It's very cold." That's real *mesirut nefesh*. Sometimes when I would get down in the dumps as a rabbi, I would think of this woman. She would inspire me with this tremendous *avodat Hashem* of hers.

S.F.: I don't quarrel with the example. But it seems to me that there are far greater demands and opportunities for *avodat Hashem* in *Eretz Yisrael*, where the person faces more demands, more mitzvot.

Rabbi Feldman: I am going to tell you something that's very revolutionary. I don't think that every Jew has to live in Israel. I think that a woman like this is making a major contribution to her community by living as she is where she is. As the lone observant person, she is doing something to those other 199 non–observant families. She's creating some doubts in their hearts as to their own non–Jewish lifestyle. So I think that she has a role to play. And I think that Hashem put her there for a reason. In my own case for example, in Atlanta thirty-nine years, I wanted many times just to come and live in Israel. I used to knock myself out, bang my head against the wall. In 1952, there were forty families not keeping anything, and thirty-nine years later there were over 600 families, many of them *shomer Shabbos*. Great. It wasn't so *pashut* ("simple"). There were tremendous problems and heartaches along the way. I said, "Listen, I can chuck all this. I can go and live in Israel." But I spoke to some of the *gedolei Yisrael*, major figures, Rav Moshe Feinstein, Rav Kaminetsky, Rav Ruderman Z"l, and my father. They told me, "You have no right to leave. You have a community that you are leading." So I don't think that every Jew has to live in Israel. I think it's a wonderful goal, if one goes to Israel for the right reason. If one goes to Israel because he wants to enhance his Jewish life, then he must make sure that his children grow up properly. But if one goes to Israel just because it's Israel, then it's not reason enough. We are all soldiers in an army. Hashem is the commander-in-chief, the *mitzaveh*. As part of the army, we have to do his mitzvot, his commands. Some people are sent to outposts, to scout out. And some must be at headquarters. Yerushalayim is headquarters. Some of us are soldiers who have to be wherever *Ha-Kadosh Baruch Hu* puts us.

S.F.: And for those of us put here in Israel now, how do you think we are doing? How is Israel as a society doing in realizing the historical challenge that God has given us?

Rabbi Feldman: Well, Torah has made tremendous strides in Israel. The Torah community is strong; it's powerful, self-confident, perhaps sometimes too self-confident. It has created a generation of people who hold Torah in high esteem. There are *shiurim* even in a small neighborhoods like Bayit Vegan every hour on the hour. It's true all over the city. We have made tremendous progress in Torah learning. But there's a long way to go. We have not made progress in human relations. There'a tremendous abyss between the Orthodox community and the non-Orthodox community, the Haredim and the non-Haredim, even the *kepah serguah* ("knitted kepot."). There's just distrust, and it doesn't have to be there. I can't speak for the secular community, But I suspect a slight opening on our part, reaching out to them, would have positive results. But we don't bother. We come across as arrogant, not caring. But we really are not arrogant, and we do care. In America, we know how to do it. Here in Israel we don't.

S.F.: I think of the lack of *derech eretz*, the lack of consideration for others showed by so many, and not necessarily in big "global issues." I don't think I have ever seen a Haredi man get up from his seat on the bus to give an elderly woman a seat. Where is the *derech eretz*?

Rabbi Feldman: But you find tremendous *chesed* in the Haredi community, under the table, privately, and also great honesty in terms of stuff lost and found. A very expensive man's sweater was found in the middle of HaPisgah a few months ago. Someone picked it up and put it on the door of the Grah *shul*. Thousands of people pass it every day, yet no one took it. It was there for 2 weeks. So there's a lot of honesty and a lot of *chesed*, but you are right when you say that there's a certain lack of ability to relate to other people, other groups, on an ordinary everyday level. They have good hearts and they are honest, and they would give you the shirts off their backs. But they have not been taught the kind of behavior you mentioned, such as getting up to give an elderly woman seat.

S.F.: It is as if, in order to retain its purity, the Haredi community feels that it must close itself off from others. Only it's odd that they have to do this in relation to their fellow Jews in Israel. And saying this, I am brought to another side of the *derech eretz* question. Did you feel, as a rabbi in Atlanta, that you had to lead your congregation in such a way as to be a model, an example to the non-Jewish world?

Rabbi Feldman: No, I didn't feel I had a particular mission to the non-Jewish world. I had limited resources and limited time. My mission was to the Jewish world, to make my Jews more Jewish. And then the rest would fall into place. A lot of colleagues who were Reform rabbis felt that their mission was to the non-Jewish world. They figured that as Jews, they were already Jewish enough. But my Jews were not Jewish enough. Still, I definitely reached out to non-Jews when the opportunity presented itself. If a church would ask me to come and speak to a class on a Sunday morning, I would do it. Or if a church wanted to come and visit our *shul*, I would show them around, and have a session with them about Judaism. I would do it for good relations, for *darkei shalom*. But that wasn't the focus of my life.

S.F.: And you do not place much store on the Noahide movement?

Rabbi Feldman: It has a possibility. I never gave it a great deal of time or energy, because I was and still am dealing in an emergency, with a crisis situation. We are losing more than 50 percent of our people to intermarriage in the United States. So I have no time to play with luxuries, which is reaching out to the non-Jews or worrying about the Noahides. I think it's fine, but our people are drowning and need to be saved. The guy's going down for the third time, and we've got to pull him up.

S.F.: In this regard, you accept the model of the Jewish people seeming to become two societies, one a small, intense, learned and learning society, the other, society less and less Jewish, rapidly assimilating?

Rabbi Feldman: If you compare it to a wheel, American Jewry is growing stronger in the hub of the wheel while the periphery of the wheel is falling off the edges. The hub, which is the Orthodox community, the mitzvah–observant community, is growing ever stronger. And the periphery is falling off; the Conservative and Reform are losing their children and grandchildren. This is a tragedy because they are two thirds of the Jewish people.

S.F.: You don't accept the figure that only 7 percent of the American Jewish community is Orthodox?

Rabbi Feldman: It's low, I believe. But I don't really know. If you go outside the major metropolitan regions you don't have Orthodox people. Outside of New York, Baltimore, Boston, and the like, we definitely have a smaller number of Orthodox Jews than there are Conservative and Reform. But that smaller number of Orthodox Jews is the most powerful unit in the United States. It's motivated. It's even got money now. Also, it's influential, and listened to. It's been a miraculous resurrection from what I saw in 1952. When I started out, Orthodoxy was dead, down for the count. The referee was about to say 'ten'. There I was, a young person going into the Orthodox rabbinate, and young people thought it was crazy. But I had good advice. My *rosh yeshiva*, Rav Ruderman *z"l*, and my father both said "Listen, you don't have to worry about the future. Just do your job every single day. Teach people. Love people. Teach them how to love Judaism. The *Kadosh Baruch Hu* will do the rest and things will fall into place. Don't get too global and cosmic. Do your daily work." And that's what we tried to do. There's no question that, right now within the American Jewish community, there's an observant, committed group and a non–committed group. Even Israel, which used to paste a lot of these non–observant Jews together, is not going to remain a glue. If Netanyahu can tell the American Congress that, in a few years, he is not going to need their money, then he certainly can tell the American Jews in a few years that he won't need their money. But if they no longer have to give money to Israel, what are they going to do? They'll have nothing. It's a tragedy.

As far as the relationship between Orthodox, Conservative, and Reform, I always try to maintain the top relationship. The Reform rabbis in my community knew where I stood religiously. At the same time, they knew I was their friend. It's a hard balance. There was a narrow ridge but I walked it. Many of them came to me with their own congregational problems. But they also knew that I would fight them tooth and nail. On patrilineal descent, I openly fought them. But I tried to keep public fights to a minimum. Also, labels are not very healthy. The fact that a person pays dues in a Reform or Conservative congregation does not mean that he is Conservative or Reform. He is not yet observant. If you train him, he will be observant.

S.F.: So the best way to define the majority of American Jews is as not-yet observant?

Rabbi Feldman: Not-yet observant—It's not an original term. Every Jewish *neshamah* wants to reach out to *avodat Hashem* except there are things that stand in the way: lack of learning, sometimes his rabbi because he does not teach him. The *neshamah* is there, you just have to feed him. The Navi says, "They are all thirsty. Give them something to drink. They'll lap it up." It's American society that American Jews often try to imitate, just as Israeli Jews started trying to imitate American society. But there's an emptiness at the core of American secular society, and American Jews make the mistake of thinking that this is the way to be. I think that even American society is hungry and would respond, and does respond, to a religious message.

S.F.: Well, there is a worldwide return to religiousness, whose negative manifestation is "fundamentalism."

Rabbi Feldman: They call Orthodoxy fundamentalism, but they are wrong. There is definitely a return to religious values in the world, even in America.

S.F.: All the great 'isms' have passed from the world.

Rabbi Feldman: They have all crashed.

S.F.: I wanted to ask you, could you say something about your experience with *Tradition* and how the magazine has developed through the years?

Rabbi Feldman: I was one of the associate editors for twenty five years, and have been editor for the past 8 of 9 years. The magazine, which appears four times a year, is designed to be a journal of Jewish ideas, so it's different from most other magazines. We don't just do current events per se. We do have opinions, *machshavot, hashkafah*. It was designed from the beginning to be a platform for the Orthodox rabbi, where he could get his ideas published. About 40 years old, the magazine today is recognized as one of, if not the premier journal of Jewish thought, the premier Journal of Orthodox Jewish thought. It's a platform for rabbis, teachers, anyone who wants to say something and can say it well. In writing circles you sometimes hear, "This guy has nothing to say, but he says it well." We hope our guy has something to say and says it well. Despite all this, *Tradition* is a money–losing deal. It takes no advertising. All of us who work at *Tradition* are volunteers. No one gets paid, including our writers. *Baruch Hashem*, it's an influential magazine. I think. I hope.

S.F.: Your years in the rabbinate, your work on the books, the contribution to Jewish thought in editing *Tradition*—is all of this *avodat Hashem*? Do you consider your own life to be *avodat Hashem*?

Rabbi Feldman: I wish it were true. You have to catch yourself up short every once in a while. "Why am I doing this? Is it for my own ego?" When I am editing *Tradition*, is it because I like to see my name as editor? Why do I write these books? Do I want to help Jews or do I get an ego trip because a man coming to see me has my book in his hand? A hard question, and a hard question to answer honestly. But ideally, we all have to start. Even *davvening* is not always *avodat Hashem*. One would think, ordinarily, "All right, my business is not *avodat Hashem*, but at least when I am in *shul*, when I say *ashrei yoshevi vaysecha*, "I am being *oved Hashem*." But it's not always true in *shul* either. It's an ongoing struggle for a Jew, even the greatest Jew. And I am talking now about rosh yeshivot. The greater the Jew, the more he struggles toward *avodat Hashem*, because he knows how important it is, and the more he sees. The closer one is to the top of the mountain, the harder it is to get there. When one wants to reach the summit, the last 100 yards are the most difficult. That's what they tell me. I have never been there. But the greater the person, the harder he works at *avodat Hashem*. And the guy who is not aware of it—it is not a big deal for him. While it's a tremendously difficult goal, we all have to strive for it. As we say in the Shema every day, "Love your Lord your God with all your heart, with all your soul, and with all your might."

Rabbi Menachem Fruman

The rabbi of the community of Tekoah Menachem Fruman is a well-known and widely respected figure in Israel. Rabbi Menachem Fruman's original ideas on the way to true peace have led him to dialogue with Islamic religious leaders. His deep faith in and love of the land of Israel are expressed in the poetry which he writes. A student of Rav Kook, he is like his predecessor a person of great mystical passion for the land of Israel.

I met with Rabbi Fruman at the Yeshurun synagogue on King George Street in Jerusalem before he was about to give a lesson in the Beit Midrash there. He seemed at the time very tired, but keeping his promise, he showed patience in answering my questions. This seemed to me just one more example of the kind of actions for others, the good deeds he is well-known for doing.

ೞ ೲ

S.F.: Could you describe your present work?

Rabbi Fruman: I am the rabbi of the holy community of Tekoah—which I pray will be built, and strengthened, and grow. I do what a rabbi does in the community. Also, I am a teacher of Torah at Yeshivat Othniel in southern Hebron mountain. I teach two classes in Othniel, one about the relation of the author of Tosaphot to Christianity, and a lesson in the Zohar.

S.F.: What is your background and education?

Rabbi Fruman: I studied in Mercaz Ha-Rav.

S.F.: And your chief teacher was Rabbi Zvi Yehuda Kook, of blessed memory?

Rabbi Fruman: After the army, I studied in his yeshiva, and with him personally. I don't know, from the other side, if I faithfully represent his teachings, if all I say and teach he would agree with. But I am of course deeply grateful to him.

S.F.: You are known not only as a rabbi but as a creative writer, a poet. How do you connect the two worlds?

Rabbi Fruman: I feel that the challenge of present reality for the people of Israel and the Torah of Israel is the challenge of freedom. The

religious community is living in a world in which there is an atmosphere of freedom. Against this background, I write what is called
"poetry," which has as its basis, or its expression, freedom. There are
of course many definitions of poetry. What is the difference after all
between poetry and prose? As I understand it, in poetry, you allow
yourself to break through the standard, limited, even prosaic means of
expression regularly used. This also expresses itself in the physical form
on the page. I often say that I do not write poetry but rather "broken
lines." In poetry, you do not finish but rather break the lines. You break
the first conventionally accepted structure. In a certain way, writing
poetry for me is a kind of *midrash*. As in a *midrash*, I take a Torah
suggiah, or "problem," and give myself the freedom of checking out all
kinds of options, which are within the *pesukim*, the verses. And my
poems are the poems of a rabbi. They are built on *divrei Torah*, on
words of Torah. For three years, I wrote for the paper *Davar*, since
closed, a weekly Torah commentary that took the form of a poem.
Each week I would write a *shir*, a poem, on the Biblical portion of the
week. It might be on one *pasuk* or on a particular idea within the
parashah. For one whole year, I did this for each Shabbat, and also for
the *chaggim* ("holidays"). My other most recent effort was a book of
love poems to *Eretz Yisrael*, between the person and the land. In both
of these works, I took a Torah idea and gave it freedom. That is, I
checked within the poems all kinds of options as to how this idea can
develop. Often, these were non–conventional and remote possibilities.
I can give examples of how this is done. For instance, in a recent poem,
the establishment of a new government is built on the idea of a wedding: "You do not know what will be, but at the wedding the Jews
dance." I take the fear of new dimensions that have opened before me,
and turn it around, make it into joy. It's analogous to Purim. For *Am
Yisrael* in that time, there was the threat of total destruction. In one
day, they wanted to destroy all of *Am Yisrael*. But they cast the lot,
the *pur*, and all turned into joy. I take elements that are from the Torah, like the "not knowing" of Purim, which connects with the tree of
knowledge in the Garden of Eden, and I check, develop them freely.
This is what I call poetry.

When I say that I do not write poetry but rather "broken lines,"
the association is with "absence of perfection." We have possibilities,
but we do not have a perfect model or idea. We try and we search. It
also relates to the "broken heart." We have not arrived—we have a

broken heart—and so we search. The freedom is connected with the search. We have not found it and we are broken, so we look. The broken lines are thus both the freedom and the incompleteness. So the poetry presents, on one side, the freedom in moving away from the conventional expression, and on the deeper level, the incompleteness and search to come closer to the *Kadosh Baruch Hu*. Poetry is thus the effort to use our freedom and heal our brokeness through coming closer to God.

S.F.: I am thinking now, and this in a political context, of Professor Avi Ravitzky's speaking of the wisdom of our being satisfied with the "part," with not attaining the whole.

Rabbi Fruman: We now go in the opposite direction. I am broken when things are not complete. One has to strive to search. One has to long and yearn all the time for perfection and wholeness. But if there is in your question a political matter, then of course there is something opposite to the position of my friend Avi in the striving to get to the perfect without narrow limits.

S.F.: But isn't there something mistaken in placing all our emphasis on freedom. Doesn't our relation to God require our binding ourselves closely within the limits of what God demands of us?

Rabbi Fruman: *Daat*, or religion, is law. Chazal says that Moshe brought to us *cherut* (freedom), but there is no *cherut* except for those who are engaged in the study of Torah. I do not feel that religious life is the life of limitation. Freedom means for me the longing, the yearning for connection with God. What I described earlier was the search for connection, closeness, to the *Kadosh Baruch Hu*. I have never felt what certain people apparently do, that the *Halachah* is something that limits me. I simply do not feel this.

Halachah is not everything. There is also an inner dimension. The *halachah* is an instrument to search for the *Kadosh Baruch Hu*. I am a *gerer Hasid* from my home. My father of blessed memory was a *gerer Hasid*. I never feel the *halachah* as limiting but rather as something that produces a home, a way of life. My father would say the *halachah* is life, producing the means to bring us closer to God. Every *keriyat shema* is a call to the *Kadosh Baruch Hu*. I believe that the *halachah* gives us means to come closer to God, but it is not enough to rely on *halachah* alone. It depends upon what you do with those instruments. You may have a violin, but what you play with the violin is another matter. The *halachah* is the violin of King David. There are those who play on it Tehillim, words of praise and psalms, and those who simply make noise. It's an instrument, and I don't feel it limits me in any way.

S.F.: How do you connect the search and the striving you talk about to *avodat Hashem*?

Rabbi Fruman: Avodat Hashem, in the words of Chazal, includes three things: Torah, *avodah*, and *gemilut chasadem*. Torah is the search, to learn to know what God wants of us. *Avodah* is the *korbanot*, and it means *mesirut nefesh*, "true dedication." You give yourself. A *korban*, a sacrifice, is like the transmission and dedicating of the *nefesh*, the soul. Rambam says that all the *nefesh* longs for is to be close to the *Kadosh Baruch Hu*. Then comes the *avodah*. Rambam ends his *Guide to the Perplexed* with *gemilut chasadem*: That which we understand, we have to do in order to give to others. To give to others. To love the creation. To give to others what we ourselves have achieved. This is *avodat Hashem*: the search in order to learn, and then to give to others in *gemilut casadem*. And all this on the back of *mesirut nefesh*, dedication in searching and in giving. *Mesirut nefesh* is also connected with *anavah*, "true humility." One of my principal things is to come to true humility: to give my soul, my ego in dedication.

S.F.: And the human being can know with certainty that he is worshiping God, serving God?

Rabbi Fruman: *Kirvat Elokim li tov* ("The nearness of God is good.") Whoever has one time tasted what it is to learn Torah as one should, experienced prayer as it should be, has tasted the Tree of Life. Who has tasted this has tasted eternal life.

S.F.: And in this, the higher service is of love and joy, rather than of fear?

Rabbi Fruman: A human being has to try to understand what the *Kadosh Baruch Hu* wants and to do this, and to give to others. For example, a person should give to his children materially, spiritually, should give to others what he has succeeded in receiving himself. You ask me what *avodat Hashem* is? *Avodah* is *mesirut*, dedication of oneself, expression of oneself. During the time of the search to become closer to God, and during the time of giving to others, one expresses oneself. This is *avodah*, and it is very much connected with humility, which is essential to *avodat Hashem*. There is a spiritual element too in the search and in the giving, and in the teaching of Torah, and simply when you help others, providing psychological or spiritual help, even a pat on the shoulder. All these things are the "body." The *neshamah* is "*Harbeh harbeh em miat miat*," as Rambam says to Chochmah. We take it one time as a wise saying "If there is more *avodah*, more *mesirut*, then the search and the giving are also greater." As with the Torah, so with the *gemilut chasadem*. The *avodah* gives the *neshamah* to the Torah and to the *gemilut chasadem*.

S.F.: I wanted to ask you a general question about the situation of *Am Yisrael* today. How do you understand our situation today?

Rabbi Fruman: I am a *tsabar*, a native born Israeli, and I know very little firsthand about what is happening outside of Israel. The dream of my life was never to have to leave *Eretz Yisrael* even once. I did not however achieve this. Rabbi Steinsaltz, as guest of the Soviet Scientific Academy, offered me an opportunity seven years ago to go to the Soviet Union to teach Torah. I remember my great difficulty in making the decision, to leave the *eretz*, the Land, to go to meet our brothers in the Soviet Union. It was such a difficult and painful decision process. Nonetheless, I traveled to the Soviet Union and met our brothers whom we so longed for and prayed to meet. I was gone for 6 weeks, but this does not mean that I have a real knowledge of the Diaspora. I don't really know the life there. I have a certain impression. There is deep sorrow for each Jewish soul that gets lost. If it's a simple piece of advice you're looking for, if Judaism will be strong and filled with life, then people will not be lost. So the effort to be stronger in Judaism goes together with the effort to prevent assimilation. What I tried to do, in my brief time there, was to teach Torah with spiritual strength and in humility, with more spirit. Again, everything is connected to humility.

S.F.: And in regard to "assimilation," or at least turning from Judaism within Israel?

Rabbi Fruman: Outside of Israel, there are people who are involved in intermarriage or simply wish to abandon the Jewish community. Here in Israel it's something different, and new. They live among Jews but wish to live, as it were, as the Gentiles do. This desire of many to live without Judaism is the great problem of *Eretz Yisrael*. All the negotiations I have engaged in with the Arabs have as their main purpose the reaching of these secular Jews.

S.F.: I don't understand the connection.

Rabbi Fruman: I will explain. I said, if Jewish life will be strong and filled with a real higher spirituality, then people will want to be a part of it. If there is a good taste to Jewish life, then there will be *teshuvah*, return. If we return to the *Kodesh Baruch Hu*, then our life will be stronger, more positive.

S.F.: How do you relate to the option raised by Rabbi Hartman? His idea is that the task is not to return all Jews to closeness to God, that secular humanism is an acceptable Jewish option.

Rabbi Fruman: Life without any connection with God is life that is lacking, severely lacking, and limited. In a more specific way, in my own life I will pray and work so that people will come closer to living by the *Halachah*. This does not mean that we cannot meet an exceptional person who tries to live without God. But the normal and right thing even for such a Jew is to live by *halachah*. How can we suffer life in which there is not the sanctity of Shabbat, in which there is no regard for the laws of *niddah*? You can say that this person is noble in spirit and acts accordingly, which is even more regretful. If a man has a wonderful loving relationship with his wife, and his wife does not maintain ritual purity, then this seems to me worse in some way. In fact, if a Jew acts rudely to his wife, then it would seem to me more natural that he does not care for "purity." For me, it's something simple. The instruments, the means that God has given us, are the instruments we must play. The *halachah* is our instrument, our violin. It can be that there is a Jew who whistles wonderfully, ignoring the violin, but this seems to me irrelevant.

S.F.: In Israel today, the majority of those in the intellectual, academic, communication elite are not *shomrei mitzvah*. What does this say about those who are *shomrei mitzvah*, about reaching others?

Rabbi Fruman: I'll tell you what I learned in Mercaz Harav. Rabbi Kook's answer was that our generation needs great things. The abandoning of religion came because religion did not answer to, respond to the great longings of a generation. The religious Jews provide something so weak, that many do not wish to be a part of it. Rabbi Zvi Yehuda would say we have to be strict to say *Shem Hashem Ha-Gadol* ("the great Name of God"). If we say something weak and not spiritual, then it does not meet the need. The analysis of Ha-Rav Kook was that the leaving of religion did not come from the *yetzer hara*, from sensual desire, but from a longing for something "greater," the *Shem Ha-Gadol*. I believe that Rabbi Kook did not mean that each secular Jew is a great person, nor did he feel that they were free from *taavaot* (desires). But the main reason that this great abandonment of faith occurred was because religion did not supply the answer to the call for something great. Now, as one who wishes to return in *teshuvah* and return others to *teshuvah*, I see that if people will live on a higher, a greater spiritual level, then those people who seek higher and greater things will find them. And this will be done by those within our spiritual movement. To speak of it in the secular language, this would allow these people to "go up a level." The goal is for us to get to a higher spiritual level. And if we get there, then the secular public that abandoned the faith because it did not find an answer in it will return to it. This is the best answer I can give to your question. What I understand as vital for my own personal direction and aim is for me to come to a life that is more refined, more modest, closer to God. This involves the desires to help others, *gemilut chasadem*. The more I can become more refined spiritually, the more I can give to others. I will have what to give them.

S.F.: People speak today of "abundance materially and poverty spiritually". . . .

Rabbi Fruman: I am from Tekoah. *Amos pesukim* can be a source for the words of Rabbi Kook. In that day, the "*bachurim hayafim v'habetulot hayafot mishottim mi'yam l'yam b'Dvar Hashem.* ("They seek *Davar Hashem*, the word of God, and faint from thirst. And our people do not give them living waters.") If our people would give them living waters, then they would drink.

S.F.: Do you sense this is happening, that the whole process of the

Jewish people's return to the land of Israel is to the return in Redemption? And that this will bring us to Shalom?

Rabbi Fruman: "Shalom" is the name of the *Kadosh Baruch Hu*. When I look at the issue of peace as when I look at the issue of Zionism, I see that there is a side of "forcing the end." There is an effort to get to a higher level; so too with the whole process of creating a people, and not simply a group of scattered '*kehillot*' communities. An effort to go up—there were greats in Israel who strongly doubted whether we had the right to try this. But in regard to this effort to make a people in the Land, this was without question right, the raising of a spiritual level. With peace, there are many problems, setbacks, obstacles; as with Zionism. But there is a will, a strong desire to come to a higher level of life, spiritually. This is another stage in the process of the complete Redemption. The search for peace is another effort to raise Judaism to a higher level. In regard to Zionism, we can say at least that a great share of the people succeeded in going up a level and living in *Eretz Yisrael*. If we will raise it another level and come to shalom, this I do not know. This has not been determined yet. But the effort to arrive at peace is an effort to bring us to a higher, a greater level of being.

Rabbi Mordechai Gafni

Rabbi Mordechai Gafni's weekly lectures in Jerusalem on *parashat ha-shavuah* draw exceptionally large crowds. He is without question not only a brilliant lecturer but an original thinker who reveals a deep concern for the situation of the Jewish people today. A graduate of Yeshiva University, formerly a communal rabbi, he too has been closely connected with the Third Way party that won representation in the most recent Knesset elections.

I spoke with Rabbi Gafni in what was then his office in one of the high-tech companies in the Har Hotzvim district of Jerusalem.

☙ ❧

S.F.: In a recent talk, you indicated that there is something problematic in the concept *chozer bi–teshuvah* (to "return in answer"—the popular idiomatic expression for one who has returned to Jewish observance), especially when it is paired with its opposite, *chozer be–shayalah* (one who "returns in question"—the popular idiomatic phrase for one who has left religion). Can you clarify why this way of making the distinction is problematic for you?

Rabbi Gafni: I hear the question. I would just like to rephrase it somewhat. What we said in terms of *shayalah* (question) and *teshuvah* (answer) is that the passionate expression of the question makes sense when it is an expression of relationship. If I am not in a relationship with you, then the question of "why" does not make sense. When I ask, "Why? Why have you done this?," there's a you and there's a me and I have a right to ask. I ask "why" as a function of relationship. If someone stops me on the street and says, "Hey, Gafni, you are a complete idiot" and I don't know him, then I'll just keep walking and think, "How does he know my name?" If a close friend makes a critique of the same nature—hopefully phrased differently—then I'll take it very seriously. Relationship allows for critique and allows for questioning. It allows for the screaming of "Why?" The paradox is that the person who is not in a relationship, such as the professed atheist, can't phrase the question because the question's substructure makes no sense. In a world in which gases and molecules and random combinations form

161

both the laws of physics and the laws of morals, in which human preference is the only standard, and in which there is no guiding force and direction—there is no reason to think that the world should be fair. So my point in that lecture was that the affirmation of the question is an expression of deep spiritual connection.

We need to be aware that facile answers aren't always available. There has been an enormous effort by the *kiruv* movement to sell *teshuvah* as a system, or as a *Weltanschauung,* which has answers to everything. The impetus for that trend is basically the desire to sell Yiddishkeit much like one sells an insurance policy. An insurance policy makes you safe. This is the working assumption of much of the *kiruv* movement. Yiddishkeit is going to make you safe. The problem arises when, within the framework of the world, Yiddishkeit does not make you safe. If it does not "work," its "not working" becomes an enormous challenge to its veracity. Who would buy an insurance policy that doesn't protect you? The system to keep *mitzvot* is called, by much of the *ba'al teshuvah* world, "Instructions for living." This is the popular mistranslation of the Hebrew phrase *Torat chaim.* The phrase really means a "Torah of life," and life is often ambiguous, nuanced, and complex. The implication of the mistranslation is that, if you follow the instructions, your life will be fine. How does this position respond, however, when communities of Jews who keep mitzvot are mercilessly destroyed? Then, the effect, or efficacy, of the "policy" is undercut. The instructions for living haven't kept us safe. Therefore, if *chazarah bi-teshuvah* does not mean "return to myself," which is what it should mean, but rather a return to having facile answers—including the answer as to why children are killed in a Petach Tikvah bus accident; that is, because people didn't keep Shabbos—then it's not authentic.

Teshuvah needs to be not a return to easy answers, or even to the spiritually arrogant assumption that we as human beings have answers to everything beneath the sun. *Teshuvah* needs to be a "return to myself," to my deepest sense of who I am. It needs to emerge from a sense of confidence in the core integrity of one's soul. The essence of a human being is *chelek Elokah mimal mamash*—a literal part of the divine substance. When the human being does return to his authentic self, there is a powerful, deep return to God at the same time. He is given guidance, given direction, given 2,000 years of wisdom, masters, and tradition.

This is precisely what Rabbi Avraham Yitzhak Kook means when he interprets the phrase *"Ani Hashem Elokechem"* as referring to my divine "I." He calls it *bakashat h'ani 'atzmi*, the search for my essential self. This, by the way, was Rabbi Kook's audacity.

S.F.: What about spiritual Jews who want to find their essential selves but instinctively feel that Judaism is not their path? And we all know, the Jewish world today is more polarized than before between a learning community that has a strengthening Jewish identity and a general community that does not feel any specifically Jewish quality or content in its life. How do we connect between these two groups?

Rabbi Gafni: There are two issues that need to be addressed. One is what I will call a technical issue, and the other is essentially existential. First, the technical issue. We haven't even begun to exhaust our resources for outreach. If every committed family in Israel or in the States invited one uncommitted, uninvolved family over for Shabbos once a month, we would close down every outreach organization. Period. We wouldn't need them.

The resources our community has available are massive and we haven't yet tapped into them. You see, the power of the community to help is enormous. Everyone knows someone at work, everyone has a friend; we just don't bring them in. I will give you an example. A *rosh yeshiva* here in Yerushalayim, who is well-known as a centrist, Orthodox, yeshiva dean, lives in a building in which a very good friend of mine lives. My friend is a single person, not committed, not involved at all. Never once did this person receive a hello, never once a Shabbos invitation. It's beyond belief. While I am not critiquing this rabbi personally, I am saying that, if our community does not say hello to the person next door, we cannot ask the dramatic existential question, "Why aren't people involved?" We have to stretch our natural abilities to the maximum because we don't yet know or realize the extent of that maximum.

As for the essential question, why do spiritual people not always come to Judaism as their natural path, I think that there is one area in which the spiritual intuition of modernity initially seems to run contrary to the intuition, or inherent impulses, of Jewish religious thought: human autonomy.

If there is one idea that is radically new in the last 150 years, it is unquestionably the internal impulse, the sense and feeling of the idea of human autonomy. There is the idea, the thought, the feeling, the notion of the creative, autonomous individual who charts his own destiny, whether it is in his or her personal or moral decisions through-out all stages of life. Religion, however, is perceived as God–father or God–king; hierarchical, commanding, heteronomous—not allowing for human autonomy.

This tension has been addressed by at least two important Jewish thinkers: Rabbi Joseph Soloveitchik and Rabbi Kook. Without going into a long discussion about them, let me just establish some broad pa-rameters. Essentially, what we need to look at is not a situation in which *ani mevatel ratzoni le-ratzon Hashem* ("I nullify my will in order to do God's will"; in other words, the idea of, above all, Thy will be done), but rather, what Rabbi Soloveitchik calls *zehui retzonot*, my will *is* God's will (see his article *"U–bikashtem mi-sham"* in *Ha–Darom*, 1977). When I reach down into the deepest part of myself, I understand or realize that my will is God's will. There is a merging between me and God's will, and its expression in *halachah*. *Halachah* is not law; the transla-tion of *halachah* as "law" is a tragedy. *Halachah* is the way. Within the Jewish Way, there is an expression of my deepest self, which emerges to become Jewish living.

We need to move away from heteronomy, toward a system in which the human being, the Jew, participates as an autonomous active partner in the creation of himself as a moral, spiritual being. The Jew who consciously forges new links in the chain and the Jew who looks to *halachah*, as a method for bringing out the deepest part of who he is, understand fully that a dialectic exists. Not only does *halachah* obli-gate me without, but it obligates me to find the place where it comes from within. I think that's critical.

Do you know Kohlberg's critical stages of human development? The lowest stage is obedience; the highest stage is autonomy. Kohlberg is expressing the core intuition of modernity. This core "movement" of modernity is not, I believe, a secular movement. It is a spiritual move-ment. Now, I know that there are important Jewish teachers who re-ject autonomy as a spiritual value. For example, Rabbi Haim Shmuelevitz of the Mir Yeshiva, in *Sichot Mussar*, rejects human au-tonomy. He is writing in the 20th century, yet he is a medieval writer in the extreme.

In contrast, Rabbi Kook understood that the unfolding of human history is the unfolding of the Divine. There is a historical process, which Rabbi Kook himself understood very deeply, that plays out or unfolds new layers of God's revelation, one of which is ideas. In a word, history is a critical arena of Divine revelation.

One of the new datum of historical revelation is new ideas. When a powerful ethical idea sweeps the consciousness of man, more often than not that idea contains a core revelatory Divine truth. Human autonomy, the emergence of human autonomy, is such an idea. We need to embrace the idea of autonomy. The modern intuition understands that a religious system that doesn't embrace autonomy is somehow religiously flawed.

Now, if we haven't allowed our religion to unfold in a way that allows for the emergence of autonomous moment within classical Judaism, then we have done Yiddishkeit a disservice. Then, we are still talking about "Thy will be done" and not *zehui retzonot,* a merging of wills.

S.F.: Two questions. If the unfolding of history is a Divine process, how do you understand the present stage of Jewish and world history? Is it possible, in your judgment, to live the kind of *halachic* life that is the Jewish way anywhere but in Israel?

Rabbi Gafni: I am going to start with the second question, actually: Is it possible outside of Israel? I think it is. But not in an ideal way. You miss a piece and, paradoxically, you gain a piece. That's one of the tragedies of Israel today. I am in Israel. I am committed to Israel and love Israel deeply. Nothing would take me out of Israel except some academic work for a short period of time. Yet, life in Israel tends to be very *menutav* (pigeon–holed). For example, when I wake up in the morning, I've got a huge pile of *yarmulkas* to choose from. Some are black, some are knitted, some are big, some are small—I just grab one. And for that day, people who do not know me will categorize me by whichever *yarmulka* I happen to be wearing. In other words, we in Israel identify people very superficially, based on an external set of symbols. There is not a lot of room for creativity or holy audacity, *chutzpah demeshichata,* the *chutzpah* of the Messiah, to borrow a mystical phrase.

Paradoxically, because in a certain sense there is less at stake in the United States, there's more room for movement and creativity. As a result, *teshuvah* in the States is essentially easier. There's more room to find a spiritual home that is more comfortable for a broader group of people who are trying to come home. In many ways, we haven't created a healthy center for grounded return in Israel outside of the Haredi context. Unfortunately, the Haredi context strikes many as

being counterintuitive. While there are many advantages to being outside of the Israeli setting, ultimately a full, rich, and existentially complete life as a Jew in the 20th Century is not possible outside the State
of Israel. Life here means to participate in the building of a country,
with all the paradoxes and with all the quandaries of a vital throbbing
society. You have to get your hands messy sometimes. That's what Judaism envisioned. The essential story of the Biblical text is one of movement towards the land, followed by creation of a society.

Back to your first question: Where are we in world history? That's
too big a question for me. I certainly don't know the answer. I may
have some preliminary thoughts. There is no question that we are definitely living in a "post" age of some sort. People are talking about post–
Zionism; people are talking about post–Modernism. Whatever this
means, there is a realization that the old categories are no longer sufficient to explain our reality. Many people are talking about a post-
halachic age too. There are Arthur Green, Zalman Schacter-Shlomi, and
any number of New Age spiritual personalities. Yitz Greenberg and
David Hartman teeter on or over the border of *halachah*. But I don't
think that we are in a post–*halachic* age; I think we are in a *halachic*
age. But in this age, *halachah* needs to embrace reality, and there needs
to be very deep interaction between text and history, between sacred
life and sacred text, between the sacred autobiography of the person—
the people—and the Torah. I am talking about continued interaction,
which took place throughout the generations and which has to an extent ceased today because we have become oriented only to text. Rabbi
Haim Soloveitchik recently wrote an excellent article for *Tradition* in
which he addressed a number of these issues. The point, to make this
more clear, is that we need to understand, when we are confronting
new realities, that we need to avoid falling back on the old paradigms.
I'll give you a very simple example. If you look at the 19th Century
texts, you will see rabbis for whom a very minor salvation took place,
and followers who were very careful to observe this date of salvation,
basically by saying "*Hallel*" on the anniversary of the event. This is
based on a Gemara in *Pesachim* (113), "*Al kol tza'ar she–lo tavo al ha-
tsibur.*" To even dream that the establishment of the State of Israel is less
important than those minor incidents of individual salvation is absurd.
It's way over the border and into the realm of fantasy and absurdity.
The establishment of the State of Israel radically changed the course of
Jewish history, and enabled Judaism to move forward into a new phase.

The entire re-flourishing of the yeshiva movement in America and Israel would have been impossible without the State of Israel. It allowed the resurgence of Torah, and it allowed the physical safety of the Jewish people. It was an expression of *kiddush Hashem* in the face of the horrible *chillul Hashem,* which was the Holocaust. To ignore that is to say that I am not living in the world anymore, that text and history don't merge anymore. It is to ignore completely the reality of the world that I live in, to say that I am withdrawing into Augustine's City of God, and I am no longer in the City of Man. When that happens, it should be no surprise that people are not returning. People understand that we want to return to a system that touches the reality of our lives. When I ignore the reality of what is going on around me, then I am lost. Then *halachah* has lost.

Take the women's movement, for instance. Is the core intuition of feminism a new and important movement? To suggest that nothing has changed, to hold up as a model women who learned during the 16th Century, is ridiculous. We point to three women from the Renaissance, four women in the Hasidic movement, and Rashi's granddaughters, and then claim that Judaism does indeed take the needs of women into account. Of course there were exceptions, but this is not even good apologetics. There is no question that there is an emergence of women's consciousness. It is real and it is part of the unfolding process of history. We need to take it seriously. To revert to 13th Century role models is essentially wrong. It ignores the history, and it means that Judaism does not take account of history anymore.

We need to look at how that works, at how text and history dialogue. We need to examine *halachic* categories, which can only change through the *halachic* process. When people are fundamentally "unintuitive" of *halachic* processes and write about them casually, then it's not relevant. *Halachah* can only change through its own internal process, parameters, and integrity. *Halachah* is about looking. It means to look at historical issues, women's issues, "*Hallel*" on *Yom Ha-Atzmaut.* It isn't a political issue or process. Much of the *halachic* community, particularly large sectors of the Haredi world, ignores the reality in which we live. Consequently, we are going to have Jews with pictures on the wall of hasidim dancing, but they will remain pictures, quaint images, and they will never dance themselves.

S.F.: And the movement of the State of Israel in history—are we moving forward toward redemption, or backward, God forbid, to exile?

Rabbi Gafni: I grew up with a sort of classical *mercaz ha–rav* image of Zionism. I viewed history as the unfolding of *geulah,* which found its expression in *"ve–atem harei Yisrael anvechem titenu u'prichem tisu le'ami Yisrael ki kervu lavo."* ("And you the mountains of Israel give forth your grapes and give forth your fruit from my nation Israel for it draws close.") The Talmud in *Sanhedrin* (97) cites this verse, which describes the physical rejuvenation of the land of Israel as the sign of imminent redemption. The Gemara refers to this as *ketz hameguleh,* the revealed redemption. There is a metaphysical notion that the process of redemption never moves backwards; that ultimately, if one sees the pattern, there is a forward motion. I have not retreated from that view essentially, but I think it needs to be expressed differently, with nuance. We are not at all sure what a backward or forward motion looks like. It does strongly appear that the process of history is such that it is moving forward. The Jewish return to the Land of Israel after 2000 years of exile is an important and critical step towards redemption, and it is clearly a partial fulfillment of prophecy. At the same time, between that and ultimate *geulah,* we don't know what the distance is in either chronological or qualitative terms. Could we be 500 years before *geulah* takes place? We could. However, let me make it clear. I understand *geulah* as an historical event. I don't agree with Rabbi Hartman's idea that the *geulah* never really takes place in history. The existential movements are critical. I speak about them often. Nonetheless, the story of the Jewish people is the story of historical people returning to historical land. Ultimately, these historical people and that historical land need to impact on the entire flow of world history in a concrete way. It means no more starving children; it means the perfection of the world in the most basic realm of human dignity. It means affirming human dignity to the maximum for every individual, so that everyone can achieve his or her Divine potential. I still believe that we will achieve it. I believe that we are on the road to achieving it. It is *be'yadenu* ("in our own hands").

Whether it will take us 50 years or 500, I don't know. When will God intervene? I certainly don't know. I think the signs are clear that we are in a process moving towards redemption. What are the signs—Global communications, the Internet, the ingathering of the exiles, the physical rejuvenation of the land, Israel's new international centrality, the empowerment of women, and other movements away from totalitarianism—these are all signs that redemption is under way.

S.F.: What about universal ethical monotheism, the Jewish light to the nations? Is there a Jewish message for humankind?

Rabbi Gafni: Absolutely. My vision of redemption is not that "everyone becomes Jewish," but that two different Jewish ideas will be embraced. The first idea is ethical monotheism, which Herman Cohen and others have talked about extensively. We reject ethics and monotheism as independent values and argue for the unique synthesis of the two. It's a classical Jewish idea, one that has been around for 2,000 years. It's an ideal—an important ideal.

The second idea is the call to holiness or the call to prophecy. Rabbi Soloveitchik, in *Halachic Man,* writes with stunning beauty that Rambam understands prophecy to be an essential goal for every human being. This transforms prophecy from a dogma to a command, a spiritual imperative. Only that which is possible is commanded. A commanded prophecy is to command to *devekut,* to passion to God. It is a command to God–consciousness.

Somebody gave me an article in which the author argued about ethical monotheism. The piece was good but not, however, completely Jewish. He totally left out *devekut,* passion in which I submit before God—the Abraham moment, in which I bow before Him. That is a powerful Jewish moment, the highest expression of who I am. Human ethics is in dialectical tension with *devekut* as primary Jewish movements.

Then again, we find streams today that only emphasize *devekut;* they also miss the point. It is the combination that is the unique system, holding tension between them that is uniquely Jewish.

What makes Judaism most true? I have been waiting to find someone to ask me that question. The answer I would probably give is "dialectic" or "balance." My experience of the Divine emerges from the kind of unique balance, dialectic, which in Jewish living takes place between values and emotional moments, between *halachic* moments and values and existential experience.

The ability to affirm opposites and find the moment of balance within: the harmony exists without needing to choose one or eradicate the other. Judaism is unique not because it is ethical or holy, not because of our cleaving to God, not because of charity or a unique ethic—

all these moments have their expression in other systems. But Judaism is radically unique, hence Divine, in its affirming and balancing the cacophony of spiritual moments into one system, into a unique whole that I think is unrivaled in the world. In every aspect of Jewish living, there is the fine-tuned sense of balance. Balance does not mean moderation. You know the saying, that you can walk on the left side of the road or on the right side, but only an ass walks in the middle. I'm not talking about a kind of *pareve*, passionless, middle–of–the–road position; I am talking about embracing both values with equal passion. Through that embrace, we find the sort of value that emerges from the two, in terms of truth and peace, in terms of physical involvement and denial, and in terms of spirituality and law. Likewise, all sorts of classical antinomies merge in a wonderful dialectical balance between man's greatness and man's insignificance. And the dialectical moment is the essence of the Jewish moment; the vessel that allows us to hold the dialectic is *halachic* Jewish Law. What *halachah* does is create a system for dialectical living in which I affirm passionately the ostensibly competing moments, and they are woven into a completely new tapestry of life. This is an important part of *halacha's* greatness.

Let's take one example. How does the "you" feel when you get up in the morning? Do you feel a basic need for *bittul*, for self–nullification that is the need to merge with the One? Or do you wake up feeling a deep need to create, a feeling of "my" individuality, "my" individuation? What is your basic moment? A different expression of the same idea: Do you experience yourself as a man or woman of simple faith or in existential struggle? These are two very different positions. How do they resolve each other?

Judaism was somehow able to affirm them both, with tremendous power. On the one hand, I am a struggler, the *Yisraeli*: "*sareti im Elokim*" (*Bereshit 32*)—meaning, I struggle with God. On the other hand, I am a *Yehudi*, a Jew, but to be a Jew means that I affirm *Hashem* (*Bereshit 29*). I *modeh* ("thank") *Hashem*. I am embraced by God, embraced in God's womb. The *Yisraeli* and the *Yehudi* moments exist in ethical dialectical tension with each other. On the one hand, I am embraced by God's shadow, which is a place of safety and love, a place where I am a child embraced by my parents. On the other hand, I am in a situation of struggle, a lovers' model in which there is constant questioning and struggle though the commitment to the relationship is powerful. These two models exist side by side. They are mutually exclusive models, *prima facie*, but within the Jewish tradition and the Jewish existential moment, they exist side by side. That is very, very, very powerful.

S.F.: Is it that, at any moment, I have the choice of which model I am to be a part of?

Rabbi Gafni: I would phrase it a little differently. At every moment, I am part of both. To a certain extent, on a subconscious level, when I embrace both moments, both moments make up a part of who I am. Even if they are not active at this particular moment, they are part of the substructure of my personality. They exist simultaneously. Within a given day, there are moments when I am more in the modality of *bittul*. Then there are other days when the lovers' model predominates and *Shir ha-Shirim* more accurately expresses my relationship to God. The ability to move between models and to exist within each one at the same time is a wonderful expression of the dialectic. This model is not found in Christian or Islamic thought. It is unique.

S.F.: Are you saying that we have a way of thought superior to others?

Rabbi Gafni: I would say that some of us are very politically correct and shy away from words like "superior." Some of us, however, are not so politically correct. The order of distinction necessitates hierarchy, redeemed hierarchy, which is destroyed and then reaffirmed after a powerful sense of egalitarianism is incorporated. In redeemed hierarchies, however, there still are notions of superiority. Our system is unique. I think that it has a powerful role to play, one which cannot be played by any other system. Part of being *ohr la-goyim*, a light unto the nations, is bringing this unique system to bear not only on Jewish religious life, but, without actually proselytizing, on the religious life of the world. In other words, we have a message that is powerful. We have a lifestyle that is powerful. We have a system that is not only for the Jewish people, but which in some shape and form we offer to the world. This is true intellectually and it is true, no less powerfully and perhaps even more so, experientially.

There's a wonderful Gemara in *Yoma*, which defines *kiddush Hashem* and *chillul Hashem*. *Kiddush Hashem* happens when a person is able to express and incorporate the learning he has acquired into the norms of daily living. You look at such a person and say, "That's how a person should be." *Chillul Hashem* is, of course, the opposite: when you look at a person and say, "That's not how a person should be." We need to bring not only intellectual argumentation to bear, but the community to bear. We need to create a community that speaks to the world, that is an *ohr la-goyim*. This is critical. To be an *ohr la-goyim* is to be able to create a community, a system, that is a model of redeemed living.

S.F.: But haven't we seen the Jews as models for the modern world in ways that are not specifically Jewish?

Rabbi Gafni: There was certainly a myriad of Jewish individuals in every field who, 50 years after the floodgates were opened, made significant contributions. Without question. Someone said that there were four great contributors to modern thought: Einstein, Freud, Darwin, and Marx. There were three who were Jewish and one who was wrong. In any case, these are contributions that emerged from the Jewish moment but are not uniquely Jewish. The Jewish community's contribution is distinctly Jewish. However, the contribution of the community as a community is far more important than the contributions of individuals. Despite the fact that we all grew up with parents who told us that there are a disproportionate number of Jews who have won the Nobel Prize, it's ultimately not what it's all about.

S.F.: It's not relevant in terms of *tikkun olam*?

Rabbi Gafni: It's peripherally relevant. Their contributions are important. Marx's grandfather was an Orthodox rabbi. Freud was a member of B'nai Brit. They emerged out of deep thought patterns—patterns needing to be transformed into broader moments—but, ultimately, they did not consciously act as Jews. They were messengers who forgot their message. We need to be messengers who know that we are messengers and know what the message is.

In other words, the primary category, the most audacious Jewish category, is *shlichut*. It's powerful, the idea that God acts through messengers. Bonhoffer talked about "discipleship"; we need to talk about "messengership." We need to be conscious of our messengership and conscious of the Torah as God's Name. We are students and teachers of the Torah, God's text. As the teachers of that Name, we need to create a community that reflects the text, an ethical community, a deeply moral community concerned with its own *tikkun olam*. Only a community that is committed to its own holiness is able to transmit that message. That is what Yiddishkeit is about. That is what we are moving toward, the goal that we need to struggle for constantly.

S.F.: The main concept of this work is *avodat Hashem*. I think you have described what you believe this to be, but could you elaborate on this further? And do you consider your own work to be *avodat Hashem*?

Rabbi Gafni: I think that everyone needs to understand their life's work as *avodat Hashem*. Whatever a person is doing, whether a person is a businessman or a *sandlar* ("shoemaker"), his work is Divine work. The greatness of the holy shoemaker stitching each stitch perfectly in the Zohar's stunning image is that of *mayeched yichudim elyonim,* causing divine unions to take place. What does the Zohar mean? The simple and stunning answer is that through stitching perfectly, through being completely present and involved in your own particular work, one engage in *avodat Hashem*.

This is true about the *sandlar,* and it's no less true about a teacher. Teachers have to view their own lives in the context of *avodat Hashem*. If they don't, then ultimately their thinking processes become distorted, because they begin trying to think in terms of originality. They try to think in order to be creative or in order to be bombastic. They lose the sense that their thinking process is a reflection, a prism, through which the channels and streams of Jewish consciousness, of Jewish thinking, of Jewish wisdom are reflected. This expression and communication are a part of one's personal *avodat Hashem*. From this perspective, it is critical not only for spiritual but for intellectual integrity. I hope that my life's teaching is a deep form of *avodat Hashem*.

What *avodat Hashem* is, I think, is implicitly clear in everything we have said. Basically, it is the ability to reach moments of holiness and remain faithful to those moments when they are not taking place. This happens through the prism of our personal story. Restatement: every person has their own story. No one person's story is anyone else's story. The ability to embrace our own story is extremely difficult but critical to Jewish thinking and living. There's a beautiful image suggested by the Rebbe of Ishpitz. He describes God walking, following along after a person. The person has lost pieces of himself along the way.

God goes after him and gathers up the lost pieces, and holds them and watches over them. Then at *layl Seder Pesach*, God allows him to re-access the pieces of the story he has lost. How does it happen? The Beit Yaakov does not explain, but I believe the way it happens is very simple: *sippur yetziyat Mitzrayim*. We tell your story, *min ha–metzarim*, from the straits, the narrow places. I can only leave my narrow places and walk in my *merchavim* ("wide spaces") by telling my story. The essence that I need to understand and embrace and incorporate is that I can only serve God through my story. I cannot serve God through anyone else's story. There is a unique moment of service available to me in my moment of life that is unavailable to anyone else. This is why there is the God of Abraham, the God of Isaac, and the God of Jacob. Abraham is not Isaac, and Isaac is not Jacob. Everybody has his own story. I first need to embrace my story; however, first I need to recognize it as my own.

There's a wonderful hasidic story that Martin Buber loved very much. It's too long a story to tell now, but it involves a bishop who had been formenting harsh anti–Jewish activity; it's a long and dramatic story—with lions and tigers and bears. At the end of the story, the Ba'al Shem Tov says, "When will you know that your *teshuvah* has been accepted? When you hear someone else telling your story and you recognize that it is yours." What is being described is the process of *teshuvah*, of coming home, of *geulah*. *Teshuvah* and *geulah*, the Maharal says correctly, are synonymous concepts and occur when we recognize our own story. Most of us walk through life not recognizing our story, not embracing our story. I can only serve God through my own story. Moreover, every person I meet in life has a piece of my story and I have a piece of theirs; true meeting is about completing each others' stories.

To restate it and make it more real, I'll add the following Jewish–Zen observation. This week's *parashah* (*Bamidbar 12*) is about Moshe, Aaron, and Miriam. It is a story about *lashon harah*, which they spoke about Moshe. Because he is separated from his wife, Miriam and Aaron complain that there is something wrong with Moshe's story. Why has Moshe separated from his wife? God's response is very strange. He says, "Don't speak *lashon harah*. I will explain to you the difference between you and Moshe." Why is God explaining to them why they're wrong? Who cares if they are right or wrong? Slander is not related to verac-ity. What God is saying is that *lashon harah* comes from *tzarut ayin*, which is translated as "envy" but literally means narrowsightedness, narrowness (Talmud, *Archin 15*). To get out of *metzarim* ("narrowness") one needs to embrace one's own story. Aaron and Miriam are unable to do this, unable to embrace their own stories as prophets. They want to embrace Moshe's story as a prophet. God says, "Moshe's story is not your story. His path is not your path." The only way you can understand the text, and it's a stunning text, is as God saying that *lashon harah* emerges from *tzarut ayin*, failure to embrace one's story.

Now, to complete the idea I can only serve God through a deep sense of my uniqueness—my unique contribution, my unique ability to come to God; to express the dimension of God, which "I" am. I need to contribute to *tikkun olam*—the perfection of God's world, or the revealing of God's light in the world, which is the same thing— through the particular spark of soul and Divine light that I have within me.

That particularly, that individuality, and that spontaneity are part of the autonomy that we talked about before. The notion that *avodat Hashem* is everyone trying to fulfill the same 613 mitzvot in the same way is completely false, because it contravenes the basic concepts of individuality and autonomy. It is true that we all have the same mitzvah structure, but we're each singing a different *niggun* when we do the same mitzvah. And it's the *niggun* in which the essence of *avodat Hashem* takes place.

It is the Zohar's most audacious claim that all *taryag mitzvot* are *etim le–devekut*, suggesting how we can achieve *devekut*. What the Zohar is saying with such great power is that mitzvot are the beginning and not the end. Rabbi Kook says the same thing in the second part of *Arpelei Toar*, his mystical diary: that being *halachic* by keeping kosher is the beginning and not the end. It's how I play the instrument, what I do with it through the prism of my own story, that is *avodat Hashem*. We get to God through the path of self, and we need to know self very, very deeply. In that sense, by the way, Freud's contribution was uniquely Jewish. He understood intuitively the notion of telling a story. The moment of free association in therapy is the moment of telling the story. It is a modern version of the idea of *sippur*. We need to take the idea of *sippur* and make it real. Only through that can we leave *Mitzrayim*, and leaving *Mitzrayim* is *avodat Hashem*. According to the kabbalistic/Hasidic model that suffuses most Jewish literature today, leaving *metzarim*—leaving *Mitzrayim*—is the image of personal redemption. The flash of insight I have into myself when I tell my story on the first night of Pesach, which the Maggid of Kosnitz calls "*it'aruta dele-ella*" ("the arousal from above"), is a Divine gift. Then I go through 49 days of *sefirah:* 49 days of counting, 49 days of regaining and making my story part of me.

S.F.: Thank you. Would you say something about the fact that some people's stories are exemplary, having great meaning—and not simply for themselves alone—while others are less so. If we look at the story of Moshe, Aaron, and Miriam that you cited, we understand their envy is because Moshe is closest to Hashem. We know there is *kinat soferim,* that even the great in serving God mar their service through demands that they alone be close to God. We also know that living one's life as a story, as a sacred text—trying to understand it as a sacred text—raises the question of how we read that text when it is flawed. And how can the person who has extraordinary gifts of insight and understanding make this story a help to others who may not have such gifts? And one more question, does the Torah you want to live come from your own life experience directly or can it also come from the reading of other stories?

Rabbi Gafni: In Hasidut, there is a strong tradition of telling the stories of others. The Maggid of Mezeritch said that the word "*ma'aseh*" in *ma'aseh merkava* is to be understood as story, the story of the chariot. He also talked about the act of storytelling as an act of prayer. The Besht talked about the telling of *sippurei tzadikim* as an act of *Talmud Torah. Sippurei tzadikim,* which tell other people's stories, can be described as virtual canonizations of the holy story, as acts of Divine service. No less important than study or prayer is telling the story of other models and being provoked to holiness, being inspired to holiness. In a sense, it is a merging with the story of another, which make their moment real to us.

I think that modernity has a particular addition to make to Hasidism, which I was implicitly trying to express. Rabbi Kook says that anyone who has within them a bit of concern for *teshuvat Yisrael* is *min ha-neshamot shel tzadikei elyon,* one of the holiest, highest *tzadikim.* That's true. If we had written a book about 36 Just Men one hundred years ago, it would have been filled with *wasser-treghers* ("water carriers"), old, pious men carrying water by day and poring over kabbalistic tomes by night. In a book about 36 contemporary Just Men, I suspect, the images of both men and women would be much different. I think that Rabbi Kook was expressing precisely this idea. The *tzadik elyon* is no longer a distant role model; we are all the *tzadik elyon*. *Kol she–yesh be'nishmato da'agah le–Yisrael*—"each person whose soul has in its concern for Israel" is among the *tzadikei elyon*. Therefore, the story we need to tell today, continuing with the idea of *sippurei tzadikim* is of course our own story. And here we come back to the last question, whether or not the *sippur* needs to come from one's own experience. We do not need to choose between the two. *Sippurei tzadikim* occupy an enormous and important place. They tell the story of the other. At the same time, if we are *tzadikei elyon*, we still need to tell our own story.

What if there are flaws in the text? It's precisely those flaws that need to be the major moments in the telling of the story. The Besht said that *ein davar rah yored min ha–shamayim*, there is nothing evil that comes down from heaven. The way the Slonimer Rebbe interpreted it is not as a statement about theodicy but rather about the human personality. A moment of wrath, a moment of pathology in the human personality, is also a moment for potential human greatness. The Besht's grandson, Baruch of Miedzybozh, suggested that only through the 49 Gates of Impurity can one reach the 49 Gates of Purity. In other words, only through telling the story of *averah*, sin, can I know who I really am.

Rabbi Kook said that we always have to take the fallen evil and return it to *shoreshav* ("to its roots"). What he meant by that, I believe, is that, only if you tell the "story of the sin," tracing it back to its source, do you begin to learn who you really are. Through the flaws, paradoxically, you are able to trace yourself back to the greatness you could be. God does not allow evil to become a part of us unless we need to own our own particular pathology (the evil) before we can move through it to the holiness that is also ours. This is precisely the idea expressed in the Talmud—"my intentional violations become my greatest merits"—not the violations per se, but the thrust that moved me to break them down. This is who I am. This is my uniqueness, my soul print, my essence. That is what I need to find and embrace. That is my story, and only through it do I achieve *yetziyat me-tzarim*, do I emerge out of the narrowness and walk in the wide places.

S.F.: In what way is that retelling done?

Rabbi Gafni: Here we come to an almost meta-*halacha,* or a substrata text just like *"kedoshim tihiyu"* or *"ve'asita et ha-yashar ve'ha-tov."* "Retelling," the idea of *sippur,* is a concept in meta-*halacha.* You don't fulfill or exhaust *sippur* in one mitzvah. There's a focus, and a beginning. There's an intense moment of spiritual therapeutic encounter, which takes place at the Passover Seder at which I am supposed to tell the national story. I am literally supposed to tell our story. But the ongoing, daily process of living is basically to be telling the story always, to be trying to understand always who I am in the deepest sense, to be tracing back always to the essence of my flaw, to use the mitzvot to do this. Different mitzvot speak to me differently. There is no such thing as equality in mitzvot; sameness doesn't exist. The Gemara speaks, in a number of places, of choosing one mitzvah. Why do I choose one? I don't ignore the rest. How do I have the right make a choice? The answer is, because it's unique to my story. The idea of mitzvah is the expression of the uniqueness of my relation to that mitzvah, the ability to let my story emerge in my "I"—in my self, in my *ani atzmi.*

S.F.: That story needs to be read and understood by myself alone or by others? By those who love me? By whom?

Rabbi Gafni: That story needs to be understood by me and myself. I need to carefully choose people who will help me understand, develop, and play out my story. In Hasidut, there's the idea of the *mashpiah,* one who impacts me and whom I allow to impact me because I have let him in. "Where is God?" the rebbe asks his Hasid. "God is where you let Him in." And God is within others where we let Him in. Everyone chooses differently, be it a friend, or a teacher, or a spouse. Here again there is spontaneity, there is autonomy. It's an enormous paradox. Within the system of mitzvah, which seems to be a uniform system, there's room for the essential movements of spontaneity and creativity that are allowed by autonomy. This is not a responsibility that we can shirk; it is a responsibility that anyone and everyone can fulfill. The signs are there, we just need to become aware of them.

S.F.: Do you perceive yourself as helping other people find their way?

Rabbi Gafni: I think that we all help other people find their way. At the risk of sounding glib, we are all teachers.

S.F.: True. But are there levels of this?

Rabbi Gafni: This is one of the stories I like to tell. When I was 16 years old, I worked at Howard Johnson's for the summer with a guy named Chris. I sat there scooping ice cream and talking to him all summer long—I brought my books with me yet didn't open a single one. Chris was a very important teacher for me. He was not Jewish and wasn't educated, but he had an intense honesty and innate wisdom.

My point is that we are all teachers. Sometimes it is more dangerous to teach directly because we make ourselves vulnerable. The absolute responsibility is heightened and so, therefore, is the culpability, being on the line. I do my best never to walk into a lecture without a great amount of respect and honor for the people sitting there. I take each lecture very, very seriously. I spend a great deal of time, hours and hours and more hours, thinking about exactly what I want to say. I try to be completely present in the moment of teaching. If this allows people to make moves in their lives, I thank God. Anytime someone calls me up to have lunch after a lecture and tells me that he was able to make this or that move in his life after hearing me, I feel very, very gratified. It's like music: When you play music, you want people to hear and appreciate it. You want it to touch their soul as it comes from yours. That's the feedback you need in order to adjust your playing. Thank God, it should only continue.

S.F.: Intellectually, Rav Soloveitchik and Rav Kook are your great guides?

Rabbi Gafni: I am certainly indebted to and have a student–teacher relationship with both Rav Soloveitchik and Rav Kook. I am heavily influenced by Hasidut and also by existential thought—Sartre, Camus, and to a certain extent Nietzsche and Kierkegaard. I have a couple of traditional degrees, but I didn't really go to school for them. That's a different story, through. I went to college for a year and got my B.A. at the end of the year. I did my M.A. at Bar Ilan University. The doctorate process is now happening at two different schools. Mostly, I am influenced by and have the greatest *hakarat ha–tov* for Rav Soloveitchik, Rav Kook, every Hasidic rebbe, and every Gemara I ever read. These are what have really shaped and formed my life-thinking. At the same time, I am indebted to life itself. There are two ways to come to a set of ideas. One is to look at a text and delve so deeply, in order to unfold the layers of text until you get to life. The other is to be in life as deeply as possible, to unfold the layers of life until you get to text. We need to do both, that is the essence of Jewish living.

Rabbi David Hartman

Rabbi David Hartman is one of the most important Jewish thinkers working today. He is also a communal leader, the founder and director of the Shalom Hartman Institute for Advanced Jewish Studies. Ordained by Yeshiva University's Theological Seminary, he has taught at the Department of Jewish Thought and Philosophy of the Hebrew University. A student of both Rabbi Joseph Soloveitchik *z"l* and of Professor Yehoshua Leibowitz *z"l*, he integrates in his work essential insights of their thought while moving toward a covenantal philosophy of his own.

I met Rabbi Hartman when he was engaged in preparations for the blessed endeavor of opening a new campus for the Shalom Hartman Institute. Brief as our talk was, I believe that it gives key insights into his thinking.

S.F.: Could you please tell me something about the Hartman Institute and the fundamental idea behind the group of institutions that you have created in Israel?

Rabbi Hartman: The idea of the institute was created in 1976, born from the recognition that Israel requires a new generation of Jewish thinkers who can bridge modernity and tradition, who are able on one level to master the Talmudic tradition, master the heritage, and at the same time be deeply *au courant* with the best of modern thought and the best of modern experience. My feeling was that Jews cannot live in the present without having a past, and can't have a past unless they have a way of integrating the present into that level of experience and understanding. The purpose of the Institute was to somehow make Torah into *Torat chayim*, which can flourish in the modern world, for Israelis who are seeking and approaching tradition, which gives them an anchor in their world. Israelis do not want to go back to the ghetto, and if the only option to live a Jewish life is to focus on the past, then I think Judaism has no future. We have to show somehow that the present can be infused with the richness of the tradition. This is what we are trying to do here.

S.F.: This is connected with your idea that *halachah* must be extended into realms of life where it was not well developed in the past, such as the political.

Rabbi Hartman: Not that the *halachah* has to be extended. I prefer to say that Jewish theology and Jewish political thinking need to be extended. I am not interested in a *halachic* state, but in the way Judaism would think about the problems of modernity in a new frame of reference. The tradition is challenged to speak to all these new issues that emerge, issues of distributive justice, issues of minority rights, issues of war and peace, and power and economic justice—all of these features. Does the tradition have something to contribute to them? Does it illuminate human life in some way, the issues that face human life?

S.F.: How does this work to bridge the great gap between secular and religious in Israeli society?

Rabbi Hartman: Well, I think that's a very serious question. That's why I mentioned that I am not interested in legislating an authoritative system of life. I am interested in creating openings to intellectually engage the Jewish tradition, to see if it has something to contribute to enrich life. The secular community in Israel is very interested in being given an opportunity to engage the tradition intellectually. What they do resent is the attempt to impose that tradition on their lives.

S.F.: But isn't there evidence that there is declining interest by secular Jews in the Jewish tradition?

Rabbi Hartman: The reason for this is because the rabbinate has not learned to communicate Torah in a meaningful way. Israelis identify religion with medievalism, with coercion, with lack of freedom of conscience, with dogmatism. They have a negative perception of what Judaism can mean for their lives. What I am saying is that there an enormous need to change that perception. That's the purpose of the Institute. And I believe that there is an hunger in the land. When they meet that new perception, they are interested. We had thirty principals of the leading secular high schools come here to study and find a way in which they can build Jewish values in their own school systems. Therefore, this indicated to me that there is in a sense potential receptivity, if the tradition is only taught properly, with a certain type of message of depth and integrity, without legislative coercion.

S.F.: The turning away from the tradition that is a great problem here is an even greater problem throughout the Jewish world. Is there hope for returning people to the tradition?

Rabbi Hartman: I would say that there's a double answer to your question. On one level, Israel is far more difficult in regard to bringing the tradition to Jews. But they have a very interesting substitute, nationalism, which serves as a feature of their identity. And there is an Israeli national culture. They speak Hebrew. There is literature. These things are capable of giving people in some way an identity, and a way of connecting themselves to Jewish history. In the Diaspora, there is nothing about nature. If there isn't Judaism, then you have nothing. In the Diaspora, there's no Jewish secular culture, therefore, a secularist in North America would have to go to a synagogue if he were to feel he has some connection with the flavor of the Jewish tradition. Here you don't have to go, in order to feel connected to your people and the family of Jews. Number one. So on the one hand, it's more difficult in Israel. On the other hand, it's much easier in Israel because the living society, the language, the land give a sense of memory and Jewish history. There is a commitment by the people who live here that they want to continue Jewish history. And they are paying a price, a serious price, to continue that history. They are interested. There's a greater receptivity because there's a greater resonance in the larger society, which would support the yearning for a deeper understanding of Yiddishkeit.

S.F.: In your writing, this deeper understanding centers on the Covenant relationship between Hashem and Israel. The subject of this present work is *avodat Hashem*. I know you very much center on the model of the marital relationship in illuminating the Covenant relationship. I wonder if in stressing this particular model, which stresses 'equality' in relationship, you do not in some sense contradict the traditional idea of *avodat Hashem* in which such great emphasis is often placed on the great gap between the infinite Divine and the finite human?

Rabbi Hartman: My notion of Covenant was not meant in some way to exclude the concept of *avodat Hashem*. What I was trying to develop was an energizing of the human partner of the Covenant to take responsibility for his life. But God and man are not two partners who have equal status. There is God and there are human beings. Worship of God grows from a much deeper impulse. What I spoke about in terms of the relational metaphor of "love" was in order to oppose those who believe that submission and authoritarianism define *avodat Hashem*. My own view is that the relational experience of the Covenant in love and mutuality is the best way to generate a type of personality who can serve God out of love. And *avodat Hashem* is a very important feature of my concept of Covenant.

S.F.: Do you understand your own life and work as *avodat Hashem*?

Rabbi Hartman: I don't like to talk about it in that way. But I would in some way say that my life's longing has been to seek to serve God out of love, and to understand the God whom I want to serve. That, clearly.

S.F.: But don't we see throughout human history, and in this century perhaps especially, that the other side of human freedom is the doing of evil?

Rabbi Hartman: I do not have a naive concept of human nature. I only said that I believe that the very meaning of the concept of "faith" is the believing in one's capacity to take responsibility. Otherwise, God would not give mitzvot to human beings. The meaning of giving a mitzvah is that God proclaims a human being is adequate to be responsible. Otherwise, the concept of *halachah* and mitzvah would not be so central in Judaism. Judaism's concept of mitzvah proclaims and liberates man from passivity to active involvement in the world.

S.F.: What is the special role of the Jewish people in terms of this active involvement in the world? Is there a special moral role for the Jewish people?

Rabbi Hartman: Our fundamental function is to survive, and to be a witness to the way of life our ancestors have given us. How that is going to improve the world is for the world to decide. Yet we offer very powerful things: the way we built our family life, the way we built our legal institutions, the way we have encouraged a critical love of God, and the way we emphasize the importance of family and community, and the particular memories of history. I have written about that. Jews bear witness to particularity, not to universality. The attempt to be universal has brought destruction to humanity. What we have to bear witness to is our own limited historical memories and own limited human capacities, and to do that with dignity, not taking up all the room. Religious faiths tend to monopolize the space. What I would like to see is religious faith making room for the other.

S.F.: In other words, you do not believe in what is called the Jewish mission of bringing ethical monotheism to humankind?

Rabbi Hartman: My concept of God is not exhausted by the ethical. There is a deep mystical dimension to man's quest for Divinity, which is beyond my comprehension. But I know that it's more than just having a foundation for ethics. There is something much more that human beings are seeking in that relationship than ethics. Worship is not just ethics.

S.F.: I did not mean to imply that it was. I meant to ask in regard to the Jewish mission to humankind.

Rabbi Hartman: I don't believe in the mission of the Jewish people to mankind.

S.F.: You don't believe this?

Rabbi Hartman: No. That's what I meant when I said that the mission of the Jews is to survive. I think that our very survival will have value to the world. I don't see the role of the Jews just to be *Ohr l'goyim.*

S.F.: Pascal said that the miraculous survival of the Jews is historical proof of the existence of God.

Rabbi Hartman: I think that Israel has to be a witness in the way a human society builds its life with the quest for holiness. Now, if that's going to be liberating for humanity, I don't know. I have to see what Jews can do. I can't claim what our mission is until I see what we do, what we make out of this society here.

S.F.: You have been in Israel for 25 years. How are the Jewish people and Israel doing in regard to the fact that Israel, in recent years, has become so great in its consumption of the universal American–inspired "world culture," what is sometimes called the "culture of nonsense"?

Rabbi Hartman: As badly as everybody else. Not worse, but as badly as everybody else.

S.F.: And what is the right response to this?

Rabbi Hartman: Torah. Unless we really fall in love with Torah and discover how Torah can make for a richer life, there is no hope. If not this, then I see us swallowed up by the assimilatory secular forces of modernity. We must build a serious Torah personality who brings the richness of his heritage to life. Without this, I see no future.

S.F.: That for you is not a denominational question?

Rabbi Hartman: No. it's not exclusive Orthodoxy. If the Reform and the Conservative want to interpret Torah in a different way, they have a right to. But they have to be Torah–intoxicated in accordance with their understanding of Torah. Fine. But it has to be Torah–intoxicated.

S.F.: One of the teachers of Torah I have spoken to in the course of these conversations, Rabbi Nahum Amsel, suggested that this will be the true division of the Jewish people in the future: on one side, all those who love "learning" and deepen in Torah, and another group who is outside the "learning" world completely. Do you see it this way?

Rabbi Hartman: My problem with that is, what do we mean by the "learned"? What is the criterion for learning? And how are the learned "learning"? That's the issue.

S.F.: In other words, it is not enough to sit and learn Gemara all day?

Rabbi Hartman: That's right. It's not enough just to learn in yeshivas. I mean, you could have a learned community with a different emphasis. I don't want the yeshiva or the *kollel* to be the only model of what serious engagement in Torah is all about.

S.F.: This means a comprehensive approach to learning?

Rabbi Hartman: Comprehensive. It means Bible. It means Talmud. It means theology. It means mysticism. It means Kabbalah. It means sociology of the family. It means a whole bunch of things, a whole range of issues. It means that we study Torah with these types of perspectives and questions. Torah is the given heritage of the vast body of knowledge that has accumulated over the past, by people who consciously wanted to serve God. Torah is the creation of people who were God–intoxicated. Now, when one touches that literature it effects him. I am not saying what interpretative strategies you are going to bring. But if one brings that type of intoxication and that type of seriousness, which is reflected in the tradition, then you are playing the game of Torah. You are not only playing *halachah*, but playing Torah.

S.F.: And how do you relate that to the traditional distinction between *limudei kosesh* and *limudei chol*? Is there a strict division in your mind? Or is it that the person who has the true attitude to Torah brings that Torah attitude to all he touches?

Rabbi Hartman: There is a difference. There is Torah and there is *chochat ha–olam*. But I think that a person imbued with the spirit of Torah brings that passion to all he studies. He tries to gleam from everything he meets and sees to enrich his *hashkfat olam* ("world view"), which is shaped by multiple melodies. Torah is the integrative power. It's fed by the best in philosophy, the best in sociology, the best in legal thinking. All this enters into the mix of Torah. Something new comes out.

S.F.: Do you have Orthodox colleagues who identify with your approach?

Rabbi Hartman: I think I do. My own teacher, Maimonides, felt this way. I don't go on a popularity contest ever. But I know that there are many serious Orthodox rabbis who have this approach.

S.F.: So you do not feel yourself in any way isolated?

Rabbi Hartman: I don't feel lonely. That's not my problem. Loneliness is not my problem. My problem is creativity. I feel that I don't do enough, as much as I could do, to create as much as I could do. I have very interesting students, very interesting colleagues in the Institute; it's a very rich community of people who are learning and thinking. It may not be for everybody. As I have said, my biggest concern is to serve God in truth, not necessarily be liked, by different Orthodox rabbis. They can like me, or dislike me. That's not my issue.

S.F.: Isn't it always those who have done much who feel the greatest obligation to do more?

Rabbi Hartman: I don't know. I know that's how I feel. My loneliness is my feeling that I haven't done all I could do with my life. I know. People comfort me by telling me all the nice things I have done. It doesn't seem to work for me enough.

S.F.: Is this related to your own desire to create a new work in writing, to extend your own thought in new ways?

Rabbi Hartman: Yes, it's very deeply related to that: the frustration that I haven't yet written the work I want to do. There is still much to do. I hope God will give me the energy to do it.

S.F.: I know that feeling very well. In terms, however, of your teaching, for instance, the principals of secular schools you mentioned earlier—you don't try to teach them a "system," do you?

Rabbi Hartman: We expose them to the tradition. And we allow them to see if the tradition speaks to them. I am teaching them now the whole section in Talmud about the family. They're finding it very rich. We teach them about Shabbos, about "*kiddushah*." In studying it, they see that it speaks to them, deep in their souls. And that's a fact. You have to come here on Wednesday and you can see it.

S.F.: You have mentioned your concern with "family" issues. Do you believe that the traditional Jewish family is the key or a key to Jewish continuity in the future?

Rabbi Hartman: The family is a carrier of memory and meaning. It's very important.

S.F.: How do you relate to the new forms of family structure that are now emerging?

Rabbi Hartman: Those are individual choices. It's too soon to tell. People should be given the opportunity to choose what they are looking for. And we will see what happens. I am fundamentally tradition-bound and very conservative about the family. But I am all for egalitarianism of a responsible kind. The sharing of responsibility between father and mother is a positive thing if it makes for greater family solidarity, family dignity, in which each one can grow.

S.F.: As I told you, one of the main reasons for undertaking this work was a 1990 survey showing increased assimilation in the United States. What is your response to this?

Rabbi Hartman: People are bored with the Jewish experience. It has ceased having a compelling music. I don't blame them for assimilating. The Jewish story is not their story. They don't know why they have to continue. We haven't given them a rootedness in their historical story, which would give them a way of organizing meaning in their lives. So what do you expect them to do?

S.F.: It's interesting that you use the word "story." There is a hasidic idea that the principal Torah a person learns is the story of their own life. I remember in 1967 how many people who were marginally Jewish felt that the threat to Israel was somehow a threat to their very being. They felt themselves then part of our story. Why not now?

Rabbi Hartman: They felt part of the drama because they did not want to see another Holocaust. I don't know if that's our story. But it lasted for exactly one week. Great events don't bring about changes. The slow process of learning Torah and the slow process of shaping people are what we need. I don't have any great faith that a great event is going to change people's consciousness.

S.F.: I agree with the basic thought that it is the long, slow process of teaching and learning Torah that is crucial to the Jewish future. But great events also have their part. The 1967 war changed the consciousness and lives of thousands, perhaps hundreds of thousands, of people. It, after all, did more than anything else to wake Soviet Jewry to its Jewishness.

Rabbi Hartman: There are stories, great moments, which may have dramatic catalytic effect. But in the long run, I have great faith in living Torah. The way one builds his family, the way one lives his daily life—you can bet on that much more.

S.F.: As you see us now in Israel, where are we in our story in terms of survival, our struggle for peace, for redemption?

Rabbi Hartman: It's a very hard question. The struggle for peace with a difficult enemy who hates us—the terrorist bombing of the bus this week only reflects in a very horrible way the vulnerability and the suffering of Jews in the face of diabolic enemies. That's one issue. And then we are a people who has to learn to live with each other in dignity and decency.

S.F.: I know how much you are concerned with dignity and respect for each individual and people. But isn't Israel now in an impossible situation, in that we can show all the respect and consideration we want to the "other" and the other goes on hating us and trying to destroy us?

Rabbi Hartman: Assymetry is a very serious issue. Where there is asymetry, it absolves people of responsibility. Responsibility requires reciprocity. And if there isn't recriprocity, then you don't have a moral claim on me. If Jews want to act with dignity to Arabs, Arabs also have to want to act with dignity to Jews. The Palestinians have to demonstrate that they want to have peace with us. And we have to demonstrate that we want to have peace with them. Each of us has to eliminate the fears of the other. Each of us has to heal the suspicions of the other. Each of us has to create good will and plant it in the soul of the other. And I hope it can work. I hope so. Some people feel as if it will never work. But we have to walk with our eyes open and be strong. We have to be careful, very, very cautious.

S.F.: Israel was created to protect the Jewish people. Here we are suffering through this, with this kind of enemy.

Rabbi Hartman: What can we do? We are a people who does not want to suffer. I think that we want peace, that genuinely the Israeli wants peace. But God blessed us and cursed us with the wrong place.

S.F.: It may be that God has given us the challenge to make peace with the most difficult kind of enemy. Maybe.

Rabbi Hartman: I hope we can respond to that challenge, and that the enemy we have had would like to stop being our enemy. I hope. But I don't know. No one knows. And each one tries. That's all I can say. We live here with the uncertainty of the future and with a great resolve to continue, a great determination to make it work. I hope that the *Kadosh Baruch Hu* does not have any diabolic schemes in mind for us.

S.F.: I pray so too. One more question. What do you feel you need to do the most in the years ahead?

Rabbi Hartman: I have to study more Torah. I have to become a bigger *talmid chocham*. I have to be a *mensch,* and live like a *mensch* in society. Those are the things that I feel I need to do.

Rabbi Israel Hess z"l

Rabbi Israel Hess z"l was a dedicated teacher of Torah throughout his life. He served as deputy mayor of Ranaana and was
founder of the Beit Ha–Midrash at University Bar Ilan. An important author and Jewish thinker, his books have reached thousands of readers in Israel. Among them are *The Way of Faith*, *The
Way of Divine Service*, *Faith in the Generation of Revival*, and, most
recently, his study of Kabbalah, *On The Threshold of Inwardness*.

I met with Rabbi Hess at his home in the Givat Shaul quarter of Jerusalem in June of 1995. Even then there were outward
signs of the great struggle he was going through against the illness
that would eventually take his life. He continued to devote himself to the dissemination of Torah through his last very difficult
months. And he truly exemplified an idea that he himself frequently taught: that through our suffering Hashem brings us closer
to Him.

This interview is published too with the hope that his works,
which to this point have not been translated from Hebrew, will
also find interest and an audience in the English–speaking world.

ೞ ೪

S.F.: The central concept of this work is *avodat Hashem*. How do you understand the *avodah* of the individual Jew and of the community of Israel as a whole?

Rabbi Hess: First of all, and above all, the service of God is the keeping of the mitzvot. This is because our very reason for being created is to affirm Hashem's rulership of the world. As is written in Adon Olam, "*L'at naaseh b'cheftzo kol, Azai Melech shemo nekrah.*" ("Who reigned before any form was created, at the time when all was made by His Will, He was at once acknowledged as King. And in the end, when all shall cease to be, the revered God alone will still be King.") In a sense, there appears to be a contradiction here because, on the one hand, He is "King" before all, yet on the other hand, He has to be "proclaimed King," His Name has to be called King by humans. This calling, proclaiming the Name (*meshichat hamahut haatzmi shel ha–adam*), is the drawing forth of the essential nature of humanity. The meaning is that our action, by calling God in Name, is to help bring His Kingship here so that He will in effect rule here. In this, He will be a King whose subjects do His Will. If He is not King, then there is no such relation. But the doing of His Will in order to be meaningful must be done through human freedom of choice. If I press a button and a robot does what I command, then I am not a King. There is true kingship only when His subjects do His Will out of their own free will. That is to say, when they make their own free will subject to the will of the King.

For instance, you may want to continue to sleep in the morning. But if the King tells you to get up early, go to a place where there is crowd of people, put two cubes on your head, say a number of words, be with Him for half an hour, directly profit nothing, then you put the Will of the King first and overcome your desire to sleep. You overcome your own desire. And so I am ruled by the King. But we do not speak continually of Hashem as King, rather of our receiving (*kabbalah*) the burden (obligation) of his Kingship on us in the future to come. Because of this, we make Him our ruler, since the purpose of all creation is Kingship, and the human being is the single creature of creation with a will of his own, free choice, and the power *mamlich* (to crown), or to assert, the Kingship of God. So the purpose of all our action is to fullfill His Will, and live by His commandments. We call the keeping of the mitzvot *avodah*, or "work," because this is the "job" that is ours in life. Everything I initiate outside this is also meant to be part of this job. And if I cannot keep the mitzvot because I do not have money for food, then I will go to work at something so there will be money for subsistence. But this action is only a means to enable me to do the true work, which is the doing the mitzvot. If I can't buy Tefillin or *Lulav*, and so am unable to fulfill his will, then I will go to work so as to be able to get the means that will enable me to do His Will. In sum, each and every human being is born for one purpose only, to do the will of God, as given in the Torah. And through the Torah, I know what God demands of me, that is, to serve Him. All our life has to be centered on and around doing the will of God.

But God wants of us, demands of us not only as private individuals but as a *tsibbur* (a "public"), a *clal* (a "community"). If the Torah is the summary, the essence of all the demands Hashem makes upon us, then there is no single individual who by himself alone can fulfill the Torah. In order to fulfill the Torah completely, one has to be man and also woman, farmer and also merchant, *Kohen* and *Yisrael*, and also king and ordinary person. The Torah is given to the community of Israel. Beyond the fact that there are mitzvot that no single individual can keep, there is the fact that Torah is meant for Israel as a whole. Only when there is the people as a whole, people of all kinds, can the Torah as a whole be kept. This still relates to individuals, for you need all the individuals to keep the Torah as a whole. There are also things that belong only to the community as a whole. The simple reason is because the *Kadosh Baruch Hu* appears, is revealed, only to the congregation: "*v'ani nekdashti b'toch Yisrael.*" It is impossible and forbidden to say any prayer of holiness without a public of ten: no "*Kaddish,*" no "*Kiddushah.*" Ten is the minimum required for forming a "public." It is written in the Gemara, "The voice of ten is the *Shechinah.*" The larger the congregation, the greater the revelation of *Shechinah.* There is a very interesting thought of Rabbi Yosi Ha–Galili in the Mishneh in *Berachot.* When three sit and eat, they can say "Let us bless," but when ten sit, they can say "Bless Our Lord." When one hundred sit, they can say "Bless our Lord the Lord of Israel," while 10,000 say, "Let us Bless our Lord our God, God of Israel, God of the Hosts, who sits upon the throne of *cherubim* for the food we have eaten." That is to say, the greater the size of the congregation, the more the revelation and appearance of the Divine. Since it is the aim of the *Kadosh Baruch Hu* to rule in the world—that is to say, to be revealed and recognized as King by those on earth, from the smallest to the greatest—and since the revelation of the Lord is only before the congregation, it becomes apparent that the main part of the service of God is that of the congregation–community. The private service I do is when I am part of and included in the congregation of Israel. If I withdraw myself from the community of Israel and do all the private mitzvot in the world, then this has no real value. It is like someone whose hand is cut off. A right hand will say, "For what reason do I have to serve the boss all the time? I bring food to the mouth. Now I want to be alone. Why do I have to serve anyone else? I want to cut myself off." But even for this, you need the other hand. That is to say, all the existence, all the life of the individual organ comes only through its connection with the whole. The human being is not built like Jepetto's Pinocchio, piece by piece, mechanically: first hand and then another; then the legs; and then the screws. For us, it is impossible to take out "the screws" and separate each organ. Our 248 organs are connected as one whole, not as 248 separate distinctly functioning, independent organs. So all the private service I do is only when I am part of the whole community of Israel. This is when I belong to the community of Israel, feel its sorrows as my sorrows, its joys as my joys. This is the way we affirm the Kingship of God, because Hashem decided that He does not appear to the individual but only to the community.

S.F.: How do you explain the fact that the great majority of Jews who live in the world today do not understand their role and relation to

God in this way, that many are completely cut off from any idea of serving God, and that even within Israel, among the most important leading circles, there is no feeling of such a relationship?

Rabbi Hess: The way this came to be is a sociological, historical story, which for our purposes is not important to explore now. What is clear is that a great share of the people of Israel are not in any way close to Judaism. The moment a person feels and thinks as a Jew, he feels his belonging to the Jewish people. If someone in France enters the Interior office and they ask him his nationality, he says "French," and for his religion, he says Catholic, Buddhist, Mohammedan, whatever. But here in Israel when they ask one's nationality, he says "Jewish," and for his religion he says "Jewish." This is precisely the story, the identity between religion and nationality. The moment there is an identity of nationality and religion, you cannot be a German of the faith of Moses. I don't speak about citizenship but about national identification. The moment you feel that you belong to the people of Israel, then you belong to the religion of Israel. This is the only religious faith that is national in this way. But in ancient times, of course, this kind of connection was usual, and total. No Philistine would worship Ammon, and no Ammonite would worship Doeg. The Greeks and Romans when they ruled did not try to force their gods on everyone—the opposite. If we wanted to worship Jupiter, they would forbid this, saying "It's our god, not yours." But then began the story of universal faiths, a very late story, 1,800 years old.

First, identification with the religion requires an identification with the nationality. Since many today, both in Israel and abroad, are far from religious consciousness, this distances them then from national consciousness. So people can come and say today in Israel, "There is no difference between Jew and non-Jew, Jew and Arab." They are able to say, "Just as the Jews are entitled to a homeland, so are the Arabs here." So there are those who can love Arabs more than they love their own people; this, because they have no connection to a national framework, and framework means something that we are confined in. This word, "Framework," is the most reprehensible word for large circles of people today. In fact, there are many who wish to open all the frameworks, all the boundaries, between man and woman, between Jew and non-Jew. This is the factual condition today, the mindset of a good share of the Jewish people. How this happened cannot possibly be illuminated in a short conversation like this one. But one thing is absolutely clear, if there is someone to be blamed for this, it is the rabbis and spiritual leaders. We must remember that, even in the better periods of Jewish history, not all Jews maintained the mitzvot on a high level. It has always been the task of the spiritual leaders to strengthen the people in their faith and observance. We have always needed leaders who will teach, influence, and help the people better crystallize their observance. If a great share of the people of Israel withdrew from observance, then this was the responsibility of the spiritual leaders who should have been instructing them. Rabbi Kook wrote that, in his generation, there were many who explained this as a result of the *galut*. But the *galut* is a non–normal situation for a people. A people, in principle, needs a land of its own. This is an ancient truth. From the moment a people is outside its own land, it is not in the atmosphere that is specially suited for it. And there is a Jewish land where the Jews need to be to be fully at home. The reasons for the exile are well–known. Leaders in the exile were often totally absorbed in "holding on to what they had" because they were under pressure and attack from the non–Jewish environment. And the surrounding non–Jewish environment penetrated, the influence of the *haskalah*, of Christianity. One of the problems was that many did not understand the importance of making *aliyah* to Israel. At the beginning of the modern period in Zionism, many in the religious establishment opposed *aliyah*. As a result, many withdraw completely from the Jewish people. If the rabbis had sent large numbers, there would be in Israel today a largely religious society, with very few not keeping the mitzvot. But if someone wanted to make *aliyah*, he often had to go against the will of the rabbis, and run away. The majority of the religious came here against the will of their own rabbis. What Rabbi Kook spoke of repeatedly 99 years ago, that the rabbis do not understand the people of the present generation, applies also today. This is because Rabbi Kook did not write sociology, but he grasped the underlying non–conscious stream of things, the real motion of reality. What he understood are not things that come and go, but rather are derived from a comprehensive and great picture of the totality of things.

Unfortunately, today, the rabbinical establishment does not bother with those who are outside their framework. They say, "If you will come to me and live by the Torah, then I will love you. And if not, then no." So these leaders do not really associate or bother will all those who do not live by the Torah. In another more general way, the decline in spirituality is connected with our coming closer to completeness, to the "final days," the Redemption. And this Redemption has to come through these pangs, these shocks. The Rabbi Kook wrote over 70 years ago a precise outline of all that will happen. He spoke of the spiritual rebellion that is to come, the tremendous destruction that will come, and also the things that will come afterwards. One thing completes the other. And someone understanding the remarkable divine transformations through the generations is not surprising. This is bound to be part of the process of redemption. But this does not cancel the personal obligations of each individual in his own generation. In the generation in which a person lives, he is responsible for his obligations in this time.

S.F.: Are you implying that the great general motions of history are "dictated from above," that we therefore have no freedom to influence them, and we then cannot as a people and as individuals err?

Rabbi Hess: What you have said is absolutely not right, a misinterpretation of what I am saying. It is necessary to distinguish between the individual and the collective, the community. It is necessary to understand what we mean by *clal*, the community of Israel, which is not merely the sum of the individuals. It is not a collection. In one of my books, '*Faith for the Generations (Emunah l'Dorot)*' I explain this. When we speak about *clal*, we do not speak about "free will." The collective, the community, does not have free will. For each individual Jew, there is freedom of choice. This is one of the foundations of Jewish religious faith. Rambam says that, if there is not freedom of choice then all the high walls of faith are destroyed. But all this belongs to the individual. To the individual within the community there remains freedom of choice. What is the meaning of this? For example, if I am a student, I go to school, or I don't—free choice of my own. Once I arrive at school, although it's the middle of winter and there is no sun, someone says, "Let's go outside and learn on the grass." We vote in class. As it turns out, I am in the minority. So immediately I decide to leave. But if I wish to be part of the class, then I have to limit the free choice I make, and go along with the majority. Then the teacher says we'll go outside, but the principal of the school says no. Now the class, which is to me "the collective," is for the school as a whole, an individual unit.

And the class already has less free choice within the school, as a whole. Next, the principal comes and says that he wants to do something. The supervisor of schools of the district says, "I have fifty schools under my supervision and it is not possible that each one will do just what it wants." Then the director of the education department says, "I have 100 cities under my supervision and I cannot allow each one to do just as it wants." So where I am as the private individual is part of a class that is part of a school that is of a municipal system that is part of a nationwide network. The greater the "communal framework," the more the private freedom of choice is reduced. I said that *Elohim* appears only in the presence of the "communal," and that everything communal is in some way Divine. And what is Divine is beyond all human choice.

S.F.: I don't want to interrupt, but there are many who say precisely the opposite, that it is only to the individual that the Divine can be known and revealed. As point of fact, it is said that many of the *gedolim* of Israel, including the Gra (the Vilna Gaon), prayed primarily by themselves alone, outside any connection with the *tsibbur.*

Rabbi Hess: These two things are not related. You are not able to draw examples from people who are beyond the scale of ordinary measurement of people like you and me, and the vast majority. I do not know if the story is true. I don't think that there are witnesses to such things. But let's say that something like this happened, that he possibly was among the very great *Admorim* in a room alongside the room in which prayer was being done. According to the *halachah*, if you are alongside a *cheder*, then it is impossible to count you as part of the minyan. But if there is a minyan, then you can be included as part of the *tsibbur.* Perhaps the crowd would disturb, or he felt they would be disturbed by his presence. All this is connected to what we were talking about. It is clear to me that, when the Gra prays alone, it is not a prayer for himself, but rather for the *clal*, for the *tsibbur.* And the fact that he prays between four or between twenty *mechitzot*, in a small room or large hall, is not connected in any way with this. The main point is that, with his prayer for the *clal*, he aims to influence the community as a whole. The Gra was the man most isolated and most alone, and yet his influence on *clal Yisrael* was far, far greater than so many who all the time were speaking before the public, trying to lead the public. In any case, because the Divine appears only before the public—and the larger the public, the greater the appearance of the Divine, the more you are 'general public communal' the less you are, and the more you are involved in the 'public' the less 'free choice' you have, But this in no way frees the individual from his responsibility for all the people of Israel. And this is because, as an individual being, one's freedom of choice is absolute. In personal matters that are our own, God does not interfere in any way whatsoever. And thus we will receive punishment for that which we have done that is not all right, and we will be rewarded for what we have done that is all right because it is we who have done and decided. But in relation to *Clal Yisrael*, if *Elokim* wants Israel to be redeemed, or the Jewish people to return to its land, then it is in no way possible that a government order will succeed in destroying the Divine Plan.

S.F.: Could you describe your own individual work in service of God?

Rabbi Hess: What do you mean by "work"? Work of livelihood? First, we spoke about *avodat Hashem*, and now you speak about *avodah*.

S.F.: You mean to say that there is in your mind a clear distinction between your *avodat Hashem* and all the other things you do? Isn't the ideal of the human being to make each and every action he does, each breath he takes *avodat Hashem*?

Rabbi Hess: We try. No person can claim that each and everything he does is *avodat Hashem*. But, along with what we said earlier, in the very beginning of my work, I felt myself devoted, obliged more to the *clal*, than to myself as a private individual. So from a relatively early age, 22, I was involved in public work. I didn't even have that much time to learn in the yeshiva. Ranaana, at the time, was a very small settlement, with almost no religious public. It is impossible to compare the Ranaana of today, which is a fairly large city with a considerable established religious community, with the Ranaana then. Yet I was involved in building the yeshiva and disseminating Torah. It was not a great *parnassah*. Were I then to have placed *parnassah* first, I would have done something else and profited more with an eighth of the effort. It was work, day and night. But since I wanted everything to be done in a true way, I was not only the head of the yeshiva but also the high school. This was at the expense, in a way, of my family, my wife and children, as I was busy day and night. Many times I was not even home on Shabbat because I had to be within the yeshiva. Because of my situation, I was not always at the synagogue either, though I was given a leadership position there too. My situation then was as it is today.

Each public needs a representative to look out for its interests, not only on a national level but on a local municipal level. This is also so that the religious public can have influence on the general public. But to my sorrow, the parties and their relations, as in many small places, are based less on ideology than on personal relations. Take the great rift between the two religious parties, Mafdal (the National Religious Party) and Aguda. This was very damaging, and of course did *Chillul Hashem*. I was not really a political person, but I was called upon to be involved in municipal work. There were certain problems, such as how people would get to the sea from Herziliya on Shabbat without driving through religious neighborhoods. I wanted a united religious front, but it was difficult. Then, when it came apart, a number of people came to me and said that the only way it would work was if I would stand as head of such a united front. I had doubts, especially in regard to the time I would give. Also, I was concerned about the effect it would have upon my image in the eyes of my yeshiva students; that is, my going from *rosh yeshiva* to political operative. The matter of *Bittul Torah* was also central. I went and spoke with my teacher and guide, Rav Zvi Yehuda Zechar Tsaddik Le–Beracha. Everyone considered him an innocent idealist, but in fact, he was in strong touch with reality. He said, "All this business will not endure long (the alliance between Mafdal and Aguda) and if your going through with elections means there won't be attacks between the religious groups, then it is necessary to do it. To bring about such unity is *Kiddush Hashem*. And if you are concerned about your image in the eyes of the students, then have them be involved too." And the *Kadosh Baruch Hu* desired it, so the alliance held for my entire term of office. But again, the whole general direction is in regard to what is necessary and possible to give to the *clal*. I build there the Yeshiva.

S.F.: I am not sure I understand. You were deputy major of Ranaana, at the same time you were *rosh yeshiva*?

Rabbi Hess: Yes, *Baruch Hashem*. Because of the alliance, we had more religious representatives than we would have had otherwise. So we entered the coalition, and I was also deputy mayor.

S.F.: You are not from Ranaana originally?

Rabbi Hess: I was born in Kiryat Shmuel, near Haifa. So after 15 years I left the yeshiva, to do something new, not only for me but for Israel as a whole. I became the rabbi of a university campus. This is not like in America where, for instance, someone outside campus provides the salary of the Hillel Rabbi. Rather, it is a university function. Today there is also in Beersheva a rabbi to help religious students, as well as many who are not *shomrei mitzvot*. For 10 years, I was the campus rabbi. It was a tremendous amount of work, which I could not continue because of the immense physical and emotional effort involved. There are, in Bar Ilan, thousands of *baalei teshuvah*, in addition to the non–religious students. I had to take care of so many, individually, to work about Shabbat for them. And I had to do something I do not love, to be a great diplomat so as not to step on toes. Also, the connection between the *halachah* and the academy is very sensitive. Formally, the university is a religious one, but not all the faculty is. There are many limitations.

For instance, one of the problems was the matter of the medical school, a prestigious element of the university. But there are difficult *halachic* questions, not only the matter of animal experimentation, but very unique problems. There was, for instance, one professor who invented a means for determining the fertility of sperm in cattle, which brought in very great sums of money. This enabled them to increase by 30 percent fertility in cattle. But the next step was with human beings. Here, the issue of *zera levatalah* ("sperm wasted") was raised. All kinds of money is involved: scholarships, grants. The professor will receive an enormous amount of money if he will patent his invention. And it will greatly increase fertility. But Jews cannot use it. It's a very interesting question, which requires much real work and thought.

At the same time I was involved there, I developed in Bar Ilan an institution, Machon Shai, for secular people that provides a means of learning Judaism outside the framework of *Beit ha-Knesset*. There are over 100 schools that come to Machon Shai each year for a day of learning. They come without fear that they are being forced into a certain framework. They see all kinds of projects involving the relationship between science and religion. This too was a contribution to the *clal*. During my conversations with students, I was asked hundreds of questions and gave *teshuvot*. During this time, I also lectured throughout

Israel before audiences of all kinds. So I began to write down my answers and put them out as a newspaper. When I gathered a little money,
I put out the newspaper *Emunot.* From the computer of the university,
I was able to identify the schools the students came from, and also their
general religious background. I made a list and sent the paper out. Who
took interest, took interest. Who wanted to throw out, threw out. After
a while, I put together the weekly copies and made a book, which
became popular not because I am wise, but because the questions asked
and answered were those that the students were truly concerned with.
I checked the answers over and over, and did not publish one until I
had lectured the answer myself perhaps 100 times. Later, I put out a
few more books. I am privileged. More than 140,000 have been sold in
Israel. Nothing has been translated; I don't have the time and the
money, though many have said that it would be important to get the
book to Jews in America, and other places. But I am not willing to
give it to any publishing house. My principle is that I do not profit from
this. I want that everyone can buy it, so I would sell it at low price.
But if I give it to a publishing house, then the price will be high and
few will buy it. To avoid this, I will have to do it myself, buying the
paper, paying for the binding. If there are 140,000 purchasers, then there
are 200,000 readers. The books by themselves have helped many make
teshuvah. I have put out seven books, all based on the same principle
of "doing for the *clal*," for the community. But after 10 years at the
university, I was worn out. So was my family For nearly 25 years, I
had been so involved in the work that I was at home very little. My
own children do not know me well. This is a point that I do not wish
to go into depth here. But the fundamental question is real: How much
can a person sacrifice family life for public work? This is a very complicated question. At Ranaana, for instance, there was a national religious school, where my wife taught, whose religious level was zero.
Now if I were the head of the Mafdal in the city, then I could not
possibly send my children to the independent school network, which
has a much higher religious level. That would be a slap in the face to
the very network I head. Also, for my children, I would have to be
accountable: what is required of them in relation to the larger public?

After Bar Ilan, I decided on, what might be called, an area of general public work. I understood that, in all of Israel, religious education
is at a low level because of the poor level of the teachers. So I was among
the people who founded the Teachers College Training Institute in

Elkana. And I went to work there, wanting to educate each and every teacher at a high Torah level in all areas, be it music, or literature, or biology. Here they learn much Torah, Tanach, Emunah, and 'Torah she b'al peh' (oral law)—very high demand. I serve as the head of the faculty of Oral Torah, and continue to lecture on machshavah (Jewish thought). We have many students. I lecture also at a baal teshuvah ye-shiva in Jerusalem, and give lectures in many different places. One of the interesting project I took on was for the city of Eilat. For many years, the city was considered outside Eretz Yisrael. There were almost no religious people there. But over 20 years, I helped establish a large and thriving religious community. At first it was very difficult to per-suade religious people to go there, but now we have a religious school, which is thriving, and a seminary for Judaism, a field seminary for Zionism and Judaism. That's about it.

S.F.: Thank you very much Rabbi. I have one more very general ques-tion. How do you see the situation of the people of Israel today in the land of Israel?

Rabbi Hess: Once again, I keep trying to tell you that we see things only on the external, superficial level. The political, economic, socio-logical realities, which people speak of as the elements that determine things, are not what I am speaking about. When we speak about the people of Israel in the land of Israel, we speak about Clal Yisrael and Shechinah. And without speaking about the fact that you must, if you believe what the government is doing is wrong, resist with all your power, we are talking on another level. Elokim will bring the Redemp-tion to Am Yisrael the way Hashem wants, but this does not free us from doing all the things we must do, as if there weren't Elokim. So the two levels, that of Divine realization and that of human action, are parallel, and do not meet. It is impossible otherwise to explain and understand this. Ha–Kadosh Baruch Hu does His Will, and we do not interfere in all these matters. We are neither able to help nor harm. But we can determine for ourselves, because the Kadosh Baruch Hu will act toward us in accordance with our actions. If we are all right, then Hashem will act accordingly. We direct His responses on the personal, individual level, but that is in regard to the connection between the private person and Hashem. In relation to Clal Yisrael, we will not harm and not help.

There are two times. When the time comes that even Am Yisrael will be evil, this will not stop the process. We cannot impede this. There is a line in the Gemara, "In the affairs of the *Kadosh Baruch Hu*, why do you intervene?" We have been told what to do. We have guidance. We do the will of God. And if we do what the rabbi says to do, we will be all right. It is written. And if the Rabbi misleads us, it is not our problem. When *Am Yisrael* does what the Sanhedrin tells it, but the Sanhedrin errs it is the Sanhedrin that is responsible. But *Clal Yisrael* is not. On a personal level, the individual should do everything possible within the Law to bring down a government that tries to cut off the people of Israel from the land of Israel. This cutting off is connected of course with the growth of *chillul Shabbat*, and sexual permissiveness, materialism, and careerism. Everything goes together. When a people is healthy, there is no Mafia and no prostitution. When a people is sick from the national point of view, it is also sick from the religious point of view. They go together. And we have to do everything so that the religious leadership will act in a way that will be an example to the public as a whole. We must do everything possible to bring us closer to our father in heaven. And we must increase the spiritual element, be unwilling to give all to material success. All of this relates to the individual side of each of the 4.5 million Jews of Israel.

In terms of the Divine process, it may be that the more that things get worse for us, the closer we come to the Redemption. I don't think there is one person who can understand today how the government does what it does. They promised that they would not leave the Golan. Do they intend to do it? They promised that they would not do this and that. We read 1,000 things in the paper every day. These are not stupid people, but people with brains. They are not haters of Israel; they intend for good. But is impossible to understand. And it is impossible to put the weight of the focus on the personal question, the character question of individuals. How do they explain this complete caving in? We can blame it, on a personal level, or each minister. But because the whole process is so unacceptable, so irrational, so non–understandable we are led in a most realistic way to see that it is something beyond reality. In other words, here we do not need faith in God; by logic, we arrive at something beyond. Understanding the Divine process is impossible on one foot only. God built the world in order to rule in it. In order for there to be rule there must be free will. And for there to be free will, there must be a *yetzer hara*, with all possibilities open for it to work. The function of the *yetzer hara* is to dis-

turb and interfere with the Divine. If *Elokim* would interfere with our
yetzer hara, then our freedom is limited. So the *yetzer hara* received free
will to disturb things to the end. Hashem wants to bring *Mosheach* and
geulah, and the *yetzer hara* has free will to resist. The single means by
which Hashem has to lead us to the desired end, after giving free will,
is through an indirect, sophisticated way: the *ikvata Mashechah* ("the
heels of Messiah"), from the word *la-akoff* ("to go around"). This is
the reason that *Melech ha-Mosheach* must come from a non–Jewess, Ruth
the Moabite. Here the *yetzer hara* does not interfere, because it does
not believe that the *Mosheach* can come from a non–Jew. So the more
it seems that everyone does the work of *yetzer hara*, the more it can sit
in a cafe smoking a cigarette. The more things seem evil, deep within
salvation is being created.

S.F.: I am not convinced. In this century, the Jewish people suffered
their greatest losses and evil in history. How can anyone be certain,
and explain on the basis of any idea, religious or not, what will be in
the next historical moment? How can anyone see danger with calm of
assurance?

Rabbi Hess: I can say with perfect certainty because I, individually,
am not involved. All that I say is not because I understand or because
I am wise. You mention the Shoah, the greatest disaster—but it is not
the greatest imaginable disaster. Look at *parashat Bechukotai*, the
tochahah ("the reproof"). People say the Shoah is the sign that there is
no God. But the Shoah is the strongest sign that there is God. According to the prophecy, "I will bring upon you Shoah," there are many
more than 6 million. At the end of *Vayikra*, we read, "This is not that
it occurs once in history. It is a way of life. In the morning, two women
arise, and the one says, 'We have an agreement. We decided yesterday.
Today I slaughter my child and eat him. And tomorrow, your turn.' "
These are the kinds of things we did not come to in the Shoah. Worse
than this is part of the treatment that was announced to us at the beginning. Theoretically you are correct. But we know everything from
our Sages, who told us that the destruction of the Third Temple will
not be. Since we have clear and decisive information from them, we
can know that it is the end of such disasters.

You surely heard the story about the *yishuv* during the second
world war, when Rommel was in Alexandria and it was sure that he

would get to *Eretz Yisrael* to slaughter the Jews. Rabbi Herzog then said that particular saying of the Sages. ("The third destruction will not be.") And in a manner that no historian can exactly describe, Rommel was stopped. But I don't speak about mysticism. From the point of view of my faith, I don't fear a new Shoah because for me everything is built on *chazal* (our Sages). This is the channel through which God speaks to me. I speak to you through *chazal*. On a personal level, what happens to someone who is not allright will be clear even if it occurs through the general process of Redemption. The Prophets tell us what will be in the days of the Messiah. Great sorrows and sufferings are foretold. Gog and Magog will be destroyed. But all these things will be suffered by private individuals, very many private individuals. And the *clal*? After the Shoah, there was the rebirth of the Jewish people in the land of Israel, the state of Israel. Without entering into the question of "why each individual receives what he receives," for each individual when the 'Shoah' happens to him it is the end of his life. But for *Clal Yisrael*, the Shoah is a stage in the process foretold by the Prophets. This is not because I am wise after the fact, and can explain it thusly, but because it's based on what is written by our Sages. Rabbi Harlap foresaw precisely what would be, based on the Sages, not because he was a prophet or sage, but because all is clearly written if we rely on *chazal*.

S.F.: In this process of redemption, are you talking about building the Third Temple?

Rabbi Hess: Not necessarily. This is part of it. We are talking about redemption of the world, and redemption of the land as a whole.

S.F.: When you look at the situation of Israel today, how do you find your own public, the national religious group? Is it capable of being the leading factor in bringing the process of transformation salvation?

Rabbi Hess: First of all, the greatest *hazarah b'teshuvah* has been done within this group, which thirty or forty years ago had difficulty keeping mitzvot. Today is a public of Torah and mitzvot. There has been a great strengthening. In general sociological terms, a reason for the great hatred on the part of some of the left in Israel is that we have taken from them the senior role in many areas of life: in settling the land, in security, and the army. In the army, for instance, the situation is completely changed today. If 30 years ago the great majority of officers were *ha-shomer hatzair* kibbutznikim, today in the School for Officers five out of six of the outstanding graduates are religious, graduates of the pre-military academies of the yeshivot. In this neighborhood alone live a number of very high-ranking officers who are religious. In this group has become a leading element in settlement, in security, in business, in building the country.

Rabbi Zev Leff

Rabbi Zev Leff serves as the rabbi of Moshav Matityahu, and is a well–known lecturer in many yeshivot and seminaries throughout Israel. He is the author of *Outlooks and Insights: on the Weekly Torah Portion.* Ordained by Telshe Yeshiva, he was for a number of years the rabbi of Young Israel of North Miami Beach. Rabbi Leff has for many years specialized in giving *shiurim* in women's seminaries. It was at one of the most prominent of these *shiurim* in Jerusalem, "Neve Jerusalem," where we had our meeting for this interview. A dynamic and inspiring teacher, Rabbi Leff's enormous enthusiasm for teaching resonated throughout the interview, and made speaking and listening to him a learning experience of the first order.

S.F.: Can you tell me about the different places in which you teach?

Rabbi Leff: First of all, my main place is where I live. I am the rabbi of Moshav Mattityahu, where I give lessons in Gemara, *halachah*, *hashkafah*, a *derash* on Shabbos, *Pirkei Avot*, *parashat ha-shevuah*. I am *rosh yeshiva* of the Yeshiva Gedolah in Mittityahu. I do not give a daily *shiur* there. We have *rebbayim* who do this. But I basically guide them, and once a week, I speak to the boys. I learn with each of them separately, *halachah*, *Shulchan Aruch*, whatever. I also am the rabbinic advisor to a girls' seminary, where I teach twice a week. Basically, I give *halachic* guidance as to how the school should develop. The thrust there is not so much what grades the girls attain, but how sincere and serious they are in their learning. These are pretty much my main responsibilities. In addition, I teach in a number of other girls' seminaries once a week. I teach in Aish Ha-Torah's women's section, because I feel that these are women who are searching, and not everybody can deal with that. There are plenty of other people who can teach at the traditional seminaries, and do that well. I do teach in "Seminary Yerushalayim" twice a week, at Sharfman's, Machon, Rifkin, and Michlalah. Each of these seminaries has its own character, to which, I think, I can add something that others there might not be able to do. I also teach in two places for English-speaking people, in Rechovot once a month and in Netanya once every two weeks. I also teach the Beit Yaakov teachers and principals in their ongoing upgrading of their education. Once a month I meet with teachers from particular areas: in Ashdod, in B'nei Brak, in Tel Aviv, in Rochovot, and in Kiryat Sefer.

S.F.: This is a series of conversations with teachers of Torah in Yerushalayim. But I see that you cover much of Israel.

Rabbi Leff: I also give a *shiur* once a month as part of a program that trains women to be family counselors, and a *shiur* at Michlalah on the *halachic* and *hashkafic* implications of the Holocaust.

S.F.: You haven't mentioned the *shiur* and lectures that you give at Israel Center in Yerushalayim.

Rabbi Leff: As in Rechovot and Netanya, there is in Jerusalem a very large group of English–speaking people. I give them a *shiur* once a week in the Israel Center.

S.F.: I know you have learned at Telshe Yeshiva. Could you tell me something about your background, particularly what distinguishes the *musar* approach in which you have been trained?

Rabbi Leff: First of all, my education did not start in Telshe Yeshiva. I was born in the Bronx and grew up in Miami from the age of eight. I attended the Hebrew Academy there, and the Mesivta High School. The teachers of the high school were from Telz and, because I was en-amored of them, I went on to Telz. There I got very close to Rabbi Gifter, who was *rosh yeshiva* at the time. The Telzer *derech* is one of the deep philosophical approaches to Torah. To try to understand what the Torah is all about is central to the Telshe approach. My rebbe had the knack of being able to put things in terms that everyone could understand. I was deeply impressed by this approach. So I began study a lot in this area, to learn midrash, to think in it, to ask the implica-tions of its meaning for daily living. How could I apply it, explain it to other people, so that they could appreciate the beauty of Torah, and make it something that speaks to them, is meaningful to them, is prac-tical for them? As I was developing there, before I got married, and afterwards also, I had a chance to teach in the community, to give *shiurim* to the *kollel* I was in. I built up a great deal of knowledge for *shiurim*, which I have developed since.

The *musar* approach? I believe that my own approach is to put a greater stress on *hashkafah*. The *musar* approach is more direct, "Do this. Don't do this." My approach is to try to understand first what we are talking about, what the idea is. Then comes the effort to put it into terms that can better be dealt with, to explore its implications. If people understand what they are talking about in a way that's real—Torah is not something that is in the heavens only—then people can live by the Torah. People can live by the Torah if they understand it is meant to be lived by, and that it is not just abstract theoretical ideas.

S.F.: In your book *Outlooks and Insights: on the Weekly Torah Portion,* you speak about two ways of serving God, two ways of loving God, and in effect living by the Torah. One is *avodah b'yirah* and the other is *avodah b'ahavah*. Can you explain the meaning of these concepts as you understand them?

Rabbi Leff: *Avodah* and *yirah* have many levels. If we delve deeply enough, then we see that they are all facets of the same basic idea. *Yirah* is a service of God out of self–concern: concern that I will be punished or lose out, or I won't gain what I could. I have come to the conclusion that if I serve God properly, then it will be best for me. *Allevai* (I hope) that most people should come to that conclusion that serving God is what's best for them. It's a nice level, the level of most people. But the higher level is relegated to individuals who are selflessly serving God. They are over–awed by a concept of a God who is so beyond them that they just want to be able to have a part in the entire workings of the world, by serving that God. That's called serving God out of love. It's totally selfless. The concern is not necessarily how it's going to effect one personally, but rather how one can be part of this God that guides and has created everything. In my book, I give the example of a person who loves herring. If one loves herring, then it really means that he loves himself, because herring tastes good. Love of another human being also involves self–love. But if it's out of admiration that one recognizes the other's greatness and wants to be close to that person, not for his own reasons, but because he feels that it's the right thing to do, that's a more selfless love. So the service of God out of love is selfless service, while the service of God out of fear is selfish service. This selfishness is not in a negative way, but only that one's main concern is "How is it going to affect me?"

S.F.: Not every Jew is specially gifted and can be a real teacher of Torah. What is the service of God for most Jews?

Rabbi Leff: First of all, everybody is a teacher. Some people teach in classrooms. Some teach by word of mouth. Some teach by being a good example to neighbors. Some even teach by giving an example of what not to do. People looking at them and say, "I don't want to be like that." They are also teachers. This is not the most positive kind of teaching, but it's also teaching. As for what service of God is for the Jew, I think that Torah says very clearly. We are to be God's representatives in the world, by living lives that are godly. One has to aspire to sanctify every aspect of his life in such a way that he exudes godliness and holiness in everything he does. This doesn't mean to separate oneself from the physical, material things of the world, because that's not godliness. My *rosh yeshiva*, Rabbi Gifter, points out that God is separate from everything, not attached to any material thing, yet connected to everything because nothing can exist without Him. A Jew has to be attached to everything in this world, be involved in business, in agriculture, everything. Not that it should drag him down; rather, he should elevate it. He should use it in a way that the world, himself, and others can see that this is how a person can function in the most mundane things, and do it in such a noble way that there must be a God in this world, because this is something that represents that holiness. That's *avodat Hashem*. It can be in every sphere of endeavor. To do it in such a way is representative of Godliness.

S.F.: But how do we bring the Jewish people to this sense of serving God in all they do? There is a sense, after all, that we are missing the mark especially in running after models that emphasize above all, worldly accomplishment. How do we bring the people back? Could you address especially the situation in Israel?

Rabbi Leff: I wish I had an answer to that question. If I did, then I would be much better off than I am now. I wish I had an answer for how to do it for myself. But let me give you a little bit, something at least. I think that the beginning is learning. We have to start with learning. People need to be aware of what Judaism is. This entails not only factual learning, but learning what it all means. What are the implications? What does God expect from me? Not just reasons for mitzvot. I am talking about the implications. For example, what is Shabbos supposed to teach me that I can take into the rest of the week and conduct my business? It is supposed to teach me that the goal of the world is not physical. We work six days—it's a mitzvah to work six days—but our goal in working six days is to achieve a spiritual end, Shabbos. We must understand that it should reflect itself Sunday to Friday in the way that we work, in the way that we deal with other people, how honest we are in our work. If it doesn't spill over, then something is missing from the whole concept of Shabbos. So we should start educating our children—I think it starts with children—in a system of education, not just a system of facts, of do's and don'ts, but an understanding that this means something. It has to affect our everyday life, not just our thoughts, not just our lofty ideas. Children—it has to start with children—must be encouraged to fulfill this, and to be rewarded accordingly. This means not just rewarded for high marks. For a child who cannot produce nineties on a test, but has shown that he has fulfilled what he has learned, and has treated his parents a little better, this should show up on a report card. Teachers should be taking this child before the class and saying, "This is what we are looking for." Because the child who gets 100 and acts in a terrible way is often given all the honor. Similarly, it has to be done with adults too. Rabbis in their *kehillah* must point out the positive things that are an example of what Torah is all about, aside from giving honor to the people who give the most money, or who are the smartest. Giving *kavod* ("honor") to things that really deserve *kavod* will give people the idea that these are positive things worth doing.

Look at *daf yomi*. When it received recognition for being the thing to do, look how many people began to learn it. If only recognition would come to being a nice person, being honest in business, whatever. If that became the thing people give *kavod* to, people would do it.

S.F.: In your book, you quote the Ramban's injunction that the task of the Jewish people is to bring all mankind to recognition of Hashem. My guess is that for the majority of the Jewish people today such a goal is not central. The secular majority is far more concerned with its own material advancement, career success, personal satisfaction. How do we move the great proportion of Jews to recognizing and accepting their historical role? Sometimes I think that perhaps Hashem wants there to be these two kinds of Jews, one who is dedicated to this great goal and the other who lives primarily for his own wordly pleasure.

Rabbi Leff: The truth is, Hashem wants many different kinds of people. But he wants people who are aware of what they are doing in this world. Somebody who thinks that he is put into this world to earn a living and to progress in his career, and that's it, is missing a good portion of what the world is all about. He is related to thinking about the 120 years that he is here, and nothing about what is going to be for him afterwards. There is nothing wrong with a person living in this world to earn a living, to be involved in the more mundane things of the world, if he knows that that's not the end, but rather a means to reach an end, if he excels in his profession, but with a feeling of mission. Aside from making a nice living and living comfortably, he has to have a sense of "Why am I doing that? Where is it going to bring me?" There is something more. Yet those things as a means can be very positive. He doesn't have to go and live in a hut and say Tehillim all day. He can be the same doctor, the same lawyer, in that same beautiful house. But if he looks at that beautiful house as his goal, as his end, then this is not what the *Ribbono Shel Olam* wants. If he looks at the beautiful house as a means to reach a greater end, and utilizes it in that way, then it's perfectly okay. It's possible to be rich and be a servant of the *Ribbono Shel Olam,* and to be poor and be a servant of the *Ribbono Shel Olam,* that is, if one realizes that neither the poverty nor the wealth is an end in itself. There's nothing *frum* about being poor. Yet when a person knows how to use that properly, he can be poor and be a servant of the *Ribbono Shel Olam,* just as there's no sin in being rich so long as one knows how to use it properly.

S.F.: When you look at our task, and the Jewish people today, what sense do you have in regards to our historical place? Are we on the path of Redemption? Are we moving toward it or away from it?

Rabbi Leff: I'll paraphrase to you what the Ponivisher Rav said in his time: Is Mosheach here? Look around. He is definitely not here. This is not the world of *Mosheach.* The world has not yet been redeemed. Do I hear his footsteps? Most certainly. Are there signs that things are reaching an end? Great people have seen that this is the case. But to say that we are redeemed yet even minimally—no, we are not redeemed yet. Things have happened that are perhaps setting the stage for redemption in the future. We returned to *Eretz Yisrael.* It's a tremendous thing. But living in *Eretz Yisrael* under the conditions we live today is not redemption. It may be the final stage of the *golut* that's preparing for that redemption. But redemption itself—unless one is selling short what redemption is, this is not the Redemption. The Redemption will come when God redeems us. It's a process. It's not overnight. And God will start the process, not us. *Yetziat Mitzrayam* was a 40-year process until we got to the Promised Land. But it did not start until we left Mitzrayim. The things that came before were not *geulah*. We were not redeemed even when we stopped working in Mitzrayim. We weren't redeemed until God took us out. So Redemption is a godly thing, though there are people who think otherwise. But my teachers taught me differently. Redemption is not something that human beings start and God finishes. Redemption is something that God starts and human beings continue. It's a different approach.

How close or far are we? Many things have happened over the millenia that indicate that Jews have been successful in bringing the world to a recognition of God. Before Christianity and Islam, the world was filled with idolators. And we know what idolatry is. We can see the kind of cruel, primitive societies there were in the pagan world. Christianity and Islam, with all their shortcomings, are a lot better than the primitive human sacrifice kinds of idolatrous societies. Islam and Christianity came from Judaism, and we influenced a good portion of the world because of that. Those who have not been influenced by us directly have been influenced by us indirectly. We haven't reached our goal of making people be the way they should be, but to a certain degree, the fact that there is a recognition that there is a God means that there are Christians and Muslims who are better people than they would be otherwise. One can use the idea of God and distort it, and be more cruel because of it. But the majority of people use the idea of God in a more positive way. I would rather have a person be a good Christian than an atheist, and this because the Christian has positive values that he has gotten from the Torah, such as the Ten Commandments. So in the framework of larger history, we have, to a degree, been that catalyst. However, if the question is whether we have reached the goal that God wants us to reach, then the answer is that we have a long way to go.

The fact is, because there is a state of Israel, people look at what Jews do and expect more from us. It would be better if the state fully represented what Judaism really is, and not be a Jewish state per se, a secular Jewish state. The more that the world could see what a true Torah state would be would be a much more positive thing. Unfortunately, because that does not exist, the world gets ideas about Jews from the workings of the Israeli government. This is a big problem, a very big problem. But there are good things. People get a chance to see the positive things in Israel. And there is always positive and negative—I wouldn't say that it's so depressing that we are failing miserably. But we are not passing with flying colors either. We are limping along like Yaakov Avenu did. We do not know how many people God needs in order to say that we are successful. The masses do not necessarily have to reach to the higher levels of goodness. But individuals who know better have to reach those levels. And if we are successful as individuals, then those individuals can change the entire world. But the world won't change totally until *Mosheach* comes. It is going to take some Divine intervention. And our getting to that point, where we deserve Divine intervention, may not depend on everybody changing, only on the people who know better changing.

S.F.: Does this mean that the Jewish people as a whole should now be in *Eretz Yisrael*, where it can work to build the ideal Torah society?

Rabbi Leff: It's like this. Ideally, every Jew should want to live in *Eretz Yisrael*, just as ideally, every Jew should want to fast on Yom Kippur. But there are circumstances that prevent every Jew from fasting on Yom Kippur. And every mitzvah has its circumstances. A person who's deathly ill is not allowed to fast on Yom Kippur. He shouldn't feel happy about it. He should feel that he's missing something. But he should know too that this is what God wants from him right now. There are definite parameters, especially before *Mosheach* comes, for how the Jew can settle in *Eretz Yisrael*. Individually, a Jew should have a goal of living in *Eretz Yisrael*. It's fulfilling a mitzvah. Whether one is required to do that mitzvah or not is irrelevant. If one lives here, then he has a chance to do more mitzvot than outside of Israel. So one can find the place here that's more conducive to that holiness. If one looks far enough, then he'll find the place. There are plenty of places here in *Eretz Yisrael* that are on par with every other aspect of any other community outside of *Eretz Yisrael*. Still, they cannot compete with the fact that it is *Eretz Yisrael*.

There are factors that would make living in *Eretz Yisrael* not only not required but even prohibited, among them, financial difficulty. If one can't get a job, he can't function, and has to take charity. This would keep one from coming to *Eretz Yisrael*. Yet everybody's needs and level of living are different. Education? Children may need special education, which is not available here. Some children would not be able to move, they are very insecure. If our ancestors who couldn't come here had the opportunity, then they would have been here. At least they would have considered it. Although we have the opportunity, the *yetzer hara* makes us not consider it. Is there a reason that every Jew, 100 percent, doesn't aspire to come to *Eretz Yisrael*? It's an individual matter that must require much discussion and advice from a competent Torah authority who is not biased.

S.F.: I once read a statement of a student of the Lubavitch Rebbe who said that the rebbe said, "The Jew should be where he is needed most, where he can do the most good."

Rabbi Leff: Okay. But I would add that there is still something positive about living in *Eretz Yisrael*. If there are factors that negate it, fine. But one cannot simply discount it.

S.F.: One reason for *aliyah* for certain families is to make sure that their children marry Jews. What is your sense of the depth of the assimilation crisis in the Diaspora? Is it, in your eyes, a great disaster?

Rabbi Leff: I can express it best with something that the Hafetz Haim says: that before the *Mosheach* comes, the Gemara says, it will be a generation totally evil or totally righteous. This doesn't mean that it's going to be one way and not the other, but rather, a polarized generation. The people in the middle are not going to be able to exist. They are going to have to make a choice. It's so clear that either one will reject it totally, or accept it totally. And the people who straddle the fence won't exist anymore. That's what's happening. The religious community is moving more and more to intense religion, this, in many areas. *Allevai,* that they should move in the areas that are really important. Basically, they are moving in the areas that are easier to do. They make sure that they have 24-hour hotlines, so one can wake up at 3:00 in the morning and eat something absolutely kosher. But there is no hotline for *lashon hara*. They are moving for sure in a direction of less compromise, more commitment. Meanwhile, the people who are straying are not being Reform or Conservative anymore. They are leaving, saying that tradition doesn't mean anything, so why do they need it? There used to be in America a middle of the road: traditional people who saw their parents were *frum*. They could not do that themselves, but nostalgically they wanted to feel that their *shuls* looked like a *shul*. The next generation said, "What the heck do I need that for? I can be in a Reform temple." And the ones in the Reform temple had no nostalgia at all. There is a drift on one side toward nothing, and on the other toward more commitment. So while we can see Torah growing in America by leaps and bounds, in very, very nice ways, there's a good majority of Jews drifting the other way. And both sides are drifting farther and farther apart, with no connection to each other. To a certain degree, that's a very scary thing.

S.F.: Is this polarization also true in Israel?

Rabbi Leff: Israel has always been polarized, but polarized in a way, with so many different factions, that's hard to say anyone's drifting anywhere. In *Eretz Yisrael*, the problem is different. The relationship between religious and non–religious has always been an adversarial one. Here they are fighting over who is going to take over the state. For forty-nine years, they have been fighting. And everybody wants the state to be their way, specifically. There are not enough people who are willing to discount the trivial things, to emphasize what's really important, and to see what there is to rally around. Also, the religious people look at people who are not *frum* as their adversaries, not as people whom they can influence. When you are in a war, you discount the enemy completely and see him only as a threat. In America, you don't see a non–religious Jew as that. You can feel that, if he behaves properly, then the other will respect him. But there's a good silent majority in Israel that doesn't of course own this adversarial attitude. Also, there are more and more religious Jews from North America who do not have this adversarial relationship because they come from another culture. And there are many more irreligious Jews who don't feel the adversarial relationship because they are totally estranged from the state itself. They are not ideologically involved, they just live here. So because there are more and more people here who don't have this adversarial relationship, it's possible to bring people closer than it was before.

S.F.: In Israel, there is strong political conflict now between the state as Jewish state and the state as democratic state, and this, when the whole question of Torah state is not really on the agenda.

Rabbi Leff: It's very hard to define what a Jewish state is if you don't define it in terms of Torah. If you define it as a state just for Jews, then you have created something that the world won't accept. And since most Jews are very fair–minded, you can't have a state just for Jews that is democratic. If, however, a Jewish state means that it's not just a state for Jews, then everyone has his place within the Torah running of the state. The Torah would allow non–Jews to live here too. It's not democracy, necessarily, but it's a fair Torah rule, which the non–Jews have no idea about because, when they let religion rule, it's total anarchy, and not fair for anyone. Torah gives everyone their place. Torah is fair. It's definitely not what we call democracy, but that does not mean it's not fair. The problem today is that they started a Jewish state, but they did not make it Jewish. If only they would make it a Jewish state that defended Jewish ideals.

S.F.: When the state was founded a great part of the vision was its being *ohr l'goyim* (light to the nations). What would *ohr l'goyim* mean in terms of a Torah state?

Rabbi Leff: It would mean a state among other states that has all the accoutrements of a state: an army, a police department bureaucracy, an economy. And the nations of the world see the way we conduct our army is different from the way others conduct their armies. They can learn from us—higher values. Not that the way we run our army is based on arbitrary things that have nothing to do with Judaism. Jews decided to borrow from this culture or that. That's not *ohr l'goyim*. Purity of weaponry? We don't shoot women and children. We do this because it's something we feel that Jews shouldn't do, not because there is some external pressure. But that is not *ohr l'goyim*, because it's not based on a Torah source but rather on subjective feeling. If only we had a system that was all inclusive. But the Torah system is all encompassing. We try to create a society where people can see the righteousness of the economy, the righteousness of the judicial system. Yet the Torah is a righteous system. Ultimately, as Rashi says, if you keep the mitzvot properly, then the *goyin* will see that there is something special to us. If we create arbitrary standards though, which have nothing to do with Torah, then those arbitrary standards eventually become contradictory to each other, become impractical. So instead of sanctifying God's name, we end up doing the opposite.

S.F.: There is a movement among non–Jews called the Noahide movement, which in a sense is trying to learn from Torah. What do you feel about this movement?

Rabbi Leff: I used to think that here were very sincere people, disillusioned with the fantasies of Christianity, who got a lot of the Judaism that's inherent in Christianity and wanted to divide it between them. In their Bible, it's obvious to them that the Jews are somebody special. These were people who were willing to be objective and accept the fact that God had a chosen people. That didn't disqualify them, make them anything less. Each nation has its purpose and they had the purpose of fulfilling the seven Noahide mitzvot. And that was their intention, which is very noble. It's something we should really have a connection to, to encourage them. Lately, I have heard from someone who has done a lot of research—and she has given me hundreds of pages of documentation—that there are missionaries behind this group, and that it's a gimmick in order to be able to make Jews feel more comfortable with good *goyim*. This enables the missionaries to get a foot in the back door. I can't say that I am convinced that that is the case, because it sounds really fantastic. But there is a lot of documentation. If that's the case, then we have to be very careful, because there are Christian groups that love Israel but with an ulterior motive. The question is, why would Christian missionary groups want to support these people who turned their backs on Christianity? And there is enough documentation that indicates they do support them. The question is "Why?"

S.F.: Excuse me if I go back now, and ask you again about your teaching. Is there some special method that you have developed in your teaching?

Rabbi Leff: First of all, I was given a gift, and I have no idea why I got it, or what it is. Someone once came to me on the street and said, "Teach me how to speak." I told him, "No one taught me." It's a gift. It's like someone saying, "Teach me to be an artist." You can enhance it. But it's just a talent you have to be given. One could go to art school for the next 20 years, but never be an artist. It's a talent. It's a God–given gift. I can speak publicly and speak well, but I never went to school for this. So I told this person, "No one taught me. I can't teach you. God gave me the gift. Go ask Him." That is a very big plus. And it's made it easier for me to articulate things. But I think that I have developed an approach to teaching Torah that puts it in very practical, readily understandable terms. It's not philosophical, theoretical, or abstract, but rather has meaning in real–life terms. I explain this so that someone can see that it is real. It applies to real life and real situations. And it makes sense.

S.F.: So that the learning enables people to live the Torah. Have you noticed through the years a change in the character and quality of your students?

Rabbi Leff: I have so many students, it's hard to generalize. But I can say I see that people now are very thirsty. And if they feel that something is speaking to them, then they want to hear more about it. They are not insulted or upset if I tell them that they are not where they should be.

S.F.: Do you have the idea that every person has a special gift, and that you can, through your teaching, bring out that gift?

Rabbi Leff: Definitely. The more people I meet, the more I am impressed that each and every person has something that he can contribute, whether it's in the family or in the community in which he lives, in the city, the country, or the world. And everything affects everything else. Some people are not meant to have an effect on the entire world. But they may affect their family and that affects the neighborhood. It's a domino effect. Everybody is very special. We simply have to open our eyes to see that special quality in each one. And this can make the world a perfect place, all working together in the right way. It's not just the people who are known and famous or speak well. *Bat pharoah* never gave a speech. She never gave a *shiur*. Bur she saved a little baby with a little mercy, and thus changed the entire history of the world. If I can be a catalyst to bring that idea out I often feel overawed at what others can do, which I cannot. If I can be a catalyst to get you to do it, then fine. Sometimes I tell people that I find it very hard to cry. But if I can get up and speak to people and bring them to tears, then I can cry through them. If I can be a catalyst to bring this out, then we are partners.

S.F.: I wanted to ask you about two specific points of your book. You talk about the fact that each of us can walk in the ways of God, *tselem Elokim*. But you say we can do this in relation to the greatness of God.

What do you mean by this, when there is the infinite gap between what we are and what Hashem is?

Rabbi Leff: I didn't mean to say that we can be as great as Hashem. Greatness is vis–a–vis us. What is a person impressed with as the greatness of God? What is God's greatness, His *gedulah,* His total selflessness at how much faith and kindness He does? This makes God great and beyond all selfish things. This we can imitate. Another of His greatness is His tremendous self–control, how even in situations where it's against His plan, He allows people free choice. A person can be great in that respect. So in those areas in which the greatness of God relates to how it affects us, not God, intrinsically we can walk in God's ways. They are not intrinsic to God. They are not *middot* that are intrinsic to God, but rather, character traits of how we see God. Greatness is something that can enhance our character if we see greatness in God.

S.F.: Another question, perhaps the most difficult of all. You speak about misfortune whose goodness we cannot at the time it happens understand. You speak about *"Gam zu la–tovah"* ("This too is for the good"), the perspective of faith through which one understands all as ultimately good. But aren't there evils so monstrously great as to make any future redemption of them impossible? The Holocaust?

Rabbi Leff: Some people feel comfortable in saying, "God did not make the Holocaust. Man made the Holocaust." I do not find this answer satisfying. He gave man free choice, but did He permit man to wreak havoc on other human beings? What kind of God is this who permits such evil? He is just a bystander, and a guilty bystander at that, if He was so insensitive as not to stop the disaster from happening. In this view, it is as if we are saying, "God let the people suffer for nothing." Such a view is much more troubling to me than the one that says God was involved, and permitted the Holocaust to happen for a reason. I don't know the reason, but God knows the reason. In the larger picture, it is for us impossible to understand, but I accept the fact that God in his infinite wisdom has a plan and a reason I cannot know. And the reason outweighs reality's having happened in a different way. I could give reasons, possible reasons, but they are in a way irrelevant. I would rather live with the idea that God did not permit such a disaster to happen for no purpose. This does not make it any less painful because, even though it may ultimately be for good, God wanted us to see it as bad. There's a reason for this too, that God wants us to react to it as if it were bad. He wants us to cry, to memorialize, to help the victims, to take revenge on the perpetrators. In that respect, I have to see it as bad. But I also have to have enough faith to believe that, if God permitted it, it ultimately has to have a purpose.

Professor Israel Levine

Professor Israel Levine is one of the world's foremost experts on the history of the Second Temple period. A teacher at Hebrew University, he has published numerous scholarly articles, and a number of important books. A graduate of the Jewish Theological Seminary and a Ph. D. from Columbia University, he was one of the founders and is director of the Rabbinical Seminary in Neve Schechter in Jerusalem and the TALI school network in Israel. The son of a communal rabbi, Professor Levine is a founder of Congregation Ramot Tzion in Jerusalem. He is also well know as a remarkable teacher who blends Torah learning and historical scholarship.

I met with Professor Levine at his home in the French Hill district of Jerusalem.

S.F.: Could you trace for me the main points in your development?

Professor Levine: In recounting the important turning points in my life, which influenced the future course of my work, the first would be my Camp Ramah experience. Thirteen years spent at Ramah, as a camper, counselor, and division head, left an indelible mark on my life, as on thousands of others. First, it brought me into direct contact with some of the finest people I have ever met: dedicated to the Jewish people, committed to maintaining and enhancing Jewish tradition, knowledgeable, and sensitive. These were people whose Jewish loyalties were balanced by broad cultural interests, and each succeeded in his or her own way in integrating those two worlds. The image of a Talmud teacher who could also excel in baseball and basketball made a deep impression on campers and staff alike. Moreover, the Ramah experience provided a total Jewish life for 2 whole months, from morning until evening, in the bunk, dining hall, on the ball field, and in classes. I relished this totality, which for me personally was absolutely necessary, as my high school years were spent in a small Ohio town of Steubenville. Moreover, camp was a major influence in my choice to attend Columbia College and, at the same time, to study at the Jewish Theological Seminary. From there, it was a natural step to continue with my graduate work at Columbia while entering the seminary's rabbinical school, with an eye to serving the American Jewish community. The Ramah experience, though it emphasized neither Zionism per se nor *aliyah,* nevertheless played a major role in my eventually making *aliyah.* The complete Jewish life that we experienced in Ramah gave us a taste of the totality of Jewish existence, and once exposed to Israel, my desire to become part of such a framework became decisive consideration in making *aliyah*—although the final decision itself was far from easy, as I will recount. I must add here that it was also at Ramah that I met my wife, Mira. Together we have shared the last 40 years, reared our four wonderful children, and already have the privilege of enjoying grandchildren these past 11 years.

The second milestone in my life came in rabbinical school, with my exposure to a number of inspiring teachers. The seminary then boasted far and away the finest coterie of scholars in every field of Judaic studies to be found anywhere in the Diaspora, and perhaps even Israel as well. Professors Lieberman, Ginzberg, Halkin, Salo Baron, Cohen, Abramson, Margoliot, Dimitrovsky, Heschel, Kaplan, Zucker, Gordis, Finkelstein, Weiss–Halivni, and many others made studying at the institution an intellectual and religious challenge. At the seminary, one was exposed to every facet of Jewish culture and civilization by the masters of their respective fields. This accumulated experience led to my decision to switch from planning a rabbinic congregational career to an academic track with teaching as a professional goal.

My third major decision was to live in Israel. Mira and I had spent 2 separate years as students in Jerusalem, one in our undergraduate days and one as graduate students. During the course of our second stay, I was invited to teach at the Hebrew University. Strange as it may seem, it was a difficult decision whether to accept this offer or not. In fact, it took us a full 9 months to decide on coming. Our hesitation was not because living here lacked attraction, but simply because we were both deeply committed to the survival and future of the American Jewish community. Just as we had so deeply benefitted from its situations, so we wanted to pass on to others what we had enjoyed ourselves. Mira and I spent endless hours weighing what we should do, and then decided to make our decision only after returning from Israel, hopefully with some necessary perspective. It is hard to say how the final decision was made. One day back in New York, it suddenly became clear what we ought to be doing, and what we indeed were interested in doing.

S.F.: Did you feel at any time a conflict between the call of the rabbinate and the call of an academic career? Or the founding of the *beit ha-midrash* and the time commitment that required, and the time required for scholarship?

Professor Levine: I assume what you mean by the call of the rabbinate is the desire to serve the Jewish people through the inculcation of Judaism as a religion and culture. The question then is whether there is a conflict between the desire to serve and do—let's call it *"tzorchei tsibbur"*—and the academic life. I don't think I would call it a conflict, but there is indeed a tension between these two callings. The academic life, as you noted, does indeed require large blocks of time to think, research, read, and write. Very few people in this world are able to dash off their thoughts quickly and effortlessly without a huge time investment. The greater the increase in bodies of knowledge available and in the incredibly accelerated pace of publication, the more difficult and time-consuming the road of scholarship becomes. Time taken from these endeavors is far more than merely time lost. There definitely is a sense of momentum, the accumulation of ideas and the pace of working, which, if broken, requires a whole new process of revving up. Two hours here and two hours there do not add up to 4 consecutive hours of research. Thus, any break is costly in terms of the quality and quantity of potential study research.

Yet for many people, and I suppose I count myself among this group, there is a need to be active in areas where one feels that he has something to contribute. Perhaps that is one of the reasons that we came to Israel: not only to enjoy the benefits of living in a Jewish society, but also to be able to contribute, however modestly, to the common good, enhancing our lives and the lives of others. This kind of involvement was not planned ahead of time. It just happened as needs arose to which we felt we had something to offer.

The first instance occurred soon after our moving to French Hill in 1973. My son, David, and I went to the local neighborhood synagogue for the first few Shabbatot. My wife and daughter stopped attending after a few weeks. The option of sitting behind a not-too-aesthetic partition, not being able to hear or see anything, was none too appealing to them. I did not suffer to the same degree, although the absence of any modicum of decorum and the quality of the sermons delivered were likewise problematic. That experience led us, together with several other friends who also happened to move into the neighborhood at that time, to start a minyan answering our particular needs. Most of these other people were likewise former Ramahniks, and the services that we created were understandably quite similar to those we had experienced and enjoyed together at camp, so much so that, for years, visitors who attended our synagogue would refer to our minyan as Ramah East.

Not long after our starting the synagogue, another challenge came, this time in the realm of education. Many of us had been painfully aware of the unhealthy polarity existing in Israeli education between the general *mamlachti* system, in which close to 75 percent of the schoolchildren study, and the religious or *dati* system, which caters to about 18 percent of the children; the reminder going to the Haredi or ultra-Orthodox schools. In the former a premium is placed on a general secular curriculum, with Jewish subjects such as Bible and history often taught only as humanistic topics of historical and national interest. The values of individualism, democracy, and respect of the other are primary. The *dati* system emphasizes the study of Jewish texts and religious observance of ritual commandments, between man and God, as well as a commitment to the Jewish tradition, the Torah, and the Land of Israel. Commitment in this framework takes precedence over tolerance, and loyalty to tradition over pluralism. The question many of us asked was whether the best of these two school systems could be integrated? Can one become a knowledgeable and identified Jew without the baggage of closed-mindedness and extremism? Or to phrase it in different, but no less cogent, terms, can Judaism survive and thrive in an open democratic system?

The first school, established on French Hill in Jerusalem, is now celebrating its twentieth year. Today there are some thirty such schools around the country. They are officially called TALI schools, which is an acronym for *Tigbur Limudei Yahadut* ("Jewish studies enrichment"). Not too many years later, there was a need to create a TALI high school for the elementary school graduates, and after a number of years of trying to work out a program within an already existing school, we finally succeeded in creating our own separate school.

On another track entirely, some of us participated in the formation of the Masorti (Conservative) movement in Israel. At first linking a mere dozen or so communities, the movement has grown in a few short years to encompass some forty-five congregations, a youth group, kibbutz, and a variegated communal life. Finally, some 13 years ago, in 1984, many of us were called upon to help found an institution of higher learning for the training of rabbis and educators, and to provide serious academic programs to a wide spectrum of Israelis and others alike. The 7 years that I spent as head of the *beit midrash* proved to be an exciting experience of institution–building, but a heavy price had to be paid in terms of academic aspirations.

Just to summarize for a moments. There certainly is a tension between the world of scholarship and other outside commitments. Although at times it might cause some frustration, often it forges a healthy tension, allowing one to contribute in very different ways to our society. I learned the blessings of such a combination of activities from my father, Harry Levine *z"l*, who himself combined the world of study and knowledge with that of the rabbinate and Jewish education.

S.F.: You have done a far more than ordinary amount in working for the community. Is there some philosophical explanation for this?

Professor Levine: I am not sure that I can point to a specific philosophical dimension to this activity. Perhaps it is best explained as being anchored in the following statements found in *Pirkei Avot*:

> R. Hanina ben Dosa said, 'Whoever's deeds are more numerous than his wisdom, his wisdom will endure. Whoever's wisdom exceeds his deeds, his wisdom will not endure' (3,12).
> R. Elazar ben Azariah said, 'Whoever's wisdom is greater than his deeds can be likened to a tree with many branches and few roots, and when a wind comes, it uproots it and turns it upside down . . . However, he whose deeds exceed his wisdom is likened to a tree with few branches but many roots, and even if all the winds in the world come and blow at it, they cannot move it' (3, 22).

Like many others, I too have a need to give and contribute, and naturally do so in areas where I feel that I many have something to offer, that is, in the fields of education and culture. As I've said, I have no game plan in this regard. Challenges arise simply in the course of events, and if I feel the ability and desire to contribute, and am asked to do so, then I have an inclination to involve myself to one degree or another. Heading the *beit midrash* for 7 years was most unusual. I have always undertaken such involvements in a lay capacity, but this I carried out as a professional. Nevertheless, this instance highlights the point I wish to make. Asked to head the institution because of an internal crisis, I did so while at the same time continuing my teaching at the Hebrew University. I must say that these years provided me with an unforgettable experience. In a short period of time, to change an institution from one serving eleven students to one of over 300 students, to supervise the development of the TALI schools all over the country through the TALI foundation operating under the aegis of the *beit midrash,* to run a teachers seminary in Budapest as well as a series of schools and summer camps in the former Soviet Union—all of this was the source of great pride and satisfaction. But at a certain point, it simply became too much to handle on a half–time basis. At first, some $100,000 a year had to be raised to keep things going, which was not too difficult a chore. However, by the end of the seventh year, we were running a budget of well over $3 million, and this required a far greater allocation of time and energy. It was clear to me that the institution needed a full–time president, and my research simply could not be kept on a back burner any longer, if I still wanted to be productive academically. Since I had never intended the position to be a long–term one, I decided that the time had come to step down and turn over the reins of the institution to someone else.

S.F.: In all your worlds, you are a teacher. Do you teach differently in the *beit ha–midrash,* for instance, than you do at the university?

Professor Levine: The answer is both yes and no. The basic academic approach to Jewish studies characteristic of the university is the basis of my, and others', instruction at the *beit midrash.* The same methodologies that govern academic inquiry in one, inform the other as well. Nevertheless, there is a difference. In my teaching, for example, I am more willing in the *beit midrash* framework to entertain questions that touch on the relevance and significance of what we are learning in regard to the modern Jew and Israeli. I might do this in the university as well, but if so, it would be in a much more circumspect way; for example, by inviting a student to discuss the matter after class. In the *beit midrash* context, through, I am more willing to devote some class time to discussing a particular issue even if it has no particular academic focus. For example, in dealing with a topic such as the encounter of Judaism and Hellenism, questions immediately arise as to the relevance of this topic in today's society. Is Judaism more or less open today to outside influences than it was in earlier periods? Is such openness good or bad? To what degree is historical Judaism a product of outside influences being incorporated and Juda–ized, or has Judaism always been wary and isolated from the outside world (a la Bilaam: "A people who dwells alone") (*Bamidmar 24:9*)? The *beit midrash* setting is far more conductive to entertaining such queries, although even there one must avoid overdoing this type of discussion in class to the detriment of the academic agenda.

But to answer your question on a deeper level, the *beit midrash* is in fact an attempt to synthesize the best of the yeshiva and university worlds. On the one hand, it resembles the latter in its commitment to the rigors of modern scholarship. On the other hand, it takes traditional sources and commentaries most seriously, and there is an attempt to create a warm and informal atmosphere through cultivating a personal tie between staff and student, through the extensive use of the *hevruta* method of study. Prayer and holiday celebrations are part of the life of the institution, thus creating an additional dimension and range of experiences to the basic study agenda.

The courses at the *beit midrash* are focused on the relevancy of the subject matter studied, even without explicitly saying so. For example, in a Biblical course, instead of our studying a particular prophetic book, the course might be called "Prophecy and the Critique of Society." The material to be covered is essentially the same, but the way the subject matter is conceptualized raises all sorts of questions and issues regarding values and behavior that have clear–cut implications for our own day. Another example would be with regard to the books of Ezra and Nehemiah. If we try to conceptualize two of the central issues of their period, ones addressed by each of these two books, then we might want to call the course "*Galut* and *Geulah*" (Exile and Redemption).

This kind of emphasis and concern, in a slightly different vein, is one of the reasons for the *beit midrash's* phenomenal growth this past decade. The institution has been able to meet the needs of a number of important constituencies in their search for a serious but meaningful and relevant course of studies leading to a M.A. degree. Let me be specific. The network of community centers here in Israel (*Matnasim*) was interested in having senior workers study for an advanced degree in Jewish studies, but wanted as much of the studies as possible to be geared to students' particular backgrounds and concerns; in this case, the areas of family and community. Thus, in addition to the strictly professional side of their curriculum, the Judaic component was to be adapted to their interests: Talmud texts would focus on issues relating to family and community, and so too their history courses. In other words, ways were found to tailor these studies so as to maximalize their relevency. The same processes of thought and adaptation held true with regard to the senior staff of the Ministry of Education's department of informal education, and other groups as well.

S.F.: In the university, you concentrate on instilling your students with certain basic knowledge.

Professor Levine: I would say that is the lowest level of university academic training. Unfortunately, it goes on all too often, but it is far from the ideal, from what should be. If university education is true to its purpose, then it should train students how to think and anaylze issues. For them to simply know facts is a sine qua non of study, but it is far from being the goal of a university education. Perhaps the accumulation of a mass of basis knowledge is important and necessary at the beginning of a course of study in a new field, but by the second and certainly the third year, the challenge should be to bring these students to a stage where they are able to think on their own, to ask the pertinent questions, to be able to carry out the research necessary in investigating an issue, and, finally, to be able to present it in a coherent and persuasive fashion, both orally and in writing.

S.F.: I wanted to ask you a bit about your scholarship. How did you chose the areas of specialization in which you work today?

Professor Levine: I chose my particular area of specialization, Jewish history and archaeology in the Greco–Roman era, owing to several teachers whom I found especially stimulating and challenging. Originally, my interest had been in philosophy, in which I majored as an undergraduate at Columbia. Despite the opportunity to continue in graduate school in that field, I opted for the rabbinical school of the seminary, for reasons already mentioned. Even my graduate work at Columbia, a few years later, began in the area of intellectual history, the study of ideas that were related to specific historical contexts in which they emerged and flourished. But slowly I moved into history itself, political, social, and cultural. The greatest influence on me in this respect was from a revered and brilliant teacher, Gerson Cohen, who was then teaching both at the seminary and at Columbia, and was eventually to become the chancellor of the seminary. Two other luminaries at Columbia also had an enormous influence on my academic career, Elias Bickerman and Morton Smith.

S.F.: And the archaeological dimension?

Professor Levine: That came somewhat later. Having decided to work on a history of the city of Caesarea in the Roman period, one of my advisors, Professor Bickerman, suggested that I spend time in Israel in order to study archaeology generally, and in particular the site of Caesarea. My year in Israel brought with it an invitation to join the staff of the Hebrew University in both the archaeology and history departments. I gained excavation experience in Caesarea itself, as well as in digging the ancient synagogue of Horvat Amudim in the lower Galilee. But field archaeology is a full-time job, and that was not my primary interest. I wished to write history by utilizing archaeological material to the hilt, while integrating it with data from literary sources.

S.F.: In reading your work, *The Rabbinic Class in Palestine during the Talmudic Period*, I was surprised by how much attention you give to social history. Do you have the sense of yourself as a social historian?

Professor Levine: Very much so. In that particular study, I focused on certain institutions in Talmudic society, especially the rabbinic elite. In a book just published in Hebrew on Jerusalem in the Second Temple period, I attempted to trace the development of this city over a 600-year period, focusing on political, social, and religious developments, while weaving the archaeological material into the narrative whenever possible: Even in the major study that I will be completing in a few months, a history of the ancient synagogue over its first 1,000 years, the focus is on a major institution in Jewish life of late antiquity.

S.F.: What date do you take as your starting point?

Professor Levine: The short answer to the question is in the Hellenistic period. But then the question becomes "Why?" And here I have a rather different approach from most scholars to date. The problem is that we have no data on the origins and beginnings of the synagogue. When it first appears on the stage of history in the first century C.E., it is as a fully developed institution that was playing a central role in

Jewish communities throughout the Roman Empire. In trying to account for the origins of this institution, scholarly views have ranged over no less than a 900–year period, from the 10th Century to the first, B.C.E. Almost all have assumed that the institution was essentially a religious one from the very beginning, and that a major upheaval in Jewish life must have generated its creation, perhaps King Josiah's reformation of 622 B.C.E., or the destruction of the First Temple, etc.

The approach I am suggesting is to begin at the other end of the spectrum, from what we know about the early synagogue, and then work backwards. In the 1st Century C.E., when the institution emerged into the full light of history, it functioned as the center of the community, fulfilling all conceivable functions. If we then ask ourselves where these functions took place earlier, than the answer is immediately evident. Every documented activity associated with the 1st Century synagogue took place formerly at the Biblical city gate. This area served as the hub of city or village life, and functioned as such politically, socially, economically, juridically, and culturally. Thus, for many hundreds of years, the role eventually played by the synagogue was fulfilled in the gate area. At some point in antiquity, the city gate stopped playing this role, losing its elaborate architectural layout featuring side rooms and open areas, and it became instead only a place for entrance and exit. This change in the plan and structure of the city gate area took place, as can clearly be seen in the archaeological evidence, during the course of the Hellenistic period, probably owing to the development of newer and more sophisticated weaponry.

S.F.: I have no real knowledge of this subject. But the need to pray is so deeply a part of us. If there were no Temple, then how would this need have been served?

Professor Levine: Prayer is a universal phenomenon of the human spirit, and according to our tradition, it goes back to the patriarchs and matriarchs, and of course to Hannah. However, fixed communal prayer was a rather late development in Judasim. What made the synagogue unique liturgically, and what set it off from other kinds of pagan religious institutions of antiquity, was the central role of sacred Scriptures. The public, communal reading and study of Torah was the primary, perhaps exclusive, activity of the synagogue for centuries, and it distinguished Jewish worship from that of their neighbors. Communal obligatory prayer for the ordinary Jew is known only from the period of Yavne, that is, following the destruction of the Second Temple.

S.F.: Do you mean that the *beit ha-midrash* precedes the synagogue?

Professor Levine: Not the *beit midrash* as an institution. That too only evolved in the Hellenistic or early Roman period. What I was referring to was the synagogue as a place of study, for children and adults alike. The most famous inscription we have from the Second Temple of Jerusalem, the Theodotus inscription, specifically singles out the synagogue as a place for reading the Torah and studying the commandments. That was the essence of the early synagogue in its religious dimension.

S.F.: Do you believe it possible to draw from your historical research lessons for the Jewish people today? I am thinking of this specifically in connection to the question of assimilation.

Professor Levine: I certainly believe that it is a valid exercise, just as one studies a text and asks about its relevancy for our day and age. The philosopher Santayana said: that whoever does not learn from the past is doomed to repeat its mistakes. Much can be learned from the past, but the question is what and how.

For example, solutions to particular situations can not, of course, be found in events of the past. Each historical moment is unique and therefore irreplaceable. However, when it comes to processes, to larger trends and more fundamental historical developments, I think that parallels and analogies can be helpful. They not only make clear what and why things went wrong in the past, but more positively, they shed light on how similar challenges in the past were successfully overcome.

Take the issue you have just raised. Assimilation is certainly a curse with respect to its negative impact on the vitality and continuity of the Jewish people. Yet assimilation is but the extreme expression of a process that is, in and of itself, a natural and healthy one among Jews, or any other people for that matter. I am referring to the dynamic of acculturation, which has always been part of the Jewish experience. Both the Bible and rabbinic literature are chock full of examples of creative borrowing of outside models and practices, then adapting them to fit into the Jewish context. In every part of the Bible, one can see that phenomenon at work, and it finds expression in the political, social, religious, and cultural realms. Certain distinctions, of course, have to be made. Jews in more open societies are more apt to be influenced than those living in more isolated and restrictive frameworks. The wealthy and those living in cities will be more affected than others and, of course, third or fifty generations are more likely to be acculturated than the first or second.

What is important to realize is that it invariably happens, and that if is not necessarily bad.

So much of what we associate as Jewish today was once taken over, in one form or another, from non–Jewish society: Biblical sacrifices, the *midrashic* rules of Hillel, the organization and structure of the Passover *Haggadah*, the writings of Maimonides and others—all are heavily indebted to the stimulation of the non–Jewish world. Just look at the ancient synagogues discovered throughout this country in the last few generations. They are filled with Greek inscriptions, figural images including those of the zodiac and the sun god Helios—and all this in the synagogue. Here is a striking example of Hellenization, which was a form of acculturation, not assimilation. These are the facts of history. Thus, when we come to confront the issue of assimilation, it is important to understand that we are dealing with a natural process of history that has gotten out of hand, rather than with a totally new phenomenon that Jewish history has heretofore never known. One of the important lessons that the study of history offers is the importance of perspective in order to form any kind of judgment, whether with respect to conflicts and tensions, or with the creativity and adaptability that the Jewish people exhibited in transcending crises in the past. Sometimes such perspective tells us that current patterns are part and parcel of well–documented historical processes. At other times, it points out truly unique developments.

S.F.: And when you look at Jewish Diaspora history today, and the interaction with Western culture, what kind of process and dynamic do you see taking place now?

Professor Levine: What we see happening today is sui generis: "It is the best of times and the worst of times." Never have Jews benefitted from so open, pluralistic, and democratic a society as they do today in the west. Jews have made inroads into almost every conceivable area of society and, as a result, we see the unsettling result in the rates of intermarriage and assimilation. However, there are also some very positive developments in Diaspora Jewry, which give cause for hope that not all is lost. The explosion this last generation of Jewish studies on the university level, the much greater attendence in day schools, and the growth of a network of *havurot* are all signs of vibrancy and vitality.

The strategy in coping with this or any such crisis is twofold: first, to build on the positive, investing heavily in those populations that demonstrate a strong and powerful will to maintain and enhance their Jewish identity and commitments; and second, at the same time, to keep channels open to others, in the hopes of winning some back while attempting to limit the damage as much as possible. Outreach programs that attempt to keep Jewishly–born adults in touch with the community are important steps to take.

Rather than bewail assimilation, therefore, I suggest seeing it for what it is, never forgetting the blessings of acculturation. To quote my teacher, Gerson Cohen, concentrate on those who remain committed, and create the institutions that will be able to attract Jews and instill them with the pride and loyalties necessary to counter the powerful centrifugal forces operating in the modern world.

S.F.: And what about the situation of Judaism in Israel, what many perceive as an increasing polarization between the religious and the non–religious?

Professor Levine: I find this no less disturbing than the Diaspora crisis. Instead of uniting us and cementing the relationships between Jews, Jewish tradition has become such a controversial issue is our society. We are too small a nation and too ideologically charged for our own good. It is absolutely necessary for everyone to step back, gain a perspective on the situation as a whole and the implications of his or her stand, and not assume that every change is bad and must be fought tooth and nail. In other words, we must work to establish the real and deep meaning of pluralism, democracy, and how to recognize the rights and legitimacy of others and their opinions even when disagreeing. The distrust among the various sectors is enormous and growing constantly.

S.F.: Isn't there a parallel between what is happening in Israel and what is happening in America, in that in both communities the center has weakened, and the extremes have strengthened; on one side moving toward fundamentalism and on the other abandoning the tradition entirely?

Professor Levine: Absolutely. I think that one of the grave weaknesses of the Jewish community today, or of any community at any time in history, is the absence of a stabilizing center. It is the existence of a strong center that gives a balance to society and allows it to integrate and synthesize, rather than to reject and negate. When you lose that center, a dangerous and fragile climate is created. Between the rampant secularization and westernization on the one hand, and a triumphalist fundamentalism, both religiously and nationalistically, on the other hand—with boundless hostility on both sides—the present situation is fraught with difficulties. While such a bifurcation is to be found in many contemporary societies, we as Jews are more vulnerable to the negative effects of such tensions because of our size. We can little afford this divisiveness, given our small numbers and ofttimes perilous circumstances.

S.F.: But the question is, "Why doesn't the 'reasonable center' speak to more people?" We speak about the death of "isms" and the return to simple fundamentalist answers. Why aren't those with the true religious dedication, uncompromised by an open, complex realistic view of the world unable to attract more followers?

Professor Levine: Let me start with an important caveat, namely, that all such attempts at forging a consensus, an ideology, and a practicum take time. A more liberal approach to Judaism—and here I make no distinction between modern, Western–nurtured Orthodox, Conservative, or Reform—is relatively new to Israel. We are talking of several decades and no more. To affect profound changes, one has to think in longer terms than this. Just look at the Yavne period following the destruction of the Temple in the year 70 C.E. Comparatively little seems to have been accomplished in the 10 or 20 years in which Yochanan ben Zakkai stood at the head. At most, he succeeded in planting seeds and laying the foundations for a new type of institution. But the real impact of Yavne was only accomplished in following generations, under Rabban Gamaliel and his colleagues.

It is difficult to create a center that attempts to be inclusive and not divisive, tolerant and not strident. It is a difficult sell, to use modern parlance. Leadership, both educational and religious, has to be assiduously trained, and then a major outreach effort has to be mounted to affect wider circles within the population. In the face of the vigorous fundamentalism that has taken root over the past decade or two, both religiously and politically, such an endeavor requires patience and an awareness that the process calls for a long haul. I have no doubt that, sooner or later, the climate that has been so conducive to fundamentalism, spiritually and politically, will change, and this will allow for other forces to make the great leap forward.

Larger issues aside, what is necessary to mount a momentum of change in the direction we are talking about? One is the simple and fundamental issue of funding. One reason for the growth of fundamentalism is not just the ideology per se, but the fact that an enormous amount of governmental and private money is being poured into these circles. Buildings are constructed, programs inaugurated, housing units financed to a degree hitherto unknown. If the same kinds of sums were to be made available to other religious and educational institutions, then you would see some amazing changes in this society within a matter of years.

A second necessary ingredient is strong and charismatic leadership. There are some such figures active in our society, but as yet they remain heads of specific institutions, and have not achieved national stature. Sooner or later, and hopefully the former, such a figure will emerge, who will begin to coalesce the various efforts and offer some sort of united national expression.

Finally, there is the question of strategy, how to best affect change in society. Are we talking about schools, youth activities, summer programs, adult outreach, and if the latter, in what form? Perhaps a wide range of initiatives has to be undertaken simultaneously; then the question arises as to their coordination and integration. There are two basic ways of trying to influence society. One is to build new kinds of institutions and frameworks, then attract people to join or affiliate. That is a necessary but insufficient road. It is also important to penetrate and infiltrate already existing institutions and affect them from within. Schools, the army, community centers, professional groups, and immigrant organizations are all important avenues in trying to re–educate the Israeli public to view Judaism and Zionism in new and different ways.

There is no end of available strategies. What is crucial is the message to be conveyed. In short, it is a different view of Judaism than that projected today in the public consciousness. It is a Judaism that includes not only a commitment to the values of Zionism, but also to the modern world and the best that it stands for: democracy, tolerance, pluralism, and a recognition of the value and centrality of the individual. There are groups in Israel that focus on one of the above three (Judaism, Zionism, modernity), and there are even some that include two of the three. But we would be hard pressed to find many people who would subscribe to all three as valid and important ingredients in forging a world view. That is precisely the challenge that faces us here in Israel as we approach the 21st Century.

S.F.: You have been speaking about contributing to the Jewish people, which is one central way of serving God. How do you understand the concept of service of God in relation to your own life?

Professor Levine: *Avodat Hashem* in my view can be expressed in a number of different ways. Let me suggest three possibilities. The first is the traditional notion of the service of God; namely, through prayer, *kashrut*, holidays, and the study of Torah. Each of these paths has its own challenges and rewards, and cumulatively they form a precious mosaic of behavior that can offer a Jew the opportunity to grow and develop throughout the day, week, and year. For me, personally, Talmud Torah is an especially important avenue, for my work allows me to spend a great deal of time studying the classic sources of our tradition, as well as other literary and cultural expressions of our people throughout the ages.

One of the important expressions of *avodat Hashem* is the search for truth. In my humble opinion, this is one of the highest religious values to which one can aspire. In all my research and teaching, and here it makes no difference whether at the Hebrew University or the *Beit midrash*, this goal is foremost.

A second area of *avodat Hashem* is what we spoke of earlier, that is, being involved in communal affairs that deal with the advancement of Jewish knowledge and practice. And here I would mention that Jewish practice does not stop with ritual observance, the mitzvot between man and God. The other area of mitzvot, between man and man, is of equal importance. I for one certainly take the prophets seriously in their continuous invoking of God's name and God's will in emphasizing the importance of moral sensitivity and justice in dealing with other people, often with no regard to whether that person is a Jew or not. Of course, it is not only the Prophets. *Vayikra* (19) clearly sees a complimentary role between ritual and social justice, and this same world view was adopted by our Sages as well. Starting a synagogue, a school, or the *beit midrash* is a way of strengthening Judasim, and each is a legitimate expression of *avodat Hashem* as well.

The third component of *avodat Hashem* is what I would call the privilege and responsibility of self–fulfillment ("*hagshamah atzmit*"). Every human being is special, a spark of the Divine. The Mishnah in *Sanhedrin* (4, 5) states this quite forcefully, when it compares God's creation to that of man. One mints coins and they all look alike, but the Holy One Blessed be He creates a boundless number of individuals and all are unique in one way or another. One way of serving God it to make the most of the gifts that He has bestowed on each and every one of us. It is self–realization that, to be truly genuine, one cannot be confined only to the individual, himself, but also to his or her context as well. To be complete this ought to include the family, the community, and the Jewish people as well. Self–fulfillment is therefore not only a humanistic goal, but, by bringing to fruition God's gift it is no less an opportunity of *avodat Hashem*.

Professor Aviezer Ravitzky

Professor Aviezer Ravitzky is one of the world's foremost teachers of Jewish philosophy. The author of numerous scholarly articles, he is, along with being a teacher at Hebrew University, a widely respected lecturer in various public forums throughout Israel. Among his books are *Al Da'at Ha-Maquom* and *Messianism, Zionism, and Jewish Religious Radicalism.* As one working to bridge gaps in the society, he is very active in the dialogue between religious and secular Zionists in Israel.

I met with Professor Ravitzky at his office in the Jerusalem Peace Institute in the Talbieh neighborhood. Because he is enthusiastic, articulate, and good-willed, it is easy to understand why he is one of the most popular teachers in Israel today.

S.F.: Could you briefly outline your educational background?

Professor Ravitzky: I was born in Jerusalem in 1945, studied at the elementary school L'Dugma and Maaleh secondary school, was a member of the B'nei Akiva youth movement, and served in the army in the framework of Nahal. After the army, I began to study medicine, but then, after a year off thinking about it, decided to devote myself to philosophy and Jewish thought. I wrote my Ph. D. dissertation on the attitude of the disciples of the Ramban to his *Guide to the Perplexed*. I spent a year at Harvard in post–doctoral studies, then returned to Hebrew University as an assistant professor. I have been chairman of the Institute of Jewish Studies and of the Department of Jewish Thought. I have been involved in the religious peace movement in Israel too.

S.F.: Do you understand your life work to be *avodat Hashem*? How do you understand this concept?

Professor Ravitzky: My first approach to this question is Maimonidean. I may not know positively what *Hashem* is or means, but I do not consider the finite, material existence as the ultimate one. Therefore, the effort of the human being—and in this context, more specifically, the Jew—is to transcend the limited aspect of life. It is to go beyond the relative and search for the Ultimate. This is the first meaning of standing in front of the *Hashem* I do not know. For me personally,

251

this effort is done as a Jew. My whole framework in regard to religious questions, in regard to the search for the Ultimate, is in a Jewish context. So I can pray only as a Jew, and I do sense that, for instance, the prayers of Yom Kippur can at times bring me to this sincere stance before God. This does not mean that I negate the approaches of other human beings toward the Ultimate. But just as I can dream and write poems only in Hebrew, so can I pray and do God's service only in a Jewish framework.

S.F.: I have the sense that you regard the service of God more in the context of Rambam's "intellectual contemplation of the Supreme Being" rather than as the Hasidic concentration on every small action of daily life.

Professor Ravitzky: It would be very pretentious to say that I live with the consciousness of having God continually before me. Yet my relationship to a world of values is connected existentially and psychologically to a religious stance, and to religious sources. So I cannot say that *avodat Hashem* accompanies me every moment, but I have the goal that such times of consciousness will be part of my life. My aim is that standing before the Absolute will be an organic part of my life. There are many aspects of Jewish religious life when, standing before the Transcendent, one must ask oneself the meaning of what he is doing. When does a person create Jewish philosophy? Only when he is in an arena, a meeting place of ideas, when there is an encounter within him or her, a confrontation between two different worlds. This is the encounter between the non–philosophical Jewish sources—Bible, *halachah*, *midrash*—and the non-Jewish philosophical sources—Plato or Aristotle, Kant or Hegel, and contemporary existentialism. The effort to create a Jewish philosophy is a result of the reflection which comes from such an encounter or confrontation.

I mentioned that I studied for a year at Harvard. There I met another Israeli, a graduate of a black hat Yeshiva, who told me of an encounter he had at a reception for the post–doctoral scholars in physics. A Japanese post—doctoral student asked him why he wasn't eating the non–kosher food. He had no conceptual reply. Needless to say, had the inquiring student been a Christian, then the Bible might have helped him explain. But without common cultural background, he could not make his own Jewish position understood universally. In this encounter then, he began making an effort at philosophizing or theologizing, of explaining his belief to another world. If I live within my own self-enclosed world, then no such effort is required. But when I meet the "other," I have to begin to make this kind of "translation." As for myself, I feel as if I am often working as translator, translating the Jewish world into the language of Western culture, or into a more universal language. Then, too, I translate the world of Western philosophy into the inner language of Judaism, trying to make a new *midrash* of our classical sources. This is what Rabbi Soloveitchik did when he explained the world of *halachic* man to the Western world, while explaining to the students of the yeshiva the meaning of Neo–Kantian and existentialist philosophical concepts.

S.F.: When you teach Jewish thought in the university, are you primarily teaching an academic discipline like any other, or is there some special inward intention on your part to contribute to the Jewish people, serve the world of Torah?

Professor Ravitzky: First of all, one must distinguish between the two roles of the university professor, roles that in a sense contradict each other, of teacher and of researcher. The role of the teacher is to transmit the body of knowledge of the human and national tradition to the next generation. The role of the scholar is to undermine the given knowledge and to suggest new revolutionary ideas. A teacher has to construct, while a researcher sometimes has to deconstruct. Now when I work as a scholar, my work is shaped by my world of values and by my existential world. I ask questions that interest me, and I investigate texts that are near to my heart. However, I try to use an objective method for investigation, for finding answers to the questions. In this sense, the value of truth in the university wins out over the value of the good. I have to tell the truth even if it may have a negative effect upon you.

In the yeshiva world, sometimes there is a reversal of values, and the greatest emphasis is placed on doing good. I may even hide a truth, or a text, in order to promote the good. For instance, one may know that there are certain sources that contradict his thesis, but if he believes that his thesis will cause one to have greater awe before God, then he will ignore them. That is to say in the Yeshiva the Good is more important than the True, whereas in the University the True is more important than the Good.

This is my scholarly side. However, as a teacher, I find the matter more delicate. For instance, I give a course, "Introduction to Jewish Thought," in which I present nine different models or paradigms of Jewish thought. These are the nationalism of Saadia Gaon, the revelationism of Yehuda ha–Levi, the intellectualism of the Rambam, the voluntarism of Hasdai Crescas, the mysticism of "Baal ha–Zohar," the critical approach to Judaism of Spinoza, the historiosophic approach of Nachman Krochmal, the existentialist–dialogical approach of Franz Rosenzweig, and the harmonizing approach of Rabbi Kook. I try to present each of these conceptions from the inside. For two or three sessions, I am the devoted follower of one particular approach, and argue in its defense. But what I am also trying to show in the course of the teaching is that there are different classical paradigms of Jewish thought. This in itself confronts the narrow dogmatic interpretation of Judaism and makes a major educational point. For some students, it is a great revelation to know that there is such a rich range of possibilities in the history of Jewish thought.

Again, precisely because I am teaching at the university, I try to emphasize the distinctions and the deep tensions between various approaches. All these differences taken together help build the normative home of Jewish thought. And I try to teach with intimacy and enthusiasm. As these subject are truly close to me—some more than others—I can speak of them with warmth.

It can be, too, that I feel paradoxically close to a position that challenges my own. When I was writing my book *Messianism, Zionism, and Jewish Religious Radicalism*, I was overwhelmed by the power of the Haredi anti–Zionist sources, the Satmar–Munkatch writings. I was even frightened by the power of these sources. Therefore, I try to bring them to my students with a sense of warmth, which I would not be able to transfer were I teaching German or French culture. I can summarize this by recalling the positions of two of my most revered teachers. The late Professor Gottlieb, who taught Kabbalah, would say, "I cannot be a professor of Tanach because I believe in Tanach. I am not a professor of Talmud because I accept the authoritativeness of the Sages. But since I do not believe in Kabbalah, I can be an objective scholar of Jewish mysticism. I remember too a lecture of the late Professor Gershon Scholem, who said "When you as a Jew see the greatest minds of the modern period—Kant, Hegel—and see what they write on Judaism, you see that they did not even begin to understand what they were talking about." So we need both great distance and great closeness if we are truly to understand. This is the paradoxical tension I try to uphold when I am involved in exploring the Jewish sources.

S.F.: There has been much talk in recent years of declining enrollments in university courses on Judaism in Israel. Would you say something about this declining Jewish interest in Jewish thought? Does it reflect the intensification of the secular–religious divide in Israel?

Professor Ravitzky: The decline in registration for Jewish studies has been halted; in the past two years, there have been increased enrollments. But there had been a decline. As for the cause, a baker of *matzot* in Tel Aviv, interviewed in the Israeli newspaper *Yediot Achronot* a few years ago, said that every year there is a decline of two percent for the *matzot* that he and his colleagues are selling. And he gave the following explanation. One percent of the decrease is due to those newly married secular couples whose parents were used to eating *matzot* during Pesach, if not for religious *halachic* reasons, than for cultural, national ones. Another percent came from those who now want *Shemurah Matzah*, not the regular kind. In a sense, professors of Judaism are in the same situation as bakers of *matzot* as we lose a certain percentage from both sides. Secular youngsters, who once came to the university to learn their culture, fear today that if they enter such studies, they will be taken over politically or spiritually. And religious students will today tend to go to a yeshiva, or even to Bar Ilan. So the polarization between secular and religious causes the decline on both sides. Yet there is a significant change in the present, which I believe anticipates a general change within the Israeli society.

S.F.: From your work in Jewish thought, do you have the sense that ideas can change the world? And are there, in your judgment, ideas that can be used to contend with the growing assimilation Jewish people are suffering through today?

Professor Ravitzky: I am a great believer in the power of words and ideas. Marx sat in the British Museum library and wrote *Das Kapital* and today there are still over a billion people living as Marxists. Rabbi Kook, who was not a successful politician, wrote books whose influence, after two generations, is enormous. From the point of view of ideas, the Jewish religious culture today is in crisis. We have a powerful literature is Israel that is secular. The four most prominent Jewish candidates for the Nobel Prize in Literature are secular Israelis: A.B. Yehoshua, Yehuda Amichai, Amos Oz, and Aharon Appelfeld. Meanwhile, today's world of religious Jews is not producing great literature. In terms of Jewish thought, I believe that Rabbi Kook was the greatest Jew of the 20th Century. I myself am not a Kooknik, but given the depth of his work as philosopher, *halachist*, mystic, and poet, he was a giant. The problem is that so much of his thought centers on concepts of wholeness and harmony, concepts that are less relevant in a contemporary world whose key concepts are brokenness and fragmentation.

S.F.: But we hear so much talk today about "holistic thinking." Isn't there an effort to create new syntheses, to overcome the "fragmented" way of seeing things?

Professor Ravitzky: A search there may be, but my feeling is that we have not gone beyond this. Many interesting things have been said by Rabbi Soloveitchik and by Yehoshua Leibowitz, but I do not believe that they can form the new Jewish generation in thought. I believe that Jewish thought is in crisis, and has to find itself. And this is in the context of a world in which all the great "isms" and faiths and doctrines are in crisis. Take for instance when Rabbi Soloveitchik speaks about the two "Adams," he is somehow speaking in the mode of the beginning of the century. On the one side, there is the optimistic conqueror of nature, and on the other, the man of faith withdrawing inside his own religious world. I remember one lecture by Dr. Eli Ben-Gal of the Shomer Ha–Tsair in which he said, "At the end of the former century and at the beginning of this one, we said 'Hurrah, there is no God.' Now, at the end of the century, we say 'Woe, there is no God.' Therefore, Eli Gal is not the first Adam, nor is he the second. He is the kind of person that Rabbi Soloveitchik did not know in his generation, but who is common in ours. The contemporary human is neither the simple conqueror of Rabbi Soloveitchik nor the man of progress of Rabbi Kook. We are looking for the thought that will find a place for the disappointment and crisis of modernity, and go toward a new synthesis. Our aim should be to show that the alternative to modernity is not fundamentalism, but rather a new kind of creative religious thought.

S.F.: What then is your view of the major Jewish systems of thought today, especially in regard to Jewish history? You write about the Haredi world, whose model is challenged by the successful Jewish return to the land not coming miraculously and messianically as they had hoped. You write about the expectation of religious Zionists, that the socialist secularists would somehow repent religiously, as not having been realized. What do you have in mind as a model, and what should we presently be aiming for in Jewish history?

Professor Ravitzky: I will begin with the criticism you hinted at. Three generations ago, the majority of the Orthodox authorities were against the very idea of a sovereign Jewish state in the Land of Israel. Now, after three generations have passed, many of them are opposed to giving up sovereignty in any part of the land. Does it reflect a contradiction? I don't think so. In the past, they spoke against the idea of a state, not simply because of its secularist character, but because for 1,900 years we held an integral, complete vision of the whole people returning to the whole land, living completely in Torah. All the people would messianically return and live in total peace. But what has been done is rather partial. Only some of the returnees observe the Torah, peace is elusive, and morality compromised. Part of the people returned to part of the land. This is the nature of any historical achievement. However, with the gradual and remarkable success of Zionism, the religious society began to identify the Zionist realization with the Messianic dream. There were more and more demands for Zionism to bring to fruition the whole Messianic dream. They expect history itself (Zionism) to transcend history (Redemption). Then comes another voice, which says, "You cannot realize everything now; you will achieve only a partial contingent fulfillment." So they become frightened because they have become accustomed to the idea that the prophetic vision will be realized by Zionism and the state.

Personally, I am not sure, but I hope that, just as at the turn of the century the Orthodox needed the socialists and secularist Zionists to make the historical breakthrough, they today need them to make it again. The religious person has the advantage of encountering the Ultimate. It is difficult for him or her to live with history. For me, I see living in the Third *Bayit* in the sense of commonwealth. Neither the first nor the second commonwealth fulfilled all the dreams. But they were endowed with positive religious meaning. The same with the third.

We have to learn to live with partial historical fulfillment, and to understand that the part has value in itself.

According to the Talmud, at the time of the return to Zion and the construction of the Second Temple, there was a conflict of values between social justice and the settlement of all the Land of Israel. When you have a non–Messianic mind, and there is a clash of values, you realize that you have to choose, to pay a price. You understand that you are within history and you must make a choice. This is the situation of Ezra and Nehemiah, and the returnees of Zion described in the Talmud. For the Rambam too, there was a legitimate model of a Jewish politic which is not Messianic. There is always the hope that the end will be redemptive, Messianic, but history is not judged by the end. As to those from Gush Emunim and the people of Mercaz Ha–Rav, I too grant the state of Israel, a religious meaning, but unlike them, not a Messianic meaning. Rabbi Reines, the founder of the Mizrahi movement, made this distinction. He thought that there is a religious meaning to part of the people returning to part of the land and having partial independence.

Now when I say *bayit*, which enables a realization of values, I do not necessarily mean all of the values. There is a revival of the Jewish people in the land, but this is not necessarily redemption. We do not measure the value of the revival exclusively in relation to the process of redemption. In the rebirth, there is value in itself. The model of Ha–Rav Soloveitchik in *Kol Dodi Dofek* is relevant. As he outlines it there, there is for one side, an opportunity, and for the other, the chance of missing the opening. There is no determinism which foresees an inevitable destruction of the Naturei Karta kind, and no necessary inevitable redemption either. We have our role to play in determining our own fate.

S.F.: What does this kind of Jewish state aspire to be? Should it be a light to the nations?

Professor Ravitzky: The State of Israel is a means that has to provide the conditions for the Jewish people to create and be revived here. What will be in the future is not certain. I see the Diaspora as a contradiction of Jewish life, as it exists without Jewish land, without a Jewish language and judicial system, without Jewish calender, and autonomy. One prays in one language and dreams in another. Meanwhile, in Israel, the hope is for autonomous Jewish creativity—this option is not a guarantee. The Rambam said that political independence is the condition for Jewish spiritual creativity in the full sense; not a sufficient, but a necessary condition. I am talking about a collective creation, the creation of the people as a whole. In this sense, the flowering of the yeshivot and the flowering of secular Hebrew literature are both parts of what Zionism should be aiming for. Paradoxically, it is Zionism and its natural products that have brought forth the greatest flowering of Torah learning since *Avraham Avinu.*

S.F.: There is the question of whether quantity is quality.

Professor Ravitzky: I have said that I am disappointed with the quality of religious literature and creativity. If we consider that ninety percent of the Torah world was destroyed in Europe, and we now have a rebirth of Torah in Israel, then this is remarkable. And I maintain that this is a result of Zionism, for it is Zionism that also produced the conditions that made possible the flowering of secular literature.

S.F.: The sociologist, Samuel Heilman, wrote a book on the revival of Orthodox Jewry in America, in which survivors were decisive. I don't dispute the growth of the yeshiva world here, but it is happening there too.

Professor Ravitzky: The Haredi world revealed an astonishing power of rebirth in a number in places. But only in Israel do we have this kind of confrontation between the religious literature and the secular literature. Outside Israel, if not in the world of Torah, you move toward assimilation. What I said is that Israel only is an area for different kinds of creation. Take the area of law for instance. Israeli law has on the one side, its sources in Jewish law, and on the other, in Western jurisprudence. The American Jew does not know this tension. The American Jew does not have to ask how the system he lives under will, on the one side, meet the demands for freedom and autonomy of the person, and on the other, the demand to serve God. He does not confront the problems of a Jewish and democratic state, of Jewish military power versus Jewish ethics, of different kinds of Jews living together, arguing together, fighting together. Here I have to be a Jew, not only in regard to the spiritual aspects of my life, but in regard to the physical ones too.

S.F.: And what about this creation as light to the nations?

Professor Ravitzky: One who does not have a message for others will eventually degenerate. Twice I spoke in forums with A.B. Yehoshua on this issue. He spoke in defense of normalcy for the Jewish people, and I in defense of our uniqueness. As I told him, if we wanted to be normal, then we did not have to take responsibility for the massacre done by so-called Christians against Palestinian refugee camps in Lebanon. True, we did have indirect responsibility, since we had control of the areas around the camps. But once you take upon yourself even indirect responsibility (where others would not) you behave in a unique way.

S.F.: For me, this is not a good example. I saw the protestors against the Israeli government as Jews joining in a worldwide chorus of hatred against Israel, condemning us for what we had not done.

Professor Ravitzky: I did not go to the demonstration to show something to the world, but rather because the Jewish tradition teaches me that, if I could have prevented it and did not, then I am also responsible for it. As for the goal of normalcy, I believe in realms such as economics, business, we can aim for this. But in terms of cultural and spiritual life, we have to maintain our own special identify and character. I believe that we have a unique message, and we have to make strong demands upon ourselves. Take the book of *The Kuzari* written by Yehuda ha-Levi, a basic text of Jewish thought. It was constructed as a dialogue between a Jewish sage and the king of the Khazars. Throughout the discussion, the Jewish sage argues for the unique advantage of the Jewish religion and people, and the Gentile king accepts his claims. There are only two places where the king makes an argument and the Jew withdraws without reply. The first time is when the sage speaks about the unique connection between the Jewish people of Israel and the Land of Israel. The sage talks about our loyalty to the land, but the Kuzari responds, "While you talk like parrots about returning, you do nothing concretely." The second instance is when the sage says, "We Jews are murdered, but do not murder." The Gentile king responds, "When you have the power, you will. You are not unique, you are only weak."

Now what did Zionism create? Both dreams, the dream of *Eretz Yisrael* and the dream of our moral uniqueness, have simultaneously been put to the test. The complexity and difficulty of our historical situation are that we have to be true to both dreams. On the one side, we have to be true to the realistic dream of living in the land, and on the other, to our unique moral demand.

For 1,900 years, the Jews lived without these challenges, without the land, without power, without having an army to defind ourselves. What we are doing here can be the model of Jewish behavior for meeting the demands of power and the demands of morality of living in the land.

S.F.: Do you believe in the idea that the best way to do this is through bringing Jews closer to the religious tradition?

Professor Ravitzky: I believe that a human being who does not have God in his heart is an incomplete person. But I also believe that the religious person who does not dignify the image of God in the other, who does not behave humanistically, is also not complete. My struggle is an educational one on two planes. On the one side, I wish that all Israelis would have in their hearts an intimate aquaintance with the Jewish religious tradition. On the other, I wish to work for the humanization of the religious community. I want dialogue with the secular Zionist Jew. We do not have to be identical to each other, but we have to be all the time in spiritual interaction, irritating and stimulating each other. The moment you cease to be irritated at that person who does not have God in his heart, you begin to lose part of the impulse for rebirth in the society.

S.F.: You speak with enthusiasm about the experience in Israel. But what about the Jews outside of Israel? How are they to be engaged and brought into the process of rebirth?

Professor Ravitzky: There are two planes, the ideological and the sociological. As for the sociological, I do not believe that I am the person with the authority to discuss this. On the ideological plane, I believe in the possibility of authentic life on the part of the Jewish individual outside of Israel. But I do not believe it in terms of collective Jewish creativity. In this sense, I would like to see a gradual regathering of the Jewish people to their home. They once said to Franz Rosenzweig, "You and the Reform make a selection of the mitzvot. But what is the difference between you and the Reform?" He answered,

"We may both stand at equal distance from the *Beit Ha-Mikdash*. But they stand with their backs toward it, and I stand facing it." I would want to feel that their experience there is one in which they are facing toward the Bayit.

I will not explain now why I do not subscribe to the Babylonian-Jerusalem model, or the model of periphery and Center. My model is that of a collective home, and something like a hotel outside. In this space outside, there can be wondrous development for the individual but not for the collective.

S.F.: Now that we are speaking of creative work for the Jewish people, could you say a few words about what you are working on?

Professor Ravitzky: I am doing two things now. I found a text, an interpretation and commentary, on Maimonides' *Guide of the Perplexed*. This 14th Century text is astonishing, the most radical from a religious point of view until Spinoza. I intent to publish this text, and write an introduction to it.

In my previous work, I explored the theme of the tension between the longing for and the fear of realization in the Haredi relationship to *Eretz Yisrael*. Now I am going to check the fear of the Holy Land in classical and medieval Jewish tradition. I intend to show how, in the texts, this dread is clear and conscious, and not as had been supposed, "subconscious" only. I hope that this will be either a long article or a book on the subject of *eretz chemda va'charadah*.

S.F.: One final question, which relates to much of our talk. What is your conception of the ideal education for Jew?

Professor Ravitzky: You already know that I am deterred by such concepts as "ideal education." I can however say what I would like to give my students and children. I would like there to be various ideal educations, and I certainly would not like everyone in the end to end up being a carbon copy of Avi Ravitzky. Berl Katznelson once laughed at the *Shomer ha-Tsair*, saying that the students emerge as "uniform pieces of pork." I want a person who is capable of living in different worlds. I don't think that it's an accident that all the concepts of religious Zionism are built on syntheses connecting *vav Torah* and *avodah*, Torah and *Derech Eretz*, Torah *u'maddah*. All the institutions have this kind of synthesis. Kibbutz Ha-Dati, Yeshiva Tikhonit, Yeshivat Hesder,

Universita Dattit. I love the synthesis, for in my eyes, it is not a passive equation. There is value both in the traditional religious world and in the modern cultural world, and in the meeting between them. Indeed, the Rebbe of Kotzk said, "On the sides people walk and in the middle in between the horses go." I say, if the middle is a lukewarm compromise, then that is one thing. But if it involves a tension between two worlds, this is another. If I lived in only one world my world would be poorer and thinner.

If Yehuda ha-Levi would have, instead of writing his poems, studied a few more pages of Gemara, then the Jewish world would not have been richer. If the Rambam in the time he learned Aristotle would have learned Tosefot, so to speak, would the Jewish world be richer for it? So those who learn only *halachah* do not walk in the way of Rambam and Yehuda ha-Levi. But it is impossible to create real culture without studying the classical sources.

Professor Eliezer Schweid

Professor Eliezer Schweid is the foremost student of modern Jewish thought living today. He has written close to thirty books tracing the work of various streams of Jewish thought. Among his works are *Jewish Nationhood, Israel at the Crossroad, Judaism and the Lonely Jew, The Faith of Israel and Its Culture, A History of Modern Jewish Philosophy, Judaism and Secular Culture,* and *From Ruin to Salvation.* Professor Schweid has received the Israel Prize for his work in Jewish thought. His teaching of Jewish thought has been both within the university framework, at Hebrew University, and in a variety of institutions and *Batei Midrash*, including Ellul, of which he is a founder.

I met with Professor Schweid in his home in the Abu Tor district of Jerusalem.

C3 80

S.F.: What is the major aim and purpose of your research?

Professor Schweid: The first purpose of research is the quest for knowledge in and of itself. In this, I am involved in examining the various streams of Jewish thought, considering the various problems in this area. This might be called Torah for its own sake. Then, there is the matter of seeking to know and understand Jewish thought in relation to those historical questions that are of particular relevance to our own times. In recent years, I have devoted much of my time to examining modern Jewish thought, to understanding what various Jewish thinkers have said about the fundamental problems of Jewish life in our own time.

S.F.: How do you define the "modern age" in Jewish thought? Where does it begin?

Professor Schweid: The developments in the world of thought are closely connected with specific historical developments. Between the time of the emancipation and the period of the Shoah and the founding of Israel, there was a whole group of very significant developments. In the last two decades of the previous century, there was a very sharp turning point. Prior to then, processes that are central and critical to modernity developed very slowly. But in these two decades, there was a major acceleration. In fact, the most important existential dilemmas that the people of Israel contend with today made themselves felt at this period. First of all, it was a time of intense anti–Semitism, which

267

raised the question of the physical survival of the people. Persecutions and pogroms had of course occurred before this time, but the appearance of those anti–Semitic movements that eventually led to the Shoah occurred first in this time. This led to the Jewish recognition for the first time of the problematic quality of the process of emancipation. The hope that Jews would at last come to be accepted in general European society began to be dashed. This is one reason for the appearance, precisely at this time, of modern Zionism. A most important part in contributing to the appearance of Zionism was the despair over the Emancipation.

At this time, the people of Israel began to go through accelerated processes of change in other ways. The center of the Jewish people, which was in Central and Eastern Europe, began to collapse. It shifted in the decades ahead to two new centers, one in the United States, the second in the Land of Israel. Also, the acceleration of the process of mass immigration began from Europe to America, and to a lesser degree to *Eretz Yisrael*. There were also economic and social changes that were deep and even revolutionary. There was the breaking up of old Jewish communal structure, which had been so central in the European Jewish world. So, as I understand it, the turning point in modern Jewish history was in these decades when Jews had to contend in a far more difficult way than ever before with the fundamental existential questions of the Jewish people. Where to go? In which direction to turn?—these were being asked in all areas of Jewish life.

S.F.: And where have those processes led us in our own time?

Professor Schweid: If I am asked to evaluate what has happened to the Jewish people 50 years after the Shoah, and close to 50 years after the founding of the State of Israel, then I can answer only in a very general way. For a time after the Shoah, and after the founding of the State, there was a brief period of Jewish unity unlike any other in the history of the people. It was absolutely clear after the overwhelming earth–shaking horror of the Shoah that everything possible had to be done to set aside differences, and to work together for the reconstruction of the people. And this reconstruction was to be toward a process of normalizing the Jewish people within the context of the political, social, and cultural circumstances of the time. There was the hope of arriving at some new modus vivendi between the Jewish people and

the surrounding world. Central to this effort was the cooperation between the Jews of the United States and those of Israel. The reconstruction of the Jewish people meant, first of all, establishing and building
a State of Israel that would be able to live in a situation of full security. This also meant building the social, economic, and cultural foundations of the state. The aim was to have a Jewish majority in the land
of Israel, and a state that would eventually come to live in peace with
its neighbors.

As for American Jews, the aim was to enable them to feel at home
in America. Today, we have arrived at a situation where the great majority of Jewish leaders feel that we have gotten more or less to the
degree of normalcy we are capable of as a people. We have not yet
reached the dream of Messianic realization, but a degree of stability that
more or less means true normalization has arrived. Unfortunately, this
process of normalization also brings with it a good degree of disinte-
gration. Jews had historically preserved their Jewishness in abnormal
situations in which they had suffered greatly. So when normalcy arrived, when we were no longer threatened, we began to assimilate. This
process occurs in Israel, though of course to a far greater degree in the
United States and throughout the Diaspora. Clearly, the moment that
one feels he has arrived at normalization, the need to preserve the unity
of the people is felt to be diminished. Each begins chasing the interests
of his own party or group, and the general Jewish situation is put in
abeyance again.

S.F.: This process of worrying about one's own well-being only seems
on the individual level to be another Israeli import from the West. The
communal ethic, the desire to help and build the community as a whole,
even at a personal price, seems to have declined here also in the past
20 years.

Professor Schweid: These are general Western processes, both on the
individual and the communal levels. One factor, which is not given adequate attention, is that Jews at one time assimilated in cultures that
were concerned with developing and preserving themselves. Jews who
assimilated into the German or French culture assimilated into a society that strongly defined and protected its national identity and culture. Today, we live in a world in which assimilation is the keynote,
where Americanization is the assimilation of the world. The Ameri-

can reality is, after all, the assimilation of all kinds of people of differing cultures and religions.

S.F.: There is talk in America of a reverse process, of, for instance, ethnic cultures such as the Hispanic striving to preserve their own cultural identity, their language, within the American world.

Professor Schweid: That process is truly highly limited. The Hispanics preserve their language because, among other reasons, their percentage of the population as a whole has grown. Once, the United States had a white Anglo–Saxon Protestant majority. They are no longer the majority, though they still make up what might be called the leadership of the United States. But there is a movement toward complete assimilation. And this is what is in effect happening throughout the world.

S.F.: But the individual does try to define himself as "belonging to" something. How do you understand the way individual Jews and the Jewish people must define themselves communally to resist future assimilation?

Professor Schweid: The great majority of Jews simply do not make a definition. Moreover, I believe that the individual's interest in defining himself as a Jew has become weaker today. In the United States, the great majority of Jews define themselves as, first and above all, Americans. As an American of Jewish origin, one does not deny his Jewishness, because he is aware that no one will persecute or bother him for it. He does not deny whatever religious, family, or ethnic connections he has, but in general will make no special effort to preserve and enhance these connections. His unique Jewish identity is not something that he will work to promote and develop. It is not what is most important for him to transmit to his descendants.

S.F.: And what is the consequence of this kind of individual's action for the Jewish people as a whole?

Professor Schweid: It means that, for the first time in our history, the Jewish people are confronted with the danger of assimilation, which will deprive us of the majority of our forces. It also means that the Jewish people is very rapidly losing its unique spiritual and cultural identity.

S.F.: Is what you have in mind here the thesis of the "Israeli" school of demographers, to the effect that through aging, late marriage, and low fertility, the Jewish people is rapidly declining in numbers in the Diaspora?

Professor Schweid: This is not a thesis, but rather a fact. And I am not convinced that the Haredi sector of Judaism, which is an impressive exception, will continue to be so in the future. This is because processes that have affected other segments of the Jewish people are also affecting the Haredi world, though more slowly. The great success of the Haredi community after the Shoah was that it was able to hold its children within the community; first of all, economically. Before the war, the Haredi communities were not able to do this. The great majority of children left the Haredi world simply because they did not have any means of making a livelihood. After the war, the Haredi movements both in Israel and in America succeeded in establishing an economic and political base that was able to guarantee the economic future of their children. But we may well be coming close to the end of this period. In order to achieve adequate economic means, they too may have to conform to the sociological and cultural conditions of the secular environment, that is, they will have to compromise their separation from modern culture. One clear illustration of this is the position of the woman in Haredi society. As she enters the modern world from more and more vantage points, she has to adjust educationally and professionally. It is impossible to go forward with this necessary sociological process without exacting a corresponding price in assimilation. In principle, I believe that Zionism was right in its claim that, in modern reality, the only way to preserve Jewish identity is through the framework of life within a sovereign Jewish society. In such a framework, individuals are able to integrate freely in modern civilization, yet preserve a cultural Jewish identity provided they do this and are ready to work creatively for that purpose.

S.F.: Are you saying here that a good share of those living within Israeli society today are not concerned with connecting to the community of the Jewish people?

Professor Schweid: To a very large degree, we are in a stage that is familiarly called "post–Zionist." This concept has more than one meaning, one of which is ideological, whose essence is anti–Zionism, and eventually also anti-Jewishness. This is the position of extreme leftist circles, who believe that the actions of Zionism inspired by Jewish nationalism were colonialistic. But this group of post-Zionists is in fact a very small minority. The majority of Jews in Israel is not post-Zionistic in this sense, but believes that Zionism was very important but has by and large realized its major goals.

S.F.: Excuse me. The majority of the Jewish people still live outside of Israel.

Professor Schweid: This is precisely the point. Even the "maximalist" Zionists did not believe in the goal of bringing all the Jews of the world to Israel. Herzl thought that it would be possible to bring the majority, but *Ahad ha-Am* thought that it would be possible to bring only a small part of the people here in order to build the spiritual center of the Jewish people. We have arrived at the situation where a great proportion of the Jewish people have come to live in Israel. And it is already clear that, due to demographic factors, the majority of the Jewish people will be living in Israel in another ten years. The *aliyah* from the Soviet Union, the positive birth rate within Israel, combined with the declining Diaspora population, guarantee that this will be the case. So in ten or twenty years, the majority of those Jews who still consider themselves Jewish will be living in *Eretz Yisrael*. This is the best realistic achievement that they who truly saw themselves as Zionists could have hoped for. They have achieved what they set out to achieve. There is a functioning state that soon, in the view of many, will arrive at peace. So now many believe that the time has come to enjoy it, to live well, and to be concerned first and above all with one's own quality of life, one's individual self-realization. This means that we are already beyond the whole historical process of implementing the Zionist ideal.

S.F.: But what about the spiritual goals of the Jewish people?

Professor Schweid: The question is how to define those spiritual goals. I maintain that, at a certain stage after the state came into being, there was a period of talking about Zionism not only as a means to save the Jewish people in the physical sense, but as a form of reconstituting Jewish identity within a particular Jewish culture. Zionism is the aspiration that Jews will have a homeland in order to create their own particular culture.

S.F.: And what of the connection with the religious aspirations of all those Jews, generation to generation, who prayed each day for the return to Zion?

Professor Schweid: The majority of secularist Zionists thought that we should not be concerned with this: "Let the Jews build their land and state, and their culture will develop as a natural result." Of course, this was a mistake. A Jewish state is only an opportunity to create, but nothing is guaranteed by this. Rabbi Kook, of blessed memory, believed that, when there will finally be a country with a Jewish majority, this majority in time will necessarily turn to religion. And this religious identity will be the heart of the Jewish identity. But this did not happen. Ahad ha–Am was more realistic. He demanded making a conscious effort to create a Jewish culture, and there was a period when there were movements to make a serious effort to do this. But also, it seems that, after the war and the establishment of the State, the effort to form a Jewish national culture—which has a deep connection with the sources, the history of the Jewish people—has been progressively diminished. Today, we do not see any real effort in this direction, and this is my great disappointment.

S.F.: But your work is precisely in this direction.

Professor Schweid: Right. And therefore, I say this to you with great sorrow and deep disappointment. For I know that, while there are still groups who speak and think about this, if you look at the general education, then you will understand the concern for general Jewish culture is not part of the main concern of the educational system.

S.F.: And you believe that a Jewish country can go on as Jewish without such a concern?

Professor Schweid: No. If you listen to the speeches of leading representatives of Israeli culture today, then you will gather that they assume that it has no connection whatsoever with Jewish sources. They are far more interested in relations with the Arab citizens of Israel and with American culture than with the Jewish people. The single thing that disturbs them is that the Arabs are not willing to abandon their own cultural identity. This forces them to remain Jews, since the Arabs will relate to them only as Jews. But in any case, it is clear that they are not personally concerned with Jewish culture or identity. They are universalistic Western men. As for *amcha*, the common people, most of them are to a certain degree traditional or ethnic Jews. But they are not active. They do not demand anything spiritual. I do not see parents who claim to care about tradition going and demanding that their children be taught more Judaism in the schools. What these parents demand is that their children receive all the preparation they need to enable them to compete successfully in a modern market economy, and to get the most financially rewarding professions. This is the general trend of the society today.

S.F.: Are there no spiritual leaders who can change this direction? Ben Gurion, though a political leader, nonetheless had a certain spiritual vision of the people of Israel as a light to the nations.

Professor Schweid: You are mistaken here. It was Ben Gurion who helped bring about this process, and it was he who was in effect the first post–Zionist. When he established the State of Israel, he wanted the complete elimination of the Zionist movement. He thought that, now that there was a Jewish state, there was no longer a need for a Zionist movement. American Jews who wanted to come here could if they wished, because there was now an open gate. Ben Gurion held an essentially Canaanite ideology, and all his slogans about being "a light to the Gentiles" were empty except that the State of Israel would show the Gentiles what it was to have a model democratic regime of equality and justice. And he did not see, except for the Hebrew language, anything specifically Jewish in this culture. He wanted a national culture, which is modern and connected with the land, and that's all.

S.F.: But isn't there one group in society that is acutely aware of the cultural problem, that is, the national religious, the students of Rabbi Kook?

Professor Schweid: Of course there are people who are troubled by this absence of a Jewish cultural dimension. I am one of those who is greatly troubled. I ask myself, however, to what degree do I, and people who share my concerns, succeed in influencing parents and the educational system? I won't say to you that I completely despair. I believe that the majority of the Israeli Jewish community is still traditionally Jewish. But I have great concern because the social and economic dynamic is pushing us towards materialism and spiritual stagnation.

S.F.: Do you mean that the prosperity that has come to a large section of the Israeli population has forced it to concentrate more and more on material goals alone?

Professor Schweid: We have indeed assimilated the ethos of the market economy society, and have come to accept its cultural conception. Such a conception speaks of individual happiness and wealth, but does not concern itself with the people as a whole. The individual forgets about his communal obligation and takes interest solely in his own private affairs.

S.F.: And what practical remedies do you offer for this situation, for instance, in regard to the educational system?

Professor Schweid: I would propose that the process of privatization of the high school system should be reconsidered and properly balanced by national directives, concentrating on concern with national and social solidarity and transmission of cultural identity. The school system and the universities should become both able and committed to adhere to cultural and spiritual contents as ends in themselves. Trying to be realistic to the degree that a philosopher can, I am not suggesting ignoring economical "hard facts." But I do believe that a society directed by economic interests alone, without balancing these with normative spiritual values, is going to stray from the true goal of every human civilization. And it is sentencing itself to moral and spiritual decline. What I propose is that the state school system should take upon itself the task of education in its fullest sense. This means teaching retraining with this goal in mind. This also means changing the way in which humanistic and Jewish subjects are taught so that they present challenges to the students, which can evoke meaningful responses. Along this line, I propose that the state schools should reclaim the responsibility of transmitting cultural inheritance in the full sense of the term. This means developing their own concept of Jewish humanism as a culture and not as religion, though it too must include and relate positively to religious content. Along with this, I believe that applying the cultural concept of Humanistic Judaism means that the curriculum of the state high school should offer a global program for understanding Jewish history, both as narrative and as sequence of classical sources. This should include Biblie, modern Hebrew, and modern Jewish literature. And it must be done through a careful selection of what is most suited for students' understanding, with the emphasis on social, aesthetic, national, and spiritual values. I believe that this kind of learning should not only be available to those who choose these subjects, but to all, as a source for creating a common culture. I also propose that the commitment to the ideal of national and social integration should not only be a matter of creating a formal equality of opportunities, but it should be the basis for creating feelings of solidarity, of personal commitments between students and society.

Dr. Daniel Shalit

Dr. Daniel Shalit is a teacher of Judaism who in recent years has regularly written for the journal of the settlements in Judaea and Samaria, *Nekuda*. He also had for a number of years a regular radio spot on the Arutz Sheva station. His book, *Sicchot Panim* ("Inside Conversations"), is both a meditation on the Jewish holidays and a reflection on the existential dilemmas of the Jewish people today.

I met with Dr. Shalit not at his home in the settlement of Kedumim but rather in a Tel Aviv apartment. Our conversation was slow and difficult, for Dr. Shalit weighed carefully every word. He seemed to me to be a person of great integrity, with a strong mystical bent. And I felt that beyond his every word and sentence was some deeper intent that I did not quite grasp. What I was sure of was that Dr. Shalit is a person who has thought long and deeply about the fundamental questions of life, and that he continues, from a deep Torah faith, to search for the answers.

๙ ๚

S.F.: In your book *Sichot Panim*, you speak about the moral crisis of the West and of the Jewish world today. What exactly is this crisis?

Dr. Shalit: The crisis is not only moral; it cuts across the whole range of Western culture. It is also not accidental, but rather the logical outcome of a long development extending from ancient Greece to our own modern culture. The development has had its constructive creative periods—namely, classical Greece, the European Renaissance, and Enlightenment—but nowadays, we are in a stage of crisis and decline. The main manifestation of the crisis is a total relativity, or lack of guidelines, in regard to values. Everything is taken to be a matter of personal preference, and there is the abandonment of the idea that anything can be objectively true or right. Paradoxically, this attitude is in itself taken to be a truth and, moreover, a virtue, since asserting "the" truth about anything is considered not only silly, but somehow aggressive. This kind of attitude has been in the past labeled "moral relativism" or "radical liberalism," but today goes under the name of "post–modernism."

The development that led to this crisis is a part of the Western endeavor to establish an autonomous human culture. Its latest phase started a few hundred years ago. The evolving Western mind divided the world in two: on the one side, the cognitive rational subject; and on the other, the external world, "the object" of rational scientific knowledge. Scientific knowledge had to be measurable (quantitative) and experimental (empirical). But to qualify it as experimental and measurable, various elements of our direct, intuitive experience had to be eliminated one by one. The first to be eliminated was the whole realm of purposes and goals.

S.F.: The world of Aristotelian physics?

Dr. Shalit: Yes. That Aristotelian world of purposes was understood to be non–scientific. Next to be eliminated was the world of qualities: smells, colors, the whole world of the senses. These were replaced by wavelengths and other measurable qualities. But this was not the end of the process. With the same logic of elimination, moral judgements too had to be systematized, quantified, formalized, or else be cast out as subjective. There were serious efforts, notably Kant's, to construct a rational ethics of this kind.

But the Romantic movement gave up on all these heroic efforts and made ethics into something free, creative, personal, almost whimsical. It was Neitzsche who brought the term "values" into use as a replacement for morals, and this with the implication that ethics cannot or should not be derived from a well–formulated system. For a well–formulated system was regarded as too rigid to take into account the wealth of human powers, our inventive genius. A further step in this development was the American popularization of Neitzsche, which was described in Alan Bloom's *The Closing of the American Mind*. Everyone is entitled to a "lifestyle" of one's own preference and making. And so today we are immersed in this Western crisis, where everything has boiled down to two primary values, "freedom" and "equality." These are usually vulgarized into meaning that one may do as one pleases, with the one important restriction, that one does not limit another's freedom. But since no one can know what the other's preferences are at any given moment, one has almost no choice but to get on with one's own self–realization. Others then have no choice but to do the same, protest and strive to protect themselves if their interests be effected. This means in effect that Western culture becomes a war of all against all.

Closely linked with the crisis in morals is the crisis in aesthetics. Instead of the classical notion of art representing reality, real or ideal, comes the Romantic idea of art as self–expression. The logical conclusion of this idea is that art becomes anything that is presented as art.

But the deepest crisis of all is the crisis of "truth." This is the gravest crisis because the foundation and pride of Western civilization was in its claim to provide dependable, verifiable, experimental quantitative knowledge. Post-modernism rejects the demands for truth, beauty, and goodness as false. It will not accept any assertions of "final truth." It sees around it only texts and narratives for unending interpretation. It will not accord even to science more than the status of a narrative— and a white, masculine one at that. This does not contradict what one hears in modern scientific circles. Science has come a long way from 19th Century self-assurance. It is true that physicists such as Hawking are making the last heroic endeavor to contract a one grand unifying system that would encompass all nature, but others such as as Arthur Eddington see science as just one language among others, albeit a precise mathematical one. In fact, scientific thought today would find it difficult to say in just what sense science is "truer" than, say, poetry or myth. Post-modernism is then just drawing its premise from the general state of Western thought. All of this amounts to an unprecedented crisis. We have a culture that proclaims itself unable to support any concept of truth, goodness, or beauty. And this opens the gates for the triumph of their opposites, the false, the evil, and the ugly. The leveling of everything into narratives gives negative forces a hitherto undreamt of legitimacy. I do not know how long such a culture can survive.

S.F.: How do you connect this to the crisis of Judaism today?

Dr. Shalit: First, there is the crisis of Jews; then there is the crisis of Judaism. As to the first, Jews play an integral part in the contemporary scene, and hence are affected. Then, there is the matter of special Jewish sensitivity. Yehuda ha-Levi likens Jews to a heart that is affected by the slighest oscillations in the body's health. One might say that the Jews often suffer the world's diseases in a more acute way.

S.F.: Why is the crisis then felt in such a strong way among the Jews?

Dr. Shalit: The actual process may be described in this way. Other peoples or cultures have their innate, deep-seated behavioral patterns that serve their survival. These include both instincts of survival and collective moral values, such as chivalry, courage, mutual help within the group. While trying to formulate rational systems out of these natural patterns, these nations or cultures always have their original patterns to fall back on should the new rational system misfunction, as manmade systems tend to do. Now with the Jews, the instinctive side of character has long been subordinated to conscious determination. We may understand this as a result of thousands of years of Torah study, in which innate drives were constantly subdued and trained to follow conscious guidance. But how did such natural instincts, which are usually so stubborn, give way to conscious guidance? Here we suggest something in accordance with the sources, that there was a previous preparation before we were given the Torah. Our sources place the preparation, historically, in the period of servitude in Egypt, and still earlier in the forefathers' roaming between various exiles and the land of Canaan—experiences that may serve to unsettle all normal, usually egocentric tendencies and instill an inner receptivity instead. Yet, understanding the deeper meaning of the preparation, we should say that what softened natural instincts was the Revelation itself, the contact with Divinity. Human patterns, both natural and manmade, form and consolidate at a distance from the Infinite Presence. And any reappearance of the Divine Presence loosens in-built former formations and prepares us for an acceptance of higher codes.

Now, when in the modern era Jews assimilated, abandoning the way of Torah, it was at first easy for them to adopt the new humanistic codes; that is, to pursue an alternative, deliberate, calculated system of thought and behavior. But when this system shows, as it is doing now, its in-built limitations, when it fails into nihilism, then there is no in-built system to fall back on, and we receive the full blow of the crisis.

One may see this general Jewish trait most glaringly in Israel. Although America has its own crisis of values, and it is fact America that exports it to Israel and the rest of the world, Americans themselves can somehow get away with it, because they have their ingrained American values, on the one hand, and general instinctive defense-and-attack mechanisms, on the other hand. In this sense, they do not quite depend on their rationally constructed systems of thought. But Israelis must and do take their imported ideologies very seriously. They now take American values as seriously as they once took Socialism or even Communism. In fact, it is the same people who shifted their ardent loyalty from leftism to liberalism. They must have some Torah to adhere to with all their heart and strength and might. But since this Torah substitute always contains its own built-in crisis, they are left during the crisis without inner strength.

Aside from the crisis of general culture, there is the crisis of Judaism itself. This is not new. We have carried it with us ever since the beginning of our confrontation with the modern world. This was a confrontation with a culture that in its depth, was godless. True, its greatest first scientists—Kepler, Newton, Pascal—were deeply religious. But its main fruits—the French Encyclopediasts, the enlightenment thinkers culminating in Kant, Romanticism that culminated in Neitzsche—closed the human vista to God, and became man–centered.

As for the Jewish people, confrontations with major historical powers, political and spiritual, were nothing new. The first definite confrontation was with paganism; then came the confrontations with Greco–Roman rationalism and with the so–called daughter religions, medieval Christianity and Islam. Each new confrontation means re-orientation, a new self–assessment vis–a–vis a new challenge. But all of these monumental confrontations could not provide a model for dealing with the modern world. As I said, this new world developed into the first non–believing culture ever. Even classical rationalism was not entirely godless: every great philosophical system, notably those of Plato and Aristotle, culminated in the concept of "Theos," the godheard. True, this (Theos) was not—as Yehuda ha–Levi made clear in the *Kuzari*—a living personal God. But it was there towering above the philosophical system. So Rambam could later in the Middle Ages express Judaism in the language of Greek metaphysics, which was the language of the general culture of his time.

But modern rationalism was different. Judaism could not be expressed in terms of mechanistic, godless, anthropocentric general culture without being severely misrepresented.

So Judaism was confronted with two conflicting options, both of which were unhealthy. Either it could wholly convert to the new humanistic creed, or else shut itself wholly from the new emerging general culture. Of course, in the lives of individual Jews, many compromises took place. But what was really wanting was a new development, an organic linkage with the past and with the new present. This did not happen, perhaps because Western culture was too self–assured, all–encompassing totalitarian.

S.F.: But aren't we on the edge of a new age of return to faith, which in a sense has gone beyond this crisis?

Dr. Shalit: Curious as it may seem, it is developments just like post-modernism that correct the situation. Post–modernism undermines the self–assuredness, the totalitarian confidence of the modern scientific–technological mind. According to post–modern Western ways of knowledge, conduct and art cannot contain the totality of being. Other modes of orientation emerge: Far Eastern, mystical, feminist. But all of these options amount at present to a considerable confusion. Post–modernism itself is nihilistic, unable to learn much from the wealth of narratives because it does not believe that there is a focal point from which to view them.

S.F.: What then is the *tikkun* that Judaism has to offer to the post-modern Western world view?

Dr. Shalit: Perhaps to return to the world its pivot point. It is not that we will come and say, "We do have the absolute truth, or the absolute criteria for knowing the truth." But we can say, "We have—we were given—the direction of the quest." Infinite goodness, wisdom, and beauty are the source and life of all being. Of course we, as finite in time, space, and comprehension, cannot contain it. But ever reaching, striving for a growing measure of truth, goodness, and beauty, is a meaningful and possible pursuit. This, because the Infinite Divine Being can be to known by us some degree.

S.F.: But isn't the traditional faith one that believes the Torah is Absolute Truth?

Dr. Shalit: What is absolute in Torah is surely its Transcendent Source, the Divine Will. But what we can know and understand from God must always be finite, inviting a further quest. The Baal Shem Tov commented on the verse from Psalms, "the teaching of God is perfect, life restoring":

> Only when the Torah is conceived as intact, untouched as virgin, only then is it life–restoring. It was given to us, but to receive it is a never-ending pursuit. Only Moses can be said to have 'received' the Torah. All the others were 'given' it, but cannot be said to have fully received it. And since each 'receiving' is only a partial manifestation, the whole of its receiving can only belong to the totality of history.

This means, on the one hand, that each generation is just a partial manifestation of the whole. But on the other hand, each such partial manifestation is Torah. And even what may seem to us now as new answers to new problems—For example, Jewish reactions to post–modern trends—are Torah and were included in Sinai.

Of course, we must open our eyes. Many such openings have occurred in the past. Rambam opened new doors in his *Hilkot Deot* in regard to the acquisition of general scientific knowledge as part of the Torah. One might think that he tried to install something new into Judaism. But this is not right. The acquisition of knowledge was there in other ways in former times. It was natural and spontaneous, and needed no special mention. It is implied in the verses of the written Torah—and in the books of Biblical wisdom such as Proverbs and Ecclesiastes, and parts of Psalms—which sum up wisdom from a Torah point of view. There are also oral parts of the Torah that treat topics in contemporary knowledge. But in Rambam's time, general science could not any longer be dealt with indirectly. It had to be explicitly encountered. First, because contemporary knowledge was specialized by then into specific "arts" and "sciences." Second since the new Greek–medieval general culture was not a natural matrix for Jewish perceptions, there was the danger that Jews might develop an aversion to general knowledge. Hence, Rambam brought to light—said explicitly—what was hitherto implicit, namely, that learning and knowing are good, and to know God's world is to know Him. Further, one must make the necessary distinctions between such living knowledge and other intellectual constructions. Rambam gave this direction of study, which he saw as Torah, a formal *halachic* formulation. For him it was a precondition for helping to fulfill the Biblical precepts of loving and fearing God. In the same way, he opened doors in regard to our understanding of the realm of physical health. And *Rabbenu Bahya* opened the doors in the "duties of the heart" in his call for personal edification as given through Torah.

One might say that, just as a child progresses from spontaneity to self-awareness and self-control, so mankind at large progresses from naive beginnings to more self-knowing and self-controlled states. So too with the Torah. What is revealed at first are the external organs, but already the forthcoming members—the mitzvot concerning emotive and conscious life, with greater and greater depth—are suggested. These will come forth to full consciousness as history proceeds, and historical events aid in bringing out their contours. I believe that today's developments may also open up to us Torah attitudes that can help in regard to social, psychological, cultural, political, and even scientific understanding. Once they are opened up, we'll see that they were always there.

S.F.: How do you relate this development to the concept of *avodat Hashem*?

Dr. Shalit: We have such a tremendous inheritance in *avodat Hashem* that it is almost frightening to attempt an answer. We had the First Temple, in which the *avodah* was mainly public, national, centering around the Temple service. Then, in the Second Temple, new elements were added: prayer and Torah learning. These were more personal activities. In the Middle Ages, with the coming of *Torat ha–sod*, the mystical teaching, individual responsibility expanded to the dimensions of responsibility for the unification and coordination of the entire Creation—of Divine, spiritual, and physical worlds. What then is the relation between these phases of *avadoh*? I think that the first contribution of our generation may be to understand the organic relation between them. In general, later manifestations of *avodah* do not come out of the void. They were there before, implicit and waiting. Also, when they come to the fore, they do not supplant the earlier ones, but are added as new centers of gravity. So maybe our generation will renew itself in a similar manner. On the one hand, we must be receivers of the entire vast inheritance, insofar as we can. On the other hand, the question is what the next center of gravity is going to be, and how all the other components will rearrange themselves around it.

I think that the next center will somehow have to be with awareness and understanding, and so bring new life to older foundations—to prayer and Torah learning on the one hand, and to the public national aspects of *avodah* on the other. Also, one may guess that such a new center of gravity will be both highly personal and highly universal. It will be highly personal because the whole historical process points in the direction of ever more individual development. The Hebrew translation, the Jewish rendering of this universal theme, will probably be a type of person whose religious awareness will flow through a highly personal experience. The Hebrew version of today's universality can be the infinitely expanding horizons of *emunah*.

What I mean is that every era in history has a certain divine "lighting" that expresses itself according to the character of the particular culture. And the Jewish people have the potential of bringing the expressions of this age closer to their Transcendent Source.

Here I am reminded of Rabbi Kook, who insisted that such an overall renaissance is possible only in the Land of Israel. Other places may give temporary shelter to disparate parts of Jewish *avodah*, but there is only one place in which all the aspects of Jewish life may reunite into a healthy whole to the benefit of all: *Eretz Yisrael.*

Dr. Gavriel Sivan

Dr. Gavriel Sivan has made great contributions to the world of Jewish learning and knowledge. He has contributed to many important publications within the Jewish world, and was one of the most productive editors of the *Encyclopaedia Judaica*. His *The Bible and Civilization* shows the influence of the Bible on different areas of Western culture. His one volume encyclopedia, in which he completed the work of Rabbi Newman *z"l* is a highly informative guide to Judaism. Dr. Sivan, a native of Liverpool and a specialist in French Renaissance studies, shifted his focus to Jewish studies after making *aliyah* to Israel at the eve of the Six–Day War.

My conversation with Dr. Sivan was conducted in his home in the Bayit Vegan district of Jerusalem. It was as full of intellectual vigor and insight into the Jewish situation as I, who had worked under Dr. Sivan's tutelage on the one–volume *Encyclopedia of Judaism*, expected it would be.

CR BO

S.F.: Could you give some details of your background and tell us about the various projects you have worked on over the years?

Dr. Sivan: Well, in fact, it's rather an odd story. As far as expertise is concerned, I am actually a specialist in European literature, with particular reference to the 16th Century (humanism and the Renaissance). I started working on my doctoral thesis in London and completed it years later at the Hebrew University—a monograph running to 600 pages about Guy Le Fèvre de la Boderie, a French poet and Christian kabbalist. As a teenager, I had studied at yeshiva while attending high school in my native Liverpool. After 2 years of national service in the Royal Air Force (RAF) as a Russian interpreter, I took a degree in Modern Languages at Oxford and then spent 3 years (1958–61) as a postgraduate student at Jews' College, London. Academic work certainly enriched my Jewish background and strengthened my religious commitment, but I never imagined that all of this would shape my career until I arrived here in Israel and found employment as a staff editor with the *Encyclopaedia Judaica* (1967-72). Gradually, over the next few years, I moved away from my original field and became increasingly involved in Jewish studies. This was not altogether accidental— my Ph.D. thesis had a great deal to do with Kabbalah and through it I developed a growing interest in Bible, rabbinic literature, and Jewish history. After serving as deputy editor of the *Encyclopaedia Judaica's* 1974 Year Book, I was appointed Director of Education and Information with the South African Zionist Federation in Johannesburg. Over the next 3 years, as an educator and administrator, I was responsible for arranging Jewish cultural programs all over South Africa and what was then Rhodesia, giving some of the lectures myself on a wide range of topics and touring the whole area. I wrote a column for the *S.A. Zionist Record*, one of the local Jewish weeklies, and came to be regarded as something of an expert on different spheres of Jewish knowledge. During my last year in South Africa, I held a "rabbinical" post and gained experience as a broadcaster, recording half a dozen talks on "The Hebrew Element in Everyday English" for SABC. That was to prove most useful once my family and I returned to Israel at the end of 1977, when I discovered that my original specialization led nowhere and that the only real alternative was writing and lecturing on Jewish subjects. Back in Jerusalem, I was invited by the late Professor Chaim Gevaryahu to take an active part in the World Jewish Bible Society, and for about a year I was his assistant. Ever since then, I have been involved in the Society's work and I'm still on the editorial board of the *Jewish Bible Quarterly*. There, I rub shoulders with far more qualified people, but from time to time, I have managed to contribute articles and ideas of my own. An experience that I look back upon with nostalgia and great appreciation was the time I spent working for that outstanding American Zionist leader, the late Dr. Israel Goldstein. During the years 1979–1986, I edited his two-volume autobiography (*My World as a Jew*) and then encouraged him to publish a collection of his addresses, sermons, articles, and radio talks (*Jewish Perspectives*), which I was also privileged to edit. We developed a very close relationship and, thanks to that great man, I became familiar with many little-known aspects of Zionist and recent Jewish history.

As for some details of my own published work: it dates from the mid-1950s, when I was in the RAF, and has steadily increased over the past 4 decades. As a matter of fact, I am now compiling my own bibliography and have been amazed to discover its extent—books, articles (both scholarly and popular), encyclopedia entries, books reviews, letters to the press, and so forth. As Divisional Editor of European Literature for the *Israel General Encyclopedia* (1986–88), I discharged a really enormous task, compiling surveys of the literatures involved (over thirty, if I am not mistaken) and writing all of the entries myself (more than 1,000 in Hebrew). That project, or course, gave me the opportunity to return to my "first love," whereas almost everything else that I have written is more specifically Jewish, ranging from book reviews in *The Jerusalem Post* to learned articles in *Judaism, Midstream, Niv Ha–Midrashia,* and the South African Board of Jewish Deputies quarterly, *Jewish Affairs.* In Britain and South Africa I also contributed a few articles to the non–Jewish press.

Educational work has sometimes been the starting point. My experiences as a teacher at King David High School, Victory Park, in Johannesburg, as a reservist lecturer in the Israel Defense Forces, and elsewhere often provided some rare inspiration. For example, there was a Passover *Seder* that I conducted for other Jerusalem Brigade reservists on a Sinai mountaintop in 1974, and my lecture tours of the Golan Heights and Lebanon during *Milhemet Sheleg* (the "Peace for Galilee" Operation) in 1982. On that last occasion, I was mentioned in dispatches for giving ten lectures or talks during one 5–day stint. We lecturers had been given the task of boosting morale at a critical time. From such events, articles of mine have found their way into the overseas Jewish press, or have been utilized here in Israel.

The Bible and Civilization, my first book, came out in 1973. It was, to some extent, a byproduct of the *Encyclopaedia Judaica,* surveying the cultural impact of the *Tanach* on religion and ethics, law and politics, society and the arts. This volume was partly based on material that I have written or edited for the *Judaica,* but its scope was broadened to include new material as well, such as the chapter about the Bible's influence on everyday speech. Needing some extra copies recently, I found that this book is now out of print and that even secondhand bookstores can no longer supply more than one isolated and expensive copy. So purchasers obviously keep it for reference. *Judaism A–Z: A Lexicon of Terms and Concepts,* which appeared in 1980, was originally commissioned from Rabbi Dr. Yaacov Newman by the World Zionist Organization's Torah Education Department. I was called in to make some "additions and improvements," which became so extensive that the book finally bore my name as well as his. Still on the market, it has gone through reprints and there have also been new editions in Spanish and, with an improved text, in French.

Thanks to an old friend, Dr. Geoffrey Wigoder, who was responsible for my first Israeli appointment (with the *Judaica*), I have become involved in several other literary projects that he headed, beginning with the *Encyclopaedia of Judaism* (1989), on which I served as deputy editor as well as a major contributor. Other works of this type have included the *Dictionary of Jewish Biography*, *They Made History*, and *Almanac of the Bible* (for which I wrote entire sections). My article on "Developments in the Orthodox Liturgy and New Editions of the Traditional Prayer Book, 1970–1990" appeared in the *Encyclopaedia Judaica Year Book 1990–1991*, and over 30 new entries of mine—now signed with my initials—are scheduled for inclusion in the *Oxford Dictionary of the Jewish Religion*.

For some years, I have developed a keen interest in Jewish liturgy. This led to my involvement in another project, a major study of the "Kaddish," to which an interesting story is attached. Rabbi David Telsner, one of Jerusalem's veteran American *olim*, spent more than 3 decades compiling a new book on the "Kaddish" that required "knocking into shape." He consulted Professor Daniel Sperber of Bar Ilan University, the Israel Prize laureate in Talmud, whom I happen to have known for over 30 years, since we were in London. Under the impression that he was doing me a favor, Professor Sperber recommended that I be entrusted with this "stylistic improvement" job. What lay in store for me was an editor's nightmare: some 50 disorganized and often repetitious chapters with a problematic text and missing footnotes. After recovering from the shock, I submitted my recommendations to the author and then proceeded to implement them, working on and off over the next 4 years. A remarkably modest scholar of Latvian birth, Rabbi Telsner agreed to all my stipulations, but unfortunately died only a year after the editing process began. His family empowered me to continue, rephrasing the text, reducing the number of chapters, correcting errors, and filling in gaps as well as expanding the material here and there.

The Kaddish: Its History and Significance finally appeared at the end of 1995 as a memorial tribute to the author. It utilizes previous works on the subject, notably the classic short study by Rabbi David do Sola Pool, but discards outdated material and includes much that is new. Part one deals with the origins and development of the "Kaddish," giving less emphasis to the "mourner's prayer" variation than to the essential hymn of praise anticipating Israel's redemption. A whole range of different texts, in the original Aramaic and Hebrew as well as English translation, has pride of place here. And, while stressing the aspect of *geulah*, the book also shows how *Kaddish Yatom* took hold of the popular imagination from medieval times onward. Part two comprises a 200–page anthology of responsa and commentaries. I have added footnotes, biographical data, a revised bibliography in Hebrew and English, and a comprehensive index.

S.F.: In editing this work, have you made use of Hasidic sources and discussed the concept of *illuy neshamah*?

Dr. Sivan: Oh yes, very much so. Let me explain. As I said, the book consists of two parts, the first being a historical–philosophical treatise dealing with the first emergence of the "Kaddish," its elaborations, their textual variations in the different (Ashkenazi, Sephardi, Yemenite, Hasidic, and other) rites, and the associated *halachic* rules governing the recital of "Kaddish" on specific occasions; for example, whether one may respond "Amen" when hearing it broadcasted on the radio or television. The second part, Rabbi Telsner's anthology, takes its starting point from Geonic literature and then proceeds through Rashi, Maimonides, *Haseidei Ashkenaz,* and the *Zohar* to Rashba, Baal ha-Turim, Abuderham, and the *Shulchan Aruch*; then, by way of the Maharal of Prague and other commentators onward to S.R. Hirsch, Abraham Berliner, the Keter Shem Tov, as well as more recent scholars. We end with an interesting *teshuvah* by the late Rabbi Yosef Eliyahu Henkin of New York, thus covering a vast area.

S.F.: With your knowledge of Jewish communal life in the Diaspora, especially in your native England and in South Africa, how do you see the Jewish world community today in relation to the problems of assimilation?

Dr. Sivan: Until recently in South Africa, the assimilation rate among Jews was one of the lowest in the world. This mainly resulted from the unique political and social climate there (apartheid), which made it virtually impossible to move from one group to another. It wasn't just the question of black and white, but of subtle divisions within the white community as well. The "English" and Afrikaans rarely mixed, and Jews formed a white subgroup of their own. When the working day ended, they went home and lived in their own Jewish neighborhoods, mixed socially only among Jews. They had Jewish golf clubs, cricket teams of their own. South African Jews emigrating to Australia have found a congenial and similar way of life there, I am told, but Australian society is more open, so there is a much higher rate of assimilation. What's happening in South Africa at the present moment is less clear. The

picture in Britain in quite different. British society has been fairly liberal for over 100 years, while Anglo-Jewry has tended to be religiously
conservative (with a small "c"). In recent years, however, assimilation
and intermarriage have increased alarmingly, and this affects all sections
of the community apart from the "right-wing" Orthodox. My own family has remained pretty well intact, thank God, and I can think of only
three relatives, on my father's side, who "married out." Those concerned
either kept their marital life a secret or disappeared from view. They
never had children, so no other problems arose. My mother's family
was dubbed "old English" Jews because they immigrated from western
Poland in the mid–19th Century, long before my father's grandparents
came over from Lithuania. A great–great–great–great–uncle of mine,
Julius Hyams, was actually a Liverpool outfitter as early as 1857. Remarkably enough, as far as I am aware, none of my mother's family
have "married out" and practically all of them belong to Orthodox congregations.

When I was an Oriel College student at Oxford, a good 50 percent of the 300 Jewish undergraduates were paid–up members of the
University Jewish Society. We ran a kosher canteen in the local synagogue, had a daily minyan, and organized regular cultural and Zionist
programs, the Friday night speaker usually attracting a large audience.
Jews played an active role in everything from Oxford Union debates
and student politics to cricket and rowing. At least ten of my contem-
poraries now live in Jerusalem—three of us here in Bayit Vagan—and
the majority are Orthodox. There must also be people who graduated
from "the other place"—Cambridge. The real drift began after my time.
I remember someone telling us about a "splendid chap" from a very
traditional family, Hebrew–speaking and once active in B'nei Akiva,
who went up to Cambridge in 1957. Within a year, he had been elected
president of the Cambridge Union and, in the process of time, became
a Conservative M.P. He rose to the position of Home Secretary in Mar-
garet Thatcher's cabinet, but was eventually sacked and then found a
key post in the EEC. That "splendid chap," Sir Leon Brittan, married
a non–Jewess and distanced himself from the Jewish community. A
British variation on the Henry Kissinger story, you might say—but I
can think of an even worse example. A girl from my home town named
Edwina Cohen also went into politics and, as Edwina Currie, became
a Tory M.P. and a junior Minister in the Thatcher government. Before an ill–advised public statement ended her career, she had joined

the Church of England in addition to marrying a non-Jew. Her Orthodox parents sat *shivah* when she did so.

The latest statistics show how the rates of intermarriage and assimilation in Britain have been going up steadily for the past 30 years. I gave a lecture a year ago to the members of *Hitachdut Olei Britannia's* Jerusalem branch on the decline of Anglo–Jewry, asking whether there is anything that we in Israel can do to offset it. The 30,000 ex–Britishers here represent something like 10 percent of the Anglo–Jewish community. The numbers of the community were greatly exaggerated until recent years. There were about 475,000 Jews in Britain at the end of the Second World War, including refugees, and this figure was quoted for decades although trained demographers and sociologists were very skeptical. As a result of more objective, scientific analysis, we can now gauge how disastrous the slump has been. Manchester, with around 30,000, is the only major community to emerge unscathed. Greater London's Jewish population is less than it once was; Leeds, where there were reputedly 25,000 Jews, has no more than 10,000 or so today; Glasgow and Birmingham have also declined; and my native Liverpool, which had around 11,000 Jews in 1918 and 7,500 in 1950, numbers less than 5,000 today. There is an overall pattern of decline stemming from a low birth rate, assimilation, emigration, and *aliyah*. The more Jewishly involved families, as do many young couples and singles, often believe that their future lies in Israel. Also a great deal of internal immigration has taken place, with families from small communities moving to the much larger ones because Jewish life is no longer viable in many provincial *kehillot*.

S.F.: But wouldn't you agree that a situation exists, parallel to that in the U.S., where a significant minority has become much more Jewish in practice and learning—the Gateshead world, for example?

Dr. Sivan: In the course of my life, I have met several people who embraced Judaism and took it very seriously indeed. For example, there was a rather bookish Cambridge graduate who had been victimized at his public school, where they dubbed him the "Jewboy." This persecution led him to abandon Christianity. I once opened a Hebrew–English dictionary of his bearing an inscription written by his father, and do think it most remarkable that this man was able to accept the fact that his son had chosen a different faith. It shows that some Gentiles are now much more open–minded and tolerant than they used to be.

In any case, the *ger tzedek* is no longer a rare phenomenon. Way back in the 1950s, a Bible-reading Christian family began attending Shabbat morning services at the Princes Road Synagogue in Liverpool, driving up in their Rolls Royce. They eventually decided to apply for *giyyur* and were referred to the London Bet Din, which arranged a period of instruction lasting for a whole 7 years. Once converted, this family became strictly Orthodox, moved to a Jewish neighborhood, and changed its entire lifestyle. How many of us would make such a sacrifice, I wonder?

S.F.: In general terms, though, do you see an increasing polarization throughout the Jewish world?

Dr. Sivan: There can be no argument about that; the polarization is unmistakable. London's Union of Orthodox Hebrew Congregations, founded by Rabbi Victor (Avigdor) Schoenfeld, once grouped together educated *yekkes* and Hasidim, Mizrahi–type Zionists and Agudists. Today, there are Haredi Jews in it to the right of Agudah, and other such congregations in Manchester and Gateshead. Their influence on "centrist" Orthodoxy has also grown.

S.F.: Does this worry you?

Dr. Sivan: Of course it does. Anglo–Jewry has lost a great deal of the Orthodox middle ground. During the Second World War, most Jewish families were registered with kosher butchers. *Shul*–going, a kosher home, and getting married in an Orthodox synagogue were the general rule. Those standards have declined, even among the supposedly Orthodox. Reform and Liberal Jews constituted a small minority, and English Reform was much more conservative than its American namesake. In fact, when the (Liberal) Jewish Religious Union was set up by Claude Montefiore and Lily Montagu, the West London (Reform) Synagogue refused to give them the use of a hall for fear that men and women would sit together at worship. Those differences are now hardly visible. I well remember Lily Montagu, in her old age, speaking to us at Oxford and becoming rather nostalgic about her parental home— her father, the strictly Orthodox first Lord Swaythling, had created a Federation of Synagogues for East European immigrants in London. To Lily Montagu, Judaism represented a Victorian social mission as well as a system of belief. On Saturday afternoons, at the West Central

Liberal Synagogue, she would preach sermons dressed in canonicals and wearing a scarf–like *tallit*. She was a real character and an earnestly spiritual person, unlike most of those Reform and Progressive women who function as "rabbis" today.

Why the old middle ground has suffered an erosion is hard to explain, whether as a result of the war, an unimaginative rabbinate, insufficient Jewish education, or the general decline of standards in Britain. People have simply been dissatisfied with the United Synagogue type of Orthodoxy and drifted either to the left or to the extreme right. True, there are now more 100 percent *frum* Jews in Britain than ever before, but there are also far fewer Jews maintaining what used to be called the religious "essentials." I'm not sure that this represents much of a gain. Within the new, more Orthodox United Synagogue congregations, you can see people using both the revised (Singer's) prayer book, expanded and newly translated under the supervision of Lord Jakobovits and his successor, Chief Rabbi Jonathan Sacks, and the American *ArtScroll Siddur*. I have to admit that the *ArtScroll Siddur* is beautifully produced and that it appeals to the non–Zionist, less broadly educated type of Jew, but I don't like its narrow–minded commentary.

S.F.: In your own work, you stand for the meeting of the worlds that a love of learning generates. How do you regard the impulse among some Jews to close themselves off from the world around them?

Dr. Sivan: *Torah im derech eretz* is my ideal. Unconsciously, perhaps I imbibed the outlook of that world. My mother created an Orthodox home environment and my father was an "enlightened" practicing Jew and a teacher of classics. He never found any problem in living in two worlds simultaneously, and made witty observations that I have passed down to my own children. Members of our family on both sides were practicing Jews and active in the professions. To observe the "essentials" and to be a good citizen were a natural part of life. The "Litvaks" on my father's side came from the birthplace of the Dubner Maggid and the Hafetz Hayim. One branch helped to establish Gateshead Yeshiva, which was not "black-hat" 70 or 80 years ago. Another branch of his family settled in Toronto. The "Polaks" on my mother's side came from the village of Dobrzyn on the Vistula decades before the Tsarist pogroms. These ancestors of mine left Eastern Europe because of economic and social conditions, Liverpool attracted them because it was a staging post between the old world and the new that offered numerous business opportunities, and it had an old established Jewish community, the most "aristocratic" outside London. Now, had my maternal ancestors sailed to New York in the 1850s, they would probably have joined Reform temples, and by now their descendants would no longer be Jewish. Orthodoxy was not respectable in America, where Reform Jews of German and Bohemian origin set the tone. A different situation prevailed in Britain at the turn of the century, when some relatives of my mother's did cross the Atlantic. One married Arthur Baruch, a nephew of the American Jewish statesman and financier, Bernard Baruch, and I visited her in New York in 1965. She and the rest of her family were very gracious, very American, but not very Jewish. Now, 30 years letter, I can no longer trace any of them.

By contrast, the English branch of my mother's family has remained at least nominally Orthodox. Harry Samuels, one of her relatives, served on the Board of Deputies and the Kashrut Commission. His daughter, Miriam Karlin, a well-known stage, screen, and television actress, is also a Jewishly involved person. In many cases, I find younger relatives—on my father's side especially—becoming more observant than their parents and more knowledgeable as well. This is also true of some younger cousins of mine in Toronto. One, who telephoned me recently, has become a Torah-observant, Orthodox Jew, very much involved in Jewish education; he and his family make regular visits to Israel. These are all educated people, mostly university graduates, and they form part of a distinct trend toward greater Jewishness, which I consider a welcome and healthy development. To my mind, it is absolutely essential that every boy and girl receive a thorough Jewish education before deciding what their religious path in life should be. Just look at all those ignoramuses, in both Israel and the Diaspora, who would never dream of pontificating on matters that they have never studied, but who claim the right to give an "expert" opinion about Judaism.

S.F.: So you do believe that there can be a viable Jewish life in the Diaspora, and don't insist on every Jew coming to live here in Israel?

Dr. Sivan: As a third-generation Zionist, I would like the vast majority if our people to live here. If a million Jews had emigrated from the West since 1948, we would have been numerous enough to block any Palestinian claim for another Arab state between Jordan and the

Mediterranean. We have failed to grasp opportunities again and again—after the Balfour Declaration, after Israel's establishment, and after the Six–Day War. The reality is that most Western Jews prefer to stay put, come what may, and we must therefore decide whether they and their descendants should be written off. I believe that everything should be done to ensure that they will have a Jewish future.

I make a point of visiting relatives and encouraging the younger ones to think seriously about *aliyah,* or at least to spend some time in Israel.

S.F.: What are the major developments that you have experienced in Israel since you have made *aliyah?*

Dr. Sivan: My wife and I came here in 1967, 2 months before the Six–Day War. The situation was far from rosy in those days: there was an economic recession, and more people were leaving Israel than coming to settle. Then, not long after our arrival, war broke out. *Eretz Yisrael* was liberated, and people thought that they heard the "footsteps" of the Messiah. We missed some of the rights granted retroactively to new *olim* by just 1 week. In Jerusalem, very few people had a car of their own. There were virtually no parking problems in those days, and we drove everywhere, even to Gaza and Jenin. As a *miliumnik* (reservist), I also took my car to out–of–the–way places and gave lifts to people who now have cars of their own, whereas now I no longer possess or need one.

The country has changed a great deal over the past 3 decades, and has become much more materialistic. Until 1978, I never worried about burglars. Most people didn't have valuables that gave rise to envy. After we came back from South Africa, an Arab-Jewish gang broke into our apartment and stole my wife's gold jewelry and an antique gold coin that my great–great–uncle gave me on my bar mitzvah. It was a traumatic experience for us both. Now people tend to judge you on the basis of the money you make. The social gap has widened—lower–paid folks are naturally resentful—and there is much more religious and political extremism than there was in the old days. The extreme left-wing Matspen and the League against Religious Coercion were marginal groups, and Israeli newspapers would not publish anti–Zionist or unpatriotic articles. The major political parties—Labor, the Mafdal (NRP), even the Likud—were more centrist than they are today. So attitudes and values have changed—not always for the better.

All the same, living in Israel is a reward in itself. This is where Jewish history is being made, where the Jewish people's growth is taking place, where Jewish family life can really prosper. I am often saddened to hear what has happened to friends and families that chose to remain in the *galut*. There are people whose children have drifted away from Jewish tradition, gone through two divorces, or married Gentiles. This kind of story can be heard over and over again. My wife, who also comes from Liverpool, is a lawyer who went into politics. She gained thirteenth position on the Mafdal list and, but for the loss of votes to another, less experienced woman candidate, might now be sitting in the Knesset. We have three sons, all born in Jerusalem, and a South African–born daughter. The fact that they were educated here in the state religious system, and have a sane outlook on life, gives us enormous satisfaction. Our boys served in the army, two of them as *hesderniks,* and our daughter went through *sherut leumi.* Our eldest son graduated from Bar Ilan University, is a practicing lawyer, and got married at the age of 22. He and his wife have three children and a beautiful house in the Gush Etzion settlement of Neveh Daniel. Our second boy works in computers and has been married for a year. He and his wife have recently moved into their own apartment in Shoham, not far from Tel Aviv. Our third son is halfway through his medical course in Beersheva, and our daughter has 1 year to go for her degree in communications at the Hebrew University. So while cousins and friends of mine in Britain are worried about the fact that their sons or daughters show no inclination to get married, I already have three grandchildren. Our observant *mechuttanim* are politically diverse, which also makes life interesting. One, a psychologist, is an extreme right–winger active in Moledet party. Dr. Yehuda ben Meir, a one–time leader of the Mafdal and Deputy Foreign Minister, is now a prominent religious dove and spokesman for Meimad. We are on good terms with them both, listen to what they have to say, but stick to our own opinions.

S.F.: After the great hopes aroused by the Six–Day War victory, do you feel a sense of disappointment?

Dr. Sivan: My Zionism has always been of the pragmatic variety. I believe that our ability to determine the course of events is limited, that some things can be foreseen while others cannot. Had our government pursued its negotiations with Arafat and the Palestinians in a much less compromising fashion, the end result might have been different. "Is this peace agreement worth having anyway?" many Israelis ask. If we surrendered all of the Golan to Syria, would that not leave us open to renewed attacks? I don't believe in Shimon Peres' vision of a "New Middle East." Nothing in this region of the world is predictable, and one dictator can repudiate any agreement reached by his predecessor. It is a grave mistake to credit Arab leaders with thinking as we do. In their thinking, "my word is my bond" simply does not apply to infidels.

That does not mean that I am against a peace treaty with Jordan or with Egypt, though Mubarak has made it a pretty cold type of relationship. I wish that we could have peace with all the Arab world but you have to take into account that fundamentalists are ready to murder any leader of whom they do not approve.

Everyone in this country was affected by the Six–Day War, and could hear "the footsteps of the Messiah." That goes for non–religious Israelis as well. We all felt that a very momentous stage in history had been reached, but we failed to seize the opportunities available. For example, had we taken control of over *Har ha-Bayit* then, the Arabs would have been in shock, but they would probably have reconciled themselves to the fact that we Jews were in control. Unfortunately, the government backed down and forbade people to go up there, while the chief rabbinate acquiesced. The IDF'S chief rabbi, Shlomo Goren, had other ideas and was prepared to give a lecture about the Temple Mount's "safe areas" at a Jerusalem conference, but at the last moment Yitzhak Rabin, then Chief of Staff, prevented him from speaking. It's all water under the bridge now. Of course, traditional Jews pray for the Temple to be rebuilt, but just how that process will come about is in the hands of the Almighty. Only He can determine how and when this will occur, not some group of messianic zealots.

On the question of *Eretz Yisrael Hashlema*, I believe that the liberated territories are rightly ours, but we may lose most of them because of our own short–sightedness. Years before the government tackled the issue of autonomy, I said that there was no reason why the Palestinian Arabs should not have their own police force, and raise their own taxes, and see to their own economy. However, we continued with the military government when no Arab, European, or American well-wishers were ready to make the Palestinians self–sufficient. In 1967–1968, during the early months after the war, my wife and I drove all over what we now call "the occupied territories"—from Gaza to

Kuneitra—with our firstborn in the car. In Jenin, we went into an Arab restaurant to ask them if they could give us some hot water to heat the baby's food. I remember how they fell over themselves to be helpful simply because we were the "victorious Israelis." However, we were not polite, but arrogant, and if Israelis in general had behaved with greater circumspection, that might have promoted better relations. Who knows? In any case, mistakes of all kinds were made, and they have caught up with us. That is also true of the Intifada, which could have been ended in a week or so with minimum loss of life if we had done what was necessary at the time.

I never believed in the philosophy of *af shaal* ("not an inch"). But I do believe that we should hold on to as much territory as possible through skillful negotiation. I also believe that we should have built many more blocks of settlement, all over the place. It was sheer stupidity to build isolated settlements that would take soldiers needed elsewhere to defend. Gush Etzion should have served as the model of how to create new facts on the ground.

In recent months, Israelis have begun to feel insecure, with terrorist outrages in our major cities, cars and buses fired upon, soldiers kidnapped and murdered, and thousands of private cars stolen by Palestinian gangs. One fears that we may end up defending the pre–1967 borders against infiltrators based in hostile villages just across the Green Line. We need a government prepared to take sterner, well–organized measures against a recurrence of the Intifada.

S.F.: There has been much criticism of the Israeli education system's failure to provide youngsters with an adequate amount of Jewish knowledge. What, in your opinion, needs to be done?

Dr. Sivan: First of all, the whole educational approach must be revised, excluding gimmicks and shortcuts. If, as people now realize, the *Mamlakhti* (General) system is turning out vast numbers of Hebrew-speaking *am ha-aratsim*, then there must be something very wrong indeed with the teachers. One can hardly expect products of the current system, who are themselves ignorant and scornful of Jewish tradition, to suddenly turn over a new leaf. Nor is it likely that a Minister of Education from an avowedly secular party will choose to promote traditional Jewish practices and values. Second, television can be an invaluable asset in the battle against Jewish ignorance, if only it is utilized in the right way. For some time, I have been campaigning for a

Moreshet (Jewish Heritage) TV channel that would educate, not brain-wash, adults and children alike. Such a channel could beam a wide variety of programs into the average Israeli home: features explaining the importance of our festivals and observances; docudramas portray-ing great figures and issues in Jewish history; imaginative serials on Jewish literature, Diaspora communities, "Jews in the news," and the specifically Jewish role in world culture. All of this could be presented in an interesting and challenging way to grip the viewer's imagination and enhance his or her Jewish self–esteem. If only one tenth of the millions that have been squandered on other "projects" were invested in this Jewish Heritage channel, both Israel and the Diaspora would reap an enormous reward. The fact that no one in authority has imple-mented such a scheme to date is absolutely horrifying.

S.F.: How do you understand the concept of *avodat Hashem* in rela-tion to your own life and the world in general?

Dr. Sivan: The basic meaning of *avodah* is "worship" and "service," and the two things go together. A good Jew is also a good citizen, whether or not the society in which he lives happens to be a Jewish or a non–Jewish one. In any civilized society, one has to do one's duty and show one's allegiance to the president, or reigning monarch, the parliament and the lawful authority. To "pray for the welfare of the government" is, after all, one of the most ancient rabbinic injunctions. If that is how we should behave in a Gentile society, then are we not obligated to do so in the Jewish homeland? Can anyone in his right senses maintain that Israel is less *kodesh* than Britain, the United States, or Russia? Unfortunately, however, there are Haredi groups in Israel that display open contempt for institutions of the state. Jews of the same type living in Washington Heights, Antwerp, or Stamford Hill would never dream of spitting on the flag, or desecrating the grave of one of the founding fathers. To my mind, such behavior betrays a measure of schizophrenia. These people evidently believe that the State of Israel, not having been created by the Messiah, is thus completely *trefah*, and they need not show any respect for it.

    Avodat Hashem involves more than simply believing in and wor-shipping God. A Jew is obligated to serve through the mitzvot between man and man, and also to do his duty by his fellow man through the mitzvot between man and God. Putting this into practice has never been easy. There are people who were raised as and claim to be reli-

gious, yet who behave unethically, with no concept of civic duty. There
are also people who are non–religious disregarding key practices of
Judaism, either because they are ignorant or because they have been
taught to flaunt them. I can understand how a Jew who survived the
Holocaust lost his or her faith. Who can judge someone who's experienced those horrors? Take Hanna Zemer, the one–time editor of *Davar*
who came from an ultra–Orthodox Slovak home, but the Shoah turned
her into a secularist. Even so, she can draw upon the Jewish education
she received in her youth. Shimon Peres too, who grew up in Belorussia,
has an appreciation of Jewish values and can find a common language
with observant Jews.

When I was at Jews College, Rabbi Dr. Isidore Epstein, who was
the principal, often quoted his favorite *mashal*. It was inspired by the
popular notion that one can be a "good Jew at heart" without observ-
ing the mitzvot. Dr. Epstein used to say that, if you keep fueling the
locomotive, then it will pull the rest of the train. But if you stop the
feeding process, then the train will continue for a while under its own
momentum, and then come to a halt. In the same way, a person who
is filled with Jewishness keeps going. Once that stops, the Jewishness
may persist for a generation or two, after which it dies out. That's what
is happening here. The old generation, Laborites who laid the foundations of the state, were mainly rooted in the Jewish heartland in Eastern Europe. They rebelled against the tradition, but a vestige survived
with them. Ben Gurion, for all his weird ideas, was still capable of discussing things with *Hason Ish* and appreciating Jewish values. Since then,
new leaders have arisen and the old common factor is disappearing. This
is true for the secular right as well as for the left. I am not sure that
Benjamin Netanyahu is more deeply involved in Jewish life than some
labor moderates are.

Avodat Hashem is an extremely complex matter, since no two
people ever think alike. After all, great rabbis objected to the Thirteen
Principles of Maimonides, and to the *Shulchan Aruch* as a compendium
of Jewish law. No one is a complete *tzadik* and few of us are perfect
believers. There is a great deal of ignorant talk about Orthodox Jews
having to observe the 613 Commandments, as if these were all appli-
cable today. People ought to make a start by obeying the *Aseret ha-
Dibrot* (Ten Commandments), or the seven Noahide Commandments.
That would make a difference to the present–day world. Faith in ourselves and in our God–given way of life is what really matters. We Jews

have had a seminal role in shaping civilization, and that role I believe will continue. When Gentiles spoke of Judaism as a "backward" religion, my father, *alav ha–shalom*, would retort, "The world still has to catch up with the Judaism practiced 1,000 years ago."

We live in a very sophisticated world with immense technological advances, yet its standards and values appear to be on the decline. Judaism's not subject to hanging fashions nor to a referendum. As a citizen, I believe in parliamentary democracy; as a Jew, I do not believe that everyone has a right to "democratize" the Jewish way of life. One's entitled to ask questions, but must listen carefully to the answers. Only the Sages could reach a "democratic" decision by majority vote. That is why I cannot accept non–Orthodox reforms and demands— there is no logic or consistency to them. A century ago, Jewish reformers abandoned prayers and rituals that their successors have now brought back. A century ago, women "rabbis" and "gay" congregations would have been unthinkable in the most radical Reform community, but now they are in vogue. Such things are divorced from *avodat Hashem* and have no basis in Torah. One Nechamah Leibowitz is worth 1,000 women posing as rabbis. The trouble is that there is too little respect for genuine authority and too much respect for the bogus, for the purveyors of superstition. I can't accept the idolization of certain rabbis and the display of their portraits.

S.F.: Surely this latter phenomenon reflects the popularity of Hasidism today, with their reverence for *tzadikim*.

Professor Sivan: Yes it does, but one also finds it in the Lithuanian yeshiva world. Rabbi Eliezer Schach, for example, has been transformed into a *Mitnagidic Rebbe*. There are, and always have been, Jewish luminaries who are worthy of our respect, but even they have their strengths and their weaknesses. If there is one democratic factor in Judaism, it's the right to discuss, debate, and criticize out of knowledge, and not out of ignorance.

We cannot tell what God's purpose is in this world. Haredi Jews maintain that the Shoah was a punishment for the secular Jews' unwillingness to observe basic mitzvot. To me, this is an outlandish piece of heretical nonsense. Can any sane person justify the slaughter of 1.5 million Jewish children by the Nazis on such absurd grounds? We simply don't know what the Almighty's plan is, nor can we read His Mind. Each of us has been given the freedom to choose between good and evil, to do or not do His bidding, and each of us most then bear the consequences. We have no collective responsibility for the misdeeds of an individual or some fringe group.

The fact that we have survived 2,000 years of hostility, that our nation has come to life again in our ancient homeland—despite whatever criticism one may have of governments and leaders—and that there are now almost 5 million Jews here is by any standard an unprecedented achievement. It is also ample reason for hope and faith in the *Ribbono Shel Olam*. How any Jew can claim to be entirely irreligious beats me. There is nothing rational about our history and survival. As Edmund Fleg once put it, "Evidence of God's existence I find in the existence of Israel."

Rabbi Adin Steinsaltz

Rabbi Adin Steinsaltz is head of the Israel Institute for Talmudic Publications and has for many years been making a new Hebrew translation of and commentary on the Babylonian and Jerusalem Talmuds. He is arguably the most well–known and influential Torah teacher of our generation. He has written a number of important works that have been translated into English. Among them are *The Thirteen–Petalled Rose*, *The Longer Shorter Way*, *The Sustaining Utterance*, and *The Strife of the Spirit*. Rabbi Steinsaltz is one of those rare figures who become legends in their own time. His remarkable erudition, great modesty, quiet ironic humor, and powerful command of many areas of both secular and religious learning have established him as a "giant" of our age.

Meeting with him (after a number of years of trying), was a great honor and a moving experience for me. Perhaps out of being awed by him and out of a great respect, I did not ask him some of the kinds of biographical questions that appear in the other interviews of this series. Instead, as a sometime student of his Thursday night *shiurim* at Hovvei Tsion synagogue, I asked him about the subject that through the years seemed to me to be at the heart of these classes, how one comes closer to God in prayer.

C8 80

S.F.: In one of your Thursday evening talks at Hovvei Tsion synagogue, you spoke about the service of the heart, which is prayer as *avodah kashah*, very hard work. Why is it such hard work?

Rabbi Steinsaltz: When we speak about an experience that comes to someone suddenly in one particular moment and incidentally, it is not difficult; but when we speak about *avodah* as something consistent and intended, then it is difficult. Why? Because in this *avodah* the person wishes and demands to arrive at a certain change within himself. Such changes are not a simple matter, especially if one continues to make them in persistent way. First of all, there is an effort that requires great concentration. Beyond that, the service of the heart is an effort to build a kind of internal structure ("*matkonnet*"). When a person wishes to do this, it is clear that many opposing things stand in his way. There is, after all, not a kind of general *avodah*. *Avodah* is always specifically of one kind or another. And there are always difficulties involved in this. If one wishes to make the changes in a persistent way, then he comes to understand that he is always involved in an inner struggle, in which he must maintain his power of concentration. There are two aspects taken together. From one side, the struggle against the opposing things, and from the other, the effort to maintain a power of concentration make the *avodah*, no matter what it specifically is, difficult.

The *avodah* becomes even more difficult when one comes to a certain crossroads, a certain point where there is strong internal resistance.

311

Sometimes one, in principle, decides to get to a certain goal, but did not think this out, did not work it through sufficiently. There are things that the person has to force, to move himself toward, in which he is involved in a struggle against himself. There are instances in which he stands against things that are evil, ugly things.

For instance, when a person is involved in a problem with someone else, in which he is required to forgive that someone—this may be the work of heart. There may thus be an external aspect, and what one does and does not do in regard to it. But then there is the internal aspect, where one has to go against himself with all the feelings and emotions that this sometimes involves. To do this is difficult work.

S.F.: But how does this difficulty relate to the injunction to "perpetually be in joy when we pray"?

Rabbi Steinsaltz: This is something that does not always come. There are people for whom prayer is always in joy. There are others for whom this sometimes comes. And there are those for whom joy comes only as a surprise. Speaking of *avodah*, it can be that the person is overwhelmed by a certain feeling, and thus comes to believe that no *avodah* is required at all. It should be clear that the service of the heart is not free meditation. It is not an effort to arrive at some kind of trance. The *simcha* ("joy") can come when a person works on something that is specifically related to *simcha*. There are lessons that are specifically related to the joy of the heart. A person may undertake this when he is in a good mood or when he has very bad feelings, and it is not simple to struggle. Suppose he sits and is thinking of something, some aspect of a problem, and supposes that he has made progress. And this brings a certain *simcha b'lev*. But this also is not so simple, for where he takes enjoyment may come from the external side; for instance, in some beautiful invention or idea he has devised. And there can be *simcha b'lev* in this, a genuine happiness. I don't deny this. But it is not the joy of *avodah*. Yet there are situations where people suddenly feel much better. There is the example of a person suddenly relieved of a great headache who feels a great euphoria. But this is not serious. This is not *avodah*, which does not always bring with it *simcha*. And there are times when the *simcha* of the *avodah* does not come immediately, but rather much later.

S.F.: The purpose of the *avodah*, the prayer, is to come closer to God?

Rabbi Steinsaltz: Yes. That's *avodah* to come to a contact, to come to make a connection. But this connection can also be something frightening. It is not always a connection of joy. And its goal is not joy.

S.F.: This is the connection that comes through *yirat Shemayim*, the fear, the awe of Heaven?

Rabbi Steinsaltz: The problem is not one of fear of Heaven, but of connection. It is a problem of coming closer to God. Everything is all right. All that I do, that the world does, is understood, straight. There is the connection between me and the *Kadosh Baruch Hu*. And there is the sign. This is more authentic. So one goes straightforwardly.

S.F.: How can the person within himself know that he has reached this point? Can he rely on his own intuition in this?

Rabbi Steinsaltz: It is not always possible to rely on intuition. It is not always the proper guide. It is often a mediocre instrument. You see, there are situations where a person makes a certain creation, a work of art, and his mood is excellent. But the work itself is not. Then there is the other situation, where the person is dissatisfied, filled with sufferings, and yet in the end there results a work that is very good. So the intuition was not the true test but simply a passing feeling. Not always do I see before me the result of my *avodah*. There may well be the true results much later. And this is written in almost all of the books that deal with this issue. One of the signs that there was true *avodah* is that it leaves something after it. Sometimes, this is simply a great tiredness. There is a great effort, and there is a tiredness afterward. If there is a result, then this is some kind of change. And sometimes this change can mean something throughout the person's life. Some point, some subject has been touched in one's relation to the world of the *Kadosh Baruch Hu*, and the change remains. This is more than intuition; rather, it is a good sign.

There is a famous story told about a Hasid who made a *Seder* twice. The first time there was a wonderful feeling. He spoke and made many *chiddushim* (new insights into the Torah). And he felt that he was there with the angels. But during the second *Seder*, he fell asleep, and it was not at all, he felt, an outstanding event. Still, the second *Seder* was a *Seder*. Precisely when there is not an overwhelming personal feeling or experience, a person can break through a great barrier. Because he is concerned with other things, and not with his own problems, he can make the breakthrough. This is like the problem with *avodah*, when the feeling of the *avodah* at one time can be much different from the results later.

There are certain people who have a great deal of control over themselves. This kind of person can control, rule over, order his own experience. He can, as it were, bring himself into a certain experience, a certain spiritual state. These are people who can put themselves in situations of joy, or of sadness. This is not always useful in *avodah*.

There are people who can make rhymes very well, but to make rhymes well is not always to write poetry. There is a certain kind of control a person may have over his soul. He may be able to guide and direct it. But this is not always advantageous. We always face the limitations given by our personal time, the time of the world. They distract our attention. To direct ourselves inwardly requires a great effort. A person can be in a situation of great poverty and deprivation, yet worship God with joy. Sometimes it is easier for him in this situation. It's a serious problem: to leave the external world and enter the world of prayer. Part of this is work, effort. There were masters of prayer who described it. Sometimes there is a moment when a man is able to direct himself in the right way. But it is difficult, very hard work.

There is a story about the *Chiddushei ha-Rim*, who would pray with very great effort for hours. One day he came out of his prayer much earlier than usual, and said, "*Zeh halach li.*" ("This time it just went right.")

S.F.: As with Honi ha-Maagel, when the prayer flowed, he knew it was accepted. And when he had great difficulty, he knew it would not be.

Rabbi Steinsaltz: Yes. Sometimes it is as if the person opened the opening by himself, and sometimes it is as if the thing has opened by itself. But it by itself on an ordinary day, then the person has to make a certain effort, and to continue with this, he has to hold on to the thread of thought. There are other days when it goes more simply, more easily. But this is not a sign that it is more perfect and complete. Sometimes, yes; sometimes, no.

S.F.: And one result of the true prayer, the true *avodah*, is that this is reflected in the person's actions in the world?

Rabbi Steinsaltz: There are also results, consequences in actions. If a man prays within himself, and this has no results in his actions, then this raises the question as to the authenticity of the prayer. If the prayer was true, then it has to find its expression in many ways. If it doesn't, then there was probably something self–deceptive in the prayer, what is called *"dimyanot"* ("false imaginings"), unreal imaginary things. There have been experiences, but they do not reflect anything real. They do not move to anything. If they do not lead to any change in his speech or his relation to others, then they were in effect not real, a dream. How do we know that a dream is not true? There remains nothing from it. And if it was a true dream, then something of it does remain. There is in *Yehoshua* that dream in which the hungry person dreams that he eats. And he wakes up hungry. This is the same kind of thing. A person prays for 3 hours and is in high, so he gets to some far point. But in the end, nothing of this remains. We see this in much Hasidic literature. The test is that a true experience cannot simply disappear. If it is authentic then it has to endure through time.

It can also be that a person prays and does not feel anything special in this experience. Yet afterwards, nothing remains the same as it was before. In that hour, something happened to him. At a certain moment, a problem may have been solved, not to return again. There are people who are disturbed for years by a certain problem, and then one day this problem ceases to disturb them again. It's like someone travelling to the North Pole and passing by without noticing. Just like that he has passed and not noticed it, and must return sometime later just to know that he was there.

S.F.: Isn't our true state though one in which we are always uncertain as to whether or not we have truly arrived?

Rabbi Steinsaltz: The problem is that a person truly does not know how stable this is. This is something that I have spoken about in my lessons. Sometimes a person receives a gift of *chesed* and he is in a situation, not always of euphoria, but of openness of heart. It seems as if everything is open for him. And it seems that he has no problem opening up things that are blocked, obstacles. But this is the sign that it comes from external influence only, because this passes, and inside himself he remains as he was before. So when is something true, a *"segulah sofi"*? Various people have given different answers. Habad answers,

"When there remains something permanent." There are people who
have said all their lives that they were not sure. There are those uncertain as to their own essence. This raises philosophical questions. Where
is the truth? Does it have to be something eternal?

There is in the *Ari* the question as to the difference between
l'hakshot ("to complicate the question"), and *v'lahaven* ("to understand").
Say I am facing a problem in my encounter with the text, and in the
text there is some internal contradiction. I give my answer and I see
there still is a contradiction. I may rest content with my answer, or
search for another. Perhaps the problem is that I do not understand
the meaning of the word. But there may have been what is called "the
irreversible experience." For example, after I have seen an angel, I cannot somehow "unsee" it, though in time my having seen it will have
less influence on me. But I cannot unsee it. I cannot erase this experience. I can to a degree cancel the influence, but I cannot cancel the
phenomenon.

Within the difficult experience of prayer, something irreversible
can occur. Someone arrives at a certain point. He cannot erase this,
and he cannot go back. I have met a number of people who speak about
this. There was a well–known writer whom I met at the time when he
still observed the mitzvot. He had many problems, and he wrote a great
deal about them. He told me that, as a young man, he was for a year
involved in awesome experiences. And he could not erase them. Yet
somehow he managed to see something, to see beyond the curtain. Now
he is afraid of this. He is not interested in this. But he cannot erase it:
it is part of him. For example, it happens that sometimes when a person dies, the effect is not really felt on us immediately. It takes time to
absorb what happened. This may be a slow change, which it takes great
time to feel.

S.F.: This is similar to the way that you describe the process of *teshuvah*
for the Jews, not suddenly and all at once, but through time and through
many small changes.

Rabbi Steinsaltz: I said that my experience with Jews is almost completely like this, for a person can have a certain experience one day,
and the result may come in 10 years. This is a process, like climbing a
mountain. Some climb swiftly, some fall on the way, and some go up
again. But the question is, what is the sum result of all the movement,

all the process? There are those who work hard and yet do not arrive because they stood before greater obstacles. I once heard an account from a person by the name of Hugo Bergman who came to my *shiurim*. A very interesting person, he told me that, from childhood, he would investigate mystical phenomena. For years he met with people who claimed to have had mystical experiences, although he himself had no such experience. Yet he told me that each time he read *Shmoneh Yisrael* his whole body trembled. This, however, he did not think of as being in the same category as the experiences he had examined. That is, he did not realize, he was not conscious of his achievement. This is simply an example of a person who has through his *avodah* gotten something, without realizing it.

S.F.: We have been talking about the *avodah* of the individual. How do you connect this with the *avodah* of *Clal Yisrael*?

Rabbi Steinsaltz: There are exceptional individuals; very, very few who are so alone that they seem to come into contact with no one, seem "out of place." It is not always a question of the influence of the individual on the community. It may be that, in certain historical times, there are problems uniquely difficult. In general, people live within a certain general historical framework. They have to find some relation to the general community. This does not depend on whether someone reads the papers or not. There is a certain atmosphere of the time.

There is a story that one day the Rebbe of Berditchev sent out messengers to all the small towns in the area with the message, "The Rabbe of Berditchev says 'There is *Elohim* in the world.'" Consider. A rav sends out this message. There is laughter. Of course he knew about the French Revolution. But what he knew, how much he knew, is not clear and not really important. He felt the problem, and because he felt the problem, he lived with the understanding that this was what was necessary to say at this time. He understood that the problem, which 100 years before had been an individual problem, had become in his time a problem for the public. And he felt that the *avodah* of the individual was to do some part of the *avodah* of the *clal*. This was his specific contribution. There are here and there people for whom he opened a *shaar* ("a gate"), thus freeing them of their being alone.

S.F.: Why are there people who seem what might be called self–sufficient in their human loneliness, who seem to have no need whatso-

ever for any connection with God? And how does this connect with
the abyss dividing secular and religious in the Jewish world today?

Rabbi Steinsaltz: There is an abyss of *haskalah,* an abyss of words that
may seem great but is not always real. There are people who are searching. And they call this search by many different names. That is, one of
the problems of two cultures, as with two individuals, is to make a
dictionary, a common language. Because what happens now in Israel—
as well as in other places—is not so much a problem of the *nefesh* as it
is of the dictionary, the common language. We are using different words
and vocabularies, and we are not able to translate them from language
to language. Many times the search is the same search, but the way in
which the things are related is different. Still the questions have to be
asked; they are the same personal questions. But the vocabularies are
different. People seek the Absolute. It is the same kind of search but
with different names. There are people who for instance, seek romantic love, or seem to seek love when what they are looking for is some
kind of Absolute answer. One may seek a woman because a certain kind
of education teaches him that through her he can find the Absolute. So
this is a question of culture as whole, culture in general.

S.F.: When you look at the Jewish people today, is there some way in
which you can compare and judge its spiritual level to that at other
periods of our history? Where are we now?

Rabbi Steinsaltz: When I look at the Jewish people today, and I do
look, I see that they have gone through a great trauma. They have
forgotten their own language except, that is, for a certain number of
religious people. Not the Hebrew language, but the language of its
thought. Between the words we use and the thoughts we think there is
a correlation. Now it can be that there is someone who calls himself
secular who is in fact absolutely religious, just as there are people for
whom it can be the opposite. And why? There is no correlation between the words and the real content of the life. This is not a problem
of the Jewish people exclusively, but of the world as a whole.

I return again to the story of Abraham: *"Krah sham shem Hashem"*
("Call out there the name of God"). By calling out the name of God,
Abraham changes the parameters of the relationship. He goes to another place, and begins to relate and perceive human relationships in a
different way. If this were a problem of philosophy or literature, then

it would be an easy problem. But it is a problem of drawing conclusions from life. If I ask how to define a triangle, then I ask one kind of academic question. But if I ask what the purpose and meaning of life are, then I have asked something completely different. There is no problem if someone asks me trivial questions and we discuss them in the afternoon during dinner. That's no problem. But when important questions are asked, questions of identity and meaning—Who am I? What am I? Where am I going?—It's not easy, because there is resistance.

S.F.: There are people in the world who believe that they know the Absolute Truth and that truth does not include a personal God. Is it the task of each and every Jew to try to bring others closer to God? Do you understand our historical role as this task of bringing all other peoples to this recognition of God?

Rabbi Steinsaltz: This was our historic task. Now we are so absorbed in *leshmor et atzmenu* to ensure our own survival that we do not have time for this. But we were the catalyst for this throughout the world. There were people who said, "Everything is okay, is in order." Then we came into the world, bringing something new, and broke that order. And people do not forgive us for this. This is one of the reasons for anti–Semitism. We came and brought these new ideas. And once they were here, they could not be taken out.

S.F.: Is this still our work today? In relation to China? India?

Rabbi Steinsaltz: This is our work in relation to Tel Aviv. We do not have to go so far. Our problem is again in relation to the pagan world. I ask, How do I relate to a child who is defined as an idiot? If I want to relate to him in accordance with his own subjectivity, then he will be happy. He has much fewer problems, less suffering. But the minute I try to build within him a different system, I break his inner wholeness. Why should I do this? It's an interesting problem. There was a film on this subject, *Charley*, based on a science fiction work called *Flowers for Algernon*. A youth is injected with a certain medicine, which raises his IQ three or four times, until finally it goes back down and he dies. This is what happens when you break a world that is whole in itself and give it a chance to develop at the cost of great suffering. It is in a way the same in relation to the pagan world. I still believe that there is a reason and advantage in affording them the chance for development, which relates to helping a child to grow. When I was 5 this was a perfect age for me. I felt no problems.

S.F.: You can remember from such an early age?

Rabbi Steinsaltz: I have memories from the age of 1. At the age of 5, I had this sense that everything is alright. The problem is that no one recognizes this as right. If you see someone who is frozen at that age, and there are cases such as this, then you relate to his as a victim of misfortune. This may be in opposition to his subjective feelings. So when you introduce a new element—this need not be a snake into Eden, an angel—it nonetheless has a disruptive effect. Harmony is destroyed, and now a new harmony must be created, which is far more complicated. This is a matter of growth, but it is not simple. And it doesn't always solve the problem.

S.F.: In an article, you spoke about the ingathering of exiles, the founding and maintaining of the State of Israel as partial incomplete actions. And you indicated that the complete Redemption can come only with the Messiah. Do you believe that there are specific actions we can take to help this? Or is this in your judgement forcing the end? Are we simply to wait? To pray?

Rabbi Steinsaltz: Our prayer too is not something passive in this matter. Sometimes it cannot be effective, but our theology today is an activist one. This is not to force the end. But it is to say that the end is not a kind of instantaneous catastrophe; rather, it can be a kind of process. And we can try to quicken the process in some way, move toward it. What are we today? As a people, we are not in very good shape. It can be that a person goes to investigate the world beyond the horizon yet does not see the world that is at home. This is what I mean when I say that our condition is not good. At times in the past, we were closer. Then there is a condition of the world as whole. There are two phenomena that occur at one and the same time. On the one hand, the world has become more pagan; on the other hand, it seems to me on a deeper level that there is something fragile and weak in all this. That is to say, the world is very ready for some kind of turn ("*tafnit*"). I see everywhere that basic things are not strong. It seems open to change.

Do you know the description in the Book of Daniel of the huge statue with the head of gold and legs of iron, yet feet of clay—how a small stone can topple it? Our world in some sense seems a world with feet of clay. On the one hand it seems that this world is not interested in religion, but on the other hand, if we look deeply, then we can see it as a world not at rest with itself, not sure of itself, not satisfied with itself, searching on all sides. And it lives with some kind of expectation of a world that will be better. This is to say, it is as if any small push will knock it over. Once there were stable foundations, but now the world is less and less stable. This characterizes all that is happening. While the world is in a sense more open, it is less stable. The problem is at least on this side for the Jewish people, what is the image of the Jewish people. There may come a time when we have a *besorah chadashah,* a new message for humankind, but don't have the people that will bring it. We can look at this in another way. How did Christianity come to the world? The world was in ruins, from an intellectual point of view. Yet something that came from one small part of the world overturned all the world.

S.F.: Many speak today of the death of all "isms," leaving a chasm of uncertainty and lack of faith.

Rabbi Steinsaltz: Right. The death of all movements and all isms would seem to show that the world is far more open to change. You can meet someone who says that he is an atheist and not really rely on this.

S.F.: But in regard to the spiritual situation of the Jewish people, specifically—there are those who point out that there is more learning being done now than ever before in history. Supposedly, in Israel alone, there are more yeshiva students than there were even at the height of Jewish learning in Eastern Europe.

Rabbi Steinsaltz: In quantitative terms this is true, but it is not necessarily an *aliyah.* A change for the good spiritually. This is another subject. Truly things grow in terms of numbers, but in qualitative terms, there is no such growth.

S.F.: Is this a question of the few who are truly "*gedolim*"?

Rabbi Steinsaltz: Sometimes there is a historical phenomenon in which the few are not able to solve the problem, change the situation. Sometimes it comes from below to above. Sometimes it is 100 little people who begin to act together. There are processes like this throughout the range of history. Sometimes it is 100, 200, 300 who make the change. Take for instance the matter of the New Science. We can connect this to all kinds of people and names, but not with one person. Take chemistry. We cannot single out any one person as inventor of modern chemistry. There were many different little people who went in the same direction; a few hundred years later, there was a new world. All that was before, in this area, ceased to exist. So I don't think that it's one person who can do everything. Rather, it's often many small people working together who bring forth change, and results. You know the opening sentence of Dickens' *A Tale of Two Cities*: "It was the best of times, it was the worst of times." This describes, from a spiritual point of view, something of our own condition.

S.F.: When you began your work on translating the Gemara into Hebrew, making it available to the "Jewish everyman" in Israel—and later too to communities in the English–speaking, Russian, and French worlds—was your aim to help bring about this kind of spiritual change, which brings each Jew somehow closer to Torah, closer to God?

Rabbi Steinsaltz: As much as was possible. This was the aim. How successful it has been is another matter. Call it a messianic ambition.

Rabbi Berel Wein

Rabbi Berel Wein, a former director of the Orthodox Union, has been the rabbi of Bais Torah synagogue in Monsey, New York, and was a founder of Yeshiva Shaarei Torah. He is an enormously popular lecturer whose Torah tapes have reached many thousands of students. His book, *Triumph of Survival: The Story of the Jews in the Modern Era*, is the narrative of modern Jewish history told from the perspective of a wholly committed Orthodox Jew. For many summers, Rabbi Wein lectured in Jerusalem, and has recently with his wife made *aliyah* to Israel.

I spoke with Rabbi Wein at his Jerusalem home. I was deeply moved by his reflections on modern Jewish history and his awareness of the ongoing struggle of the Jewish people to survive in a world that has throughout history often been so hostile and cruel. The Rabbi's quickness of mind, humor, and great intelligence seemed to me a personal exemplification of some of the very qualities that our people have used in past struggles and may need in present and future ones.

S.F.: Since our principal writing is about the history of the Jewish people as a whole, I would like to know what you think is the *avodat Hashem* of *Am Yisrael?*

Rabbi Wein: To be a light unto the nations. To be a special holy people. To bring the ideas of monotheism to the world, the ideas of a personal God, the ideas of morality and basic values. To inject a spirit of optimism in life. To show that life and its incidents can be transcendent over the disappointments and pain that automatically come with life. The Jewish people are meant also to be a blessing to the world. Through the Jewish people, good things are meant to come to the world, whether that's in the realm of the spirit, or medicine, or music, or politics, in every facet of human behavior. That's the task that the Lord placed before us. At Sinai, He said, "You will be for Me a treasure amongst all the nations, a Holy people, a kingdom of priests." That sums it up. That's the constitution of the Jewish people.

The fact that we may not be perfect, and unable to achieve all of these goals, does not in any way change the challenge, or the goal itself. We try. And if we are not 100 percent successful, then we will be 90 percent, 80 percent. But this goal should never be lost, never lost sight of, be ignored. When people look at the Jew, they should see a godly person; they should see more than the person himself or herself.

S.F.: How are we doing historically? Do you see Christianity and Islam as, in a sense, signs of our success? And how do we relate to that

325

vast mass of the world in China and India that seems not to have been so influenced by Jewish teaching?

Rabbi Wein: There is no question that Christianity and Islam are a great step forward from paganism, and that both religions possess a bedrock of human and godly values that is common to Judaism and common to the Jewish ideal. They both spring from the Jewish people and from Judaism. There is no doubt therefore that it is a great and important thing. Certainly a step forward. As for the East and the Oriental religions, I am not an expert. I am not an expert on anything. But it seems to me, from the few times that I have been in the Orient, that even though the form of the religion is paganism, the attraction that it has is not necessarily belief in the idol that helps or harms. I don't think it's the primitive paganism that once existed, for instance, in Roman and Greek times, in Canaanite and Philistine times. It's much more sophisticated, perhaps even spiritual. It has just kept these ancient forms that have been common in the Orient for thousands of years. In fact, in *halachah* we find that the concept, "The customs of their forefathers still remain with them, even though they don't believe in it." One could say that Christianity is, so to say, a more refined Buddhism, because it also has idols and symbols, all sorts of pagan rituals that have remained within Christianity for centuries. Nevertheless, we do not think of Christianity as paganism because of the sophistication and spirit of ideas that lie behind it. I think to a certain extent that can be said about the Oriental religions as well. There are undoubtedly millions of people who believe in the idol as the idol. That's sad because it's not logical, it's not true, and it's really not productive. But I think that the intellectual sophisticated classes in the Orient who worship (their religion), do it in the form in which the religion has been for centuries, although their thoughts and ideas behind it are far more sophisticated, almost monotheistic. Buddhism is not that far from being a monotheistic religion. Shintoism in Japan is not far from being monotheism, insofar as having concepts of an Almighty. But it's the form that is definitely pagan. So it's the form that hinders them more than the idea.

S.F.: The question is often raised as to how we can be a light to the nations when we are not living that ideal itself. How do you see the spiritual situation of the Jewish people today—in the golden *golus* of

America and in Israel, which seems to have imported so much of American thinking these past years?

Rabbi Wein: The American exile is a separate chapter in Jewish history. In my opinion, it has no antecedent in terms of the opportunities that exist for Jews: to be part of society without any constraints or inhibitions, and also to remain Jewish at almost no cost. There was a time in the United States when, if you wanted to be a Sabbath observer, it knocked you out of a lot of professions. Today it does not knock you out of anything. There was a time when, if you wanted to eat kosher, you couldn't take a purchasing agent out to dinner. That doesn't exist anymore, in most of the United States. Paradoxically, I think that the United States affords Jews the easiest ride anywhere in the world, even compared to Israel, in being an observant Jew. Because there is almost no sacrifice. The sacrifice that is involved—you want to send your child to school, it costs you $20,000 tuition—is voluntary. But if people don't have the money, somehow the kids go to school anyway. Also, American Jewry has an affluence that the Jewish world has not known probably since the Golden Age of Spain. Even greater than that, there's a lot of Jewish money for a lot of things. That being said, I think that is what causes the extremes. Because it's so easy to be assimilated, people assimilate. I don't think that people assimilate out of choice; they assimilate out of ignorance. If you know more about Christmas that you do about Chanukah, if you know more American history than you do Jewish history, if you know about Marx but do not know about Maimonides—how do we expect a person to be Jewish? And the friction that has destroyed American Jewry is ignorance. When we speak about the state of Israel, I think that's the most important problem in this country too. It's not Meretz provoking riots on Bar Ilan Street. It's the fact that secular Israeli youth are completely ignorant—not that they made a choice—of the Jewish past, Jewish values, Jewish traditions, and ignorant in such a way that they are rootless because of it. They never attend the synagogue, ever. Can you imagine being a Jew and never walking into a synagogue? Leading Israeli government officials who visited the United States were forced to attend the synagogue for diplomatic, whatever, communal reasons. Many of them have said that it's the first time that they have been in a synagogue. Moshe Dayan, when he was in Washington for the Camp David Agreements went to the synagogue for the first time. He was very impressed by it. But that ignorance is a very, very difficult thing to overcome.

What happens in the United States is that, to a great extent, the rich get richer: the educated Jews, the committed Jews. And I am not just speaking about Orthodox Jews. There's a small segment of Conservative Jews that is committed. Unfortunately, it's a small segment. But they have programs and camps and seminars, schools of higher learning, and *collelim*. They have an intensive Jewish life today that never existed in the United States before. As for the other Jews, who are ignorant, they have nothing, absolutely nothing. And when one has nothing, why shouldn't he marry a non-Jew if that non-Jew is personally appealing? Why shouldn't he participate in the national holidays, Christmas and Easter? Even though they are religious holidays, they are seen as national holidays. What's wrong? Because he has nothing else to supplant them, no inner sense of who he is, he has to adopt the coloration of the society in which he lives. I think that's what brings about extremism. Because of these different, extreme circumstances, we have a large section of the Jewish people that is scholarly, intellectually aware, committed to Judaism, flaunting its Judaism. And we have a large section of Jews who don't have a clue what it is to be Jewish, and therefore they are not Jewish.

Here in the State of Israel, because of the troubles and the wars, and all of the other things, being Jewish takes on another meaning. The suicide bomber is not interested in whether you are a yeshiva student or a professing Communist. Everybody here is Jewish. That's one positive thing. On the negative side, such a large section of the population, perhaps half, is completely unaware of any Jewish values, traditions. The school system here is a shambles. Television is far worse than in the United States. It's much more childish, much more primitive. It emphasizes all the wrong things. There are so many great things to learn from America, and here they took all the garbage. All of this taken together, we have a great problem here, a problem 100 years, if not more, in the making. It's not going to be solved in 3 or 4 years.

But I think that steps are being taken, slowly, slowly. The State of Israel is much more attuned to its inner self than any outside manifestation. Because of this, therefore, I think that things will get better. But it's a long, long process.

S.F.: Are your historical works, your books, your tapes aimed largely at reaching the *frum* learned audience, which really does not have the historical dimension within traditional Gemara learning? Or are they too directed to those who are not within the world of traditional learning?

Rabbi Wein: It may be arrogant of me, but I have always prided myself on the fact that I say the exact same speech to an Aguda convention as I do to a group of Conservative Jews or to a Federation meeting, or to an Israel Bond dinner that I am invited to speak at. I don't make a different speech. I may translate the words differently, my mannerisms may be different, but basically the message is the same. When I wrote the history books, I felt that I wrote them for every Jew, even for non–Jews. And I think that's the effect that they've had. I think that they have confirmed, for the observant world, their belief in the Divine Hand that has guided us and brought us to this day. But they have also been informed of events and facts, historical personalities and historical patterns of which they were unaware; this, simply because the subject is not really dealt with in the traditional school system—until now. For the non–observant world, I think that they received not only those facts and patterns, but a sense of the spirituality of Jewish history. And Jewish history is the greatest aid to one's inner belief in the special role of the Jewish people. Just by reading Jewish history and knowing it, one should become a believer. So I am always surprised that Jewish historians are not believers. I am surprised that the great scientists are not believers. This apparently is part of the gift of free will given them by God. They become immune to what they are studying and seeing, and that presence of God which overwhelms most people is missed by them.

I wrote the book across the board. When I wrote I did not tailor it for anyone. The truth is, every book is somewhat tailored because publishers and editors are involved. The author rarely has the final word on every word in the book. So there was a minimum of compromising, mostly on personalities. But overall, the book is not tailored for anyone or to any particular audience. Yet it has sold widely and well among all circles, even amongst non–Jews. Having thought about it, I think that also should be expected. There's a tremendous interest in the world regarding the Jewish people. Jewish people are very interesting, and the non–Jewish world would like to know more about us. They would like to know about us from us, not necessarily from others. So I think that's basically what I have tried to do. And I am pretty happy with the result.

S.F.: Your work on the modern era is entitled *Triumph of Survival.* Is that the main theme of Jewish history?

Rabbi Wein: The main theme of the modern era for the Jewish people is that they have survived, beginning with the persecution of Jews in Czarist Russia and through the first world war, and through the Communist persecution, through the Holocaust, through the attempts of the world to destroy the State of Israel. I think that it's pretty remarkable that in 1996 there's a Jewish people, a State of Israel, that we are still making noise. There are two central points to the book. First, in spite of all odds, the Jewish people have survived, and to a certain extent prospered. We are better off than we were 250 years ago when the process started. Second, within the Jewish people, Torah has survived, which is also an unlikely thing after all the assaults of the Enlightenment and socialism, secularism and nationalism, and everything else that has happened to us, and the assimilation. It's also a remarkable thing that there should be a great thirst for Torah and a great deal of Torah, and an appreciation of Torah. That's why it is called *Triumph of Survival.* The mere survival itself indicates the triumph.

S.F.: And what about the relation to Redemption? The overall story of the Jewish people is a story of redemption. Are we closer to that now than we were at the outset of the modern era?

Rabbi Wein: Every day we are closer. I, for one, am very wary of speaking in Messianic or redemptive terms. Maimonides said that all these things are hidden, that they will happen at the right time, and that only God knows how they will happen, so we should not delve into it. Throughout the long history of the Jewish people, dealing with situations in Messianic or redemptive terms has always been counter-productive. We have to behave as if tomorrow is going to be normal. And that's how we have to live our lives. We have to believe that today the Messiah can come. It's interesting, but it's not clear to me exactly how the world is going to look when the Messiah comes. We may have to go to work the next day anyway. Still, we have to leave something for the next generation to do. I always say in the rabbinate, "My shoulders are not broad enough. I have to leave something for God to do also." I can't do everything. As for redemptive qualities and time, I hope too. I would like that Tisha B'Av should be cancelled. I'd like that it should be the holiday that it will be. But I bought a pair of gym shoes anyway. I think that this metaphor, however inexact it is, is a healthy understanding of how Jews should look at life.

S.F.: In our struggle to strengthen the Jewish people today, what about the two worlds of learning, the yeshiva and the university? Are there ways to better integrate the worlds of learning?

Rabbi Wein: It's not dependent upon me. In the United States, it's been proven—in the last 50 years, especially over the last 30 years that not only can it happen, but when it happens, we produce an extraordinary human being. There are so many doctors of medicine who are scholars in *halachah*. I don't think that's ever happened before in Jewish history: mini–Maimonides; very mini. There are great *talmidei chachamim* who are in every avenue of life. There are great *roshei yeshiva* who have graduated from the greatest universities. Not all of them will admit to it, but nonetheless that's a fact. So I don't think that we have to reinvent the wheel. The problem is in this country, but not quite so great as it was 20, 30 years ago. Slowly, slowly, slowly, we are seeing the change. It will come about. Not everybody need go to university. I think it's an individual choice. I think that the opportunity to make that individual choice should be present. And institutions that allow this individual choice should also be present.

S.F.: I was thinking of the university in other terms, as, what some have called, the disaster area of modern Jewish life, the place where assimilation had its great impetus. To go back and ask again, what do you believe has moved people away from Judaism, both historically and now?

Rabbi Wein: People historically moved away from being Jewish because of persecution, because of lack of opportunity. Heinrich Heine said, "Becoming Christian is the entrance ticket into Western civilization." That's not true anymore. What moves people away from being Jewish today is, first, that they are ignorant of what it means to be Jewish. We can't therefore say that they are moving away. They don't even know what we are talking about. Second, the entire culture of "having a good time," of being unfettered, creates a climate that makes it very difficult to be Jewish. To be Jewish, one can't sleep until 12 o'clock on Sunday morning. Rabbi Feldman in his excellent book on Judaism mentions that one of his congregants came to this startling realization. It means that one can't do everything. It means that one's sexual life is inhibited. It means that one's dress is inhibited, one's speech is inhibited. There are a lot of barriers. In current American life, which has few barriers, it's hard to sell that type of life to people who have no knowledge and appreciation of why they should even consider it.

S.F.: But isn't there something else? Jews, people born as Jews, are found in almost all the cults way out of proportion to our numbers. There is some kind of spiritual hunger, which somehow is not being answered or met for many. Are there tactics, means that we should be using, which we are not? What more should be done?

Rabbi Wein: Every facet of communication should be used to reach people. In our time, this includes print media, computer media, CD-ROM, movies. I think that movies that explain Judaism in an entertaining fashion to millions of people would be very important. People say that movies are no good because they are pornographic, etc. But movies are neutral. It depends on what is done with them. Audiotapes, videotapes—I don't think that there is any realm of communication we should leave untouched. I think of my experience with my audiotapes, how the yeshiva has sold close to 400,000. I estimate that at least three people hear every tape. So that's a lot of people we've reached, and it's had a profound effect on some. People have written to me. People have come to talk to me. It's not without effect. There's a whole genre now of Torah tapes that are on the market. I am not the only one, thank God. But the other areas of media are just as important. I think that there should be more books, more effort at reaching masses of people through the mass communications that exist today. If one had more money, then one could buy a half hour of television time once a month and have a good program of Jewish content. If one could do that in Israel, then it's worth having 300 schools opened. There are a lot of Jewish radio programs in the United States now. And they've been quite successful: in south Florida, in the New York area. I think it can be syndicated nationally, and it will be. Here in Israel, there are lot of little radio stations.

S.F.: Arutz Sheva has made a tremendous difference, politically and educationally, here.

Rabbi Wein: That's one example. But if we had an Arutz Sheva on television, it would make an even greater difference. I think that's how we have to go. Little segments of the Orthodox world may oppose. But when it happens and it's successful, then it will prove itself.

S.F.: One of the problems we also have today is the division within the Orthodox world. There are, it seems, many good Jews deep in their own world who simply cannot see or value what anyone else does. Is there some solution to this? Or is this an internal problem that we will always have to live with?

Rabbi Wein: It's always been that way, which doesn't mean that we should not try to improve it. I think that it's especially true among Jews. We are such a minority in the world, 12 million out of 6.5 billion. So we are in effect saying that most of the world doesn't know what the heck it is talking about. That's part of the ethos of being Jewish. The "I am the only one who's right" syndrome is built into the Jewish psyche. And that gives sustenance to these types of views. Again, there are people who have broader views. These are the people who are obligated to write and to speak and create, and do something. The mere fact that not everyone is going to agree does not in any way mitigate the importance of what's being done.

S.F.: I know that you are an optimistic person by nature, and that the Jew is required to see good in creation and work for greater good, and to try and finish with something good. How do you see our time in relation to other times the Jewish people have known?

Rabbi Wein: This generation is a transitional one. European Jewry is gone. Basically, the people who created the state are gone. To a large extent, even the great non-believers are gone. And this is a generation of the desert. We left one place, but did not get to the other yet. So it's hard to tell. But I think that the Jewish people and the Jewish state, 50 or 100 years from now, will be much more deeply rooted in Jewish values. I think that the Jewish people are on the verge of a renaissance in all areas of life, physical and spiritual. But there are a lot of hard things that we have to go through, none of which come easily. There are great physical dangers to the State of Israel. But while we have to do our best ultimately God has to save us from the scuds. I think that the inner fiber of the people, the inner devotion, is stronger now that it was. For instance, I find Reform Judaism moving in two different directions at the same time. On the one hand, they have become much more radical. Every current, politically correct position has become theirs. But on the other hand, there's a large section of the Reform leadership that would like to have more ritual, more tradition. Also, the movement of *baalei teshuvah*, even though I don't think that it will be a tidal wave, is a river that continues. And I think that traditional Jewry, though not without losses, is no longer hemorrhaging the way it once was. I would say that it is able to keep the vast majority of its youth, 75 or 80 percent. In our hearts, we would like it to be 100 percent. That's not the case. But the vast majority is there today, which was not the case 30, 40, 50 years ago. So, as in every generation of change, it's hard for us to see the future. And it's a scary time. But on the whole, in many respects, we are headed in the right direction.

A Few Preliminary and Partial Conclusions

How do we serve God?

Rabbi Menachem Fruman when he speaks about the traditional threefold way through Avodah Shel B' Lev (prayer), Torah (Learning), and Gemilut Chasadem (acts of kindness) adds another element, i.e. through doing all this with humility. He gives us then a hint at what Rabbi Eliahu Avichail will make clear in talking about his own individual service of God, that there are distinctive individual ways in serving God, styles, if you will of serving God. And as Rabbi Avichail indicates, this means through finding one's own special path and work in serving God. This insight connects up well with the brilliantly expounded Kookian thesis of Rabbi Moredechai Gafni that each one through his own life-story finds a way to serve God, i.e. that each one in finding and making a unique path in life and with this a true meeting with their own self finds the way to serve God. This too is affirmed by Professor Israel Levine when he connects the Service of God with the development of an individual's potentials and abilities. We serve God by bringing out the best in ourselves and by developing our powers in service of God.

It is not surprising then that for most of those interviewed in this work who are, after all, teachers of Judaism, the path to service of God is best found and exemplified in teaching others. As for traditional Jews Torah learning is the highest activity of all, the supreme human way to come near to God so teachers like Rabbi Eisen, Phil Chernofsky, Rabbi Aviner stress this way in learning as the true path in service of God.

Another group of teachers would however place less emphasis on traditional Yeshiva Gemara learning, and work for a conception of Jewish knowledge and teaching which is in their eyes truer to Jewish creation through the generations. So Rabbis Amsel, Berman, and Hartman advocate a curriculum for Jewish learning which encompasses Tanach and Midrash and Gemara and Kabbalah, and Jewish thought and culture. They would otherwise wish to develop a kind of Jewish mind in service of God which encompasses the best the Jews have thought and done through the ages. Along with and perhaps beyond this Professor Ravitzky would see that only through meeting with 'outside forces' can one truly explain and develop Jewish thought. And this idea by no means contradicts the conception of Rabbis Eisen and Levine, of Phil Chernofsky and Professor Schweid and Dr. Shavit that the search for truth in all areas of life, in all fields of study is the service of God. And this when this search for truth as in the research of Rabbi Wein and the explorations of Dr. Shavit has its historical dimension. If after all, all is the Creation of God, then the wonders of God's creation can be made apparent in all fields of study and learning.

If however the concentration of these teachers in their own work and service is naturally in the world of learning this does not mean that they understand the service of God as privilege of a caste or elite. In opposite many of the teachers interviewed here go out of their way to stress that the service of God is open to each and everyone no matter how great their 'learning.' Both Rabbis Eisen and Gafni have often evoked the image of the simple shoemaker who effects 'unifications of God's names' through stitching with devotion and dedication. Prof. Ravitzky in a modest declaimer makes it clear that he by no means holds himself to be one who can dare to claim continually holds God before him. The goal of serving God in all which one does with all one's mind and consciousness may be close to impossible to perfect achievement. But each one has his way and his opportunity.

In this Rabbi Adin Steinsaltz indicates how difficult and unsure in results we can be in our service of God. He teaches how the effort to come nearer to God in prayer is an effort which always leaves room for our deepening humility, as it may well be that the closer we come the farther away we sense we are. In this, of course, the service of God is an unending task, an infinite opportunity open before us.

As in prayer, so too in our action in the world, the ways are many and the results not always clear. Miriam Adahan, whose lifework is in helping others, frequently teaches that our one real commandment is to walk in God's ways, to follow God's most prominent trait and be compassionate. Acts of goodness and helping others are the way to serve God. And many of the teachers of Torah interviewed here have devoted much of their lives to helping others, often in communal work. If in the past many of the greatest Jewish thinkers, Saadia Gaon, Rambam, and Ramban among others were also communal leaders, so too today, many of the teachers of Judaism are also people of action in the world.

This communal dimension is emphasized by Rabbis Berman and Levine, Aviner, Hess, Avichail each in his own way. And their action raises the question of what the true communal service of God is not only for individuals but for the Jewish people and the people of Israel as a whole. Is it congregation building in America which Rabbi Feldman has done so admirably? Is it being a communal leader and builder in Beit El as Rabbi Aviner has done? Is it in the building of educational institutions? Or is it in a work like Rabbi Avichail's which is educating to Jewishness those uncertainly Jewish?

One clear answer and central theme of this work is that the service of God for many in this generation has involved returning the Jewish people to the land of Israel, and helping build Israel as a people and as a nation. And while there are questions as to the direction this effort has taken (witness Prof. Schweid's lament over the lack of development of true Jewish culture in Israel) there is on the part of many of the teachers such as Dr. Sivan, Rabbi Aviner, Avichail a great sense of the religious and redemptive power of the Jewish people's return to the land of Israel. And this without anyone here having the illusion that the service is complete, and that the work wholly done, and that we have even for one instant the right to take for granted our presence in the land, and God's presence among us.

After all many of the teachers here argue that our real service and task is to shape ourselves into a holy people, one who God will be present among. And if it is impossible to begin to outline here all the transformations in life this requires still it is clear that the path to this is along the traditional commandment to love justice, do mercy, and walk humbly with our God. The service of God is in other words in making our people the living exemplification of that ethical monotheism, that moral light which we have been commanded to be.

This view it must however be made clear is not the view of all

the teachers here. Many, perhaps those especially aware of how Messianic claims have led to disaster in Jewish history, urge more modest conceptions for Jewish service. Rabbis Hartman and Wein, sensitive to the
sufferings of Jewish history, feel that the great accomplishment and goal
is 'survival as a people' and survival in learning Torah. Rabbi Berman
too whose work has involved understanding the meaning of the Holy
Temple's symbolism has a sense of us being far from ready for the
reinstitution of Temple rite. His emphasis is on building community
service even at the most local level. And this when he does see Israeli
and Jewish accomplishments for excellence in diverse areas of life as a
basis for sanctification. And this when too there is a whole group of
thinkers who feel that we are in the midst of a historical redemptive
process, and that our service to God means building the land and people
of Israel now in our generation. And this toward a more complete and
true service of God in the future. And this when clearly we are in the
middle of the work, forbidden to desist from undertaking it even though
we know it is not for us alone to complete it.

Afterword: A Concluding Dialogue with Myself, on My Own Conception of, and Story, in Avodat Hashem

Q: You have interviewed over forty-five rabbis and teachers of Torah on the subject of 'Service of God'. You have studied the subject for a number of years now. What is your conclusion? What do you understand about it? What do you have to tell the world about it?

S.F.: I don't know at the moment. I will need some time to think. I want to also reread what others have said, study the notes I have collected for the past few years. I also want to try and somehow come to terms with the strong reluctance in me to say anything. There is in me now and there has been the sense that I may not have any real 'right' to speak on this subject.

Q: But you have already published one book on this subject. And your thought is to a degree revealed there? You weren't shy then.

S.F.: I had then and I have now the fear that I may be 'presuming' and that I might be punished for this presumption. For who am I? After all I am not a 'learned person' in Jewish terms. I am not a rabbi. I have no authority.

Q: It's clear. You are saying what you think. This is your view of the subject. You do not have to fear that the whole world is automatically going to adopt your conclusions, and have its fate decided by them.

S.F.: It is not only that. There is some truly deep feeling in me that I do not know anything really. There is in me a deep uncertainty as to

343

whether I have any right to say anything.

Q: But you have defined your own life purpose as service of God? You have made it the leading ideal of all your work?

S.F.: I know that. But who am I after all?

Q: You keep on protesting your own humility. And yet you have written these works, have asserted yourself.

S.F.: The choice was between 'doing nothing' and 'trying to do what I thought God wanted.' It was not a choice in which I was certain of being right.

Q: The service of God means choosing, means using our freedom to choose to walk in God's way?

S.F.: As I write this now I sense I am striving to serve God. That is my intention.

Q: But you also question and doubt your own intention. You all the time live with the question of whether you are really serving God, or in fact 'using God' to serve yourself.

S.F.: I cannot answer this, I cannot be my own judge. God is the judge. I can strive to make a connection between the will of God, and my own good. In other words not to live with the 'either for God or for myself' ideal, but with the 'for God, and for myself ideal': But again it is for God to judge.

Q: So all that you are doing now 'in service of God' might conceivably be judged by Hashem as 'wrong,' as 'evil,' as 'something you are to be punished for'?

S.F.: I cannot know for certain. I again can only strive to do what I believe to be the will of God.

Q: But this makes you much different from most of the teachers of Torah you have been speaking with. Many of them speak with authority and certainty, with a tone of deep faith and understanding, with a sense that they definitely know what it means to serve God, and that they are doing this.

S.F.: They have more right to authority than I do. They are much more learned than me. They are in most cases rabbis with semichah.

Q: And yet you by listening to more than one of them, by bringing them together, you who know so much less than each of them in effect make some kind of critique of each one, undermine his absolute authority, juxtapose him with other authorities?

S.F.: That was not my idea. My idea has been to 'learn' from each one their idea of Service of God, and bring all I have learned together. It is to make a composite definition. And not to make this definition as if it were final, closed, complete. But rather to present it to the reader as a package of possibilities from which the reader can learn and choose. For after all the aim of the work is to HELP THE READERS IN THEIR SERVICE OF GOD. And this with the idea that just as the teachers of the Torah have a 'service of God' to do, so do each and every one of us.

Q: But behind all this is a presumption; and the presumption is that the main goal of our lives is to serve God? How do you know this? How do you prove this? How are you sure that this is what God demands of us?

S.F.: I read this assumption as central to, flowing through Tanach: and through the works of the Mishneh and Gemara. And I read it as central to the Jewish religious tradition. God is Above, God is the Ruler and Commander, God is the King, God is the Creator, God is the Judge. And it is our task to do not what we ourselves feel we want to do, not what our Yetzer Hara pushes us to, but rather what God demands of us.

Q: But most people in the modern Western world would laugh at such an idea. We all know the first rule of our own world is that the person does what will make him happy, or will make him most fulfilled, or what will bring him to what he conceives as best for himself. Each individual takes himself, and his own life as the highest end.

S.F.: And I in my life and experience have come to the conclusion that such an approach is ultimately self-defeating. It is short-sighted. I have come to the conclusion that living such a way leads to ultimate failure. And that therefore the only true way to best serve oneself is to serve the Transcendent, the Eternal, that which lives beyond our lives.

Q: But what if that service is of an imaginary idea and concept?

S.F.: It still might be to one's advantage. But I do not really hold such a cynical idea. I truly believe that God has created us, does move us, does demand our showing a certain kind of relationship.

Q: The concept of service of God sounds as if it belongs to another era, one in which there were slaves. Don't you find it 'degrading' to in this day and age think of yourself as a 'servant'?

S.F.: I think of the meaning of LA-AVOD and connect it in my mind and heart with the English word 'work.' I connect it with the idea of one's principal life activity, what one does for livelihood, what one has a duty to do. And I recognize that in 'working for Someone' I am subordinated to the commands, the demands of God. I do not feel in any way humiliated by this because the subordination itself comes out of a 'recognition' of reality, a recognition of the true position and place of the Creator and Ruler of the Universe in relation to one small mortal. In other words what I am saying is that this recognition and relationship does not involve degradation for me but rather comes out of what I know to be true, as to my own 'place' in the world.

Q: But why do you have to see it this way? Who says God created you? Where is your proof, that God rules? Isn't it possible that you are simply 'inventing a power' which is to somehow be able to overcome the limitations which you yourself cannot? Your invention of God may serve you, but it is nonetheless an invention.

S.F.: I have never put much effort in proving objectively the existence of God. This has never concerned me. I just feel that those without God are as Miriam Adahan teaches somehow defective in personality. They lack a dimension that those who have a relationship with God do not.

Q: Perhaps you so believe in and need God because you experience your own inadequacies in an acute way. Perhaps the 'higher class' of people are those with such a large degree of self-confidence, that they really do not need God. They are happy to enjoy themselves, live their own lives.

S.F.: I cannot speak against them or prove anything to them. Rabbi Gafni teaches our service of God is the unique story of our own lives.

I believe strongly that my service of God is connected with my life-story. I think of my deep need for God coming out of the sufferings of my childhood. I think of how God has been to me consolation and answer when certain people could not be. I believe, too, that I am simply the kind of character who so greatly needs God, that I cannot manage my world without God.

Q: But in this work, you do not concentrate on telling the story of your own life, but rather try to have others tell their own stories?

S.F.: I have a part in much of what I have met. Their stories may become part of my story. And again there is the idea of the service of God as something which each one of us does as an individual and yet all do taken together as part of Israel, or in a wider sense as a part of mankind.

Q: But what exactly do you do in your life which makes it a 'service of God'?

S.F.: I think 'kavvanah' is important, is essential. Clearly those who are continually engaged in the effort to serve God must concentrate in mind to do so. They should be 'trying' to serve God. And most important for the Jew there is the direction, the guideline of the Halachah. The service of God is in living by the traditional Jewish way of walking in the way of God.

Q: Are you saying that the eighty percent of the world's Jews who do not live strictly by Halachah, and the ninety-nine plus percent of the world's people who do not live by Halachah are not serving God?

S.F.: Not at all. I am not the judge of others in this. I am just saying that the religious Jew considers the 'will of God' expressed, embodied in both the Written and the Oral Law. And that means that for this kind of person that there are directions. It is against the will and service of God to murder, to commit adultery, and to steal one's neighbor's property. Moreover it is understood, commanded that the Jew as part of his service of God know this law, learn.

Q: Don't most of the teachers of Torah you speak with glorify themselves and their own activity, argue that the highest activity of life, the truest way of serving God is through learning Torah?

S.F.: Clearly 'learning' is essential, but it is learning 'for action's sake'. To learn alone is not enough. And many of the teachers of Torah speak about each one in his own activity doing it with 'mesirut' with such dedication and such 'devekut' to God, that it too is service of God in the highest way. So many Rabbis (Rabbi Tropper, Rabbi Gafni, Rabbi Feldman etc.), talk about each one in his own work can serve God. So I don't feel that for most there is this self-enclosed exaltation of Torah learning alone.

Q: You are not being completely honest here. So many do talk about Torah learning as highest, not only as form of learning but as service of God in every way.

S.F.: Clearly the Avodah shel b' Lev (Prayer), and Learning Torah, and Gemilut Chasadem (through which we try to follow the Middot of the Compassionate God) are the traditional formula for serving God. And clearly individuals, according to their situation, character are engaged in varying degrees in these activities. I for instance feel myself much stronger in prayer than in learning.

Q: Aren't you being very modest? You are a gabbai. You are often involved in helping others in all kinds of small ways. You really do feel for others and want to help them whenever you can. Your soul and spirit are filled with 'ahavat chinam.' You do greet people generally with 'a shining and welcoming countenance.' Wherever you are you find some way to help others.

S.F.: It is true I 'love to give to and help others.' This is a great source of joy in my life. But it is important for me to be fair and not exaggerate here. Most of my deeds of kindness are small. I am not really anything like a tsaddik: I make no great sacrifices in helping others. I can think of hundreds of ordinary people who do much more than me.

Q: You are saying you serve God when it is convenient for you to do so?

S.F.: No. There are many things I do which I would often rather not do. But I know that it is commanded.

Q: The idea of the person 'giving up something,' 'sacrificing something' to serve God is one which appeals to many. How do you view this?

S.F.: There are Jews who 'gave up their lives' in the service of God. This today can be soldiers fighting to defend the land of Israel, as it in the past was great individuals who 'stood against idolatry' or 'forced conversion'. There is no doubt that Kiddush Hashem is one of the highest ways of serving God.

Q: But it is not the main way for most?

S.F.: Our religion is a religion of life, not of death. Judaism stresses the making of a good life in this world. But it is senseless for me to try to imagine what I would do. I don't know. I would like to think I would choose the way of God.

Q: But aren't there cases where your need for convenience overrules your sense of Halacha?

S.F.: I do not claim I am without error or sin. I do not claim to be the exemplary servant of God.

Q: But what do you give God then?

S.F.: I agree that one essential part of serving God is giving. I most often do what I do without making an accounting. Clearly I would like my work in writing to serve God. I would like to serve God through giving to others, helping others in their service of God.

Q: So for you the work on this book is a form of, perhaps the main form in your life of service of God?

S.F.: Clearly I have in mind the idea of serving God through this work. And this is another reason I went to 'learn' from others. I understood that I by myself alone do not know enough, am not strong enough in insight and wisdom and learning to really do the work in the best way.

Q: You bring others into your work, and so in effect 'sacrifice' some of the credit you would get if the work were all your own. You moreover defer to others and in this 'act of self-abnegation' aim to serve the idea of service of God.

S.F.: I know there is a less generous way of interpreting my asking others. It is arguable that what I am doing is 'making use' of them. I will take what I can from them, and then in the end subordinate them to my work, idea, name.

Q: You did not have to make that accusation against yourself. A Jew is forbidden to testify against himself.

S.F.: Many of the academic people I spoke with, Prof. Ravitzky, Prof. Levine spoke of the great value of the search for truth. This has been a central value of my life. I sense myself in this SERVICE OF GOD searching for the 'truth' about the 'subject' even when the truth does not always flatter me.

Q: But where is it written that this kind of continual self-examination, this inner exploration which you have engaged in for close to thirty years in writing is what God demands of us as service of God? Where is it written that the Jew should be so preoccupied with 'inner self' and idea?

S.F.: A number of the teachers of Torah cite Rav Kook and talk about the importance of finding the ANOCHI, the essential self. There is the sense that being in touch with our authentic self is the way to true service of God.

Q: Which authentic self? The pure 'soul' which exists before our birth? The self we are conscious of all the time in our everyday life in consciousness? The self we make through our work, our lifestory?

S.F.: There is always the sense that for the Jew it is not enough to save himself alone. And that the true emphasis of the Jew must be in the whole network of his life relationships. The true self is found in the way one is a child, and the way one is a spouse and a parent. And it is in the way one relates to one's fellows. And in one's work. It is the whole action of our being. And our aim of serving God should be reflected in all these relationships. In each we should aim at the highest degree of holiness possible, the highest degree of blessedness possible.

Q: But how can the person possibly be a 'blessing' wherever he goes and in whatever he does? Are you such a blessing?

S.F.: I am so far from this I somewhat reluctantly relate it as an ideal. But I know that this striving to realize the ideal is too our service of God. And this when I do know how much of my life has been, and is, waste, stupidity, trivial and senseless thoughts, clowning vulgarity, lust, envy, ill-will, sin.

Q: You are saying that a key element in the service of God, is the struggling against our own inner impulses, the overcoming of our own yetzer hara, the transforming of our life moments from profane to sacred?

S.F.: Imagine a mind which was totally devoted to loving God. A mind as a poem, or continual sacred learning. One can imagine such a mind. But I myself know how far I, and most are from this. What I do have, and this is a strong element in my own service of God, is a SET OF IDEALS AND INTENTIONS FOR SERVICE OF GOD.

Q: You are saying that one essential element in serving God is an inner intention, will to serve God.

S.F.: Perhaps many assume this. But I believe it should be made most clear. The consciousness of the will to serve God is key to serving God.

Q: And why do you have such a will? And how can others be made to have such a will who do not have it?

S.F.: I again came to this idea after years of serving primarily an idea of my own greatness. I came to see the vanity of such self-worship. I came 'logically' to understand that only with God's help and will could most of my own 'goals' be realized.

I too, and this is an important element, came to this need to serve God out of my love for and desire to help and save others. We are all mortal. We see what happens to those we most love. We long for their continued life. Only God can bring us to a higher world of blessedness. So out of love for other human beings one comes to a recognition of the need of God. And one begins to serve God. And this with the idea that a service which begins in difficulty and overcoming one's own reluctance will become in time a service of joy.

I believe my own experience with prayer is the best testimony I have here. I began reluctantly, slowly with difficulty. Now I so much need and so much love to pray. There are days when prayer is the blessing of my life.

Q: So what in effect you are saying is you are prescribing that others' work in your path make some kind of 'teshuvah' and make the service of God central to their life?

S.F.: I cannot presume to prescribe for anyone. I can give my example, including the example of 'my change in thought.' But I know people's situations and characters are highly varied. I imagine they can come to their relationship to God in many different ways.

Q: You are very liberal. And what if the person says they do not need or want to serve God, that this adds nothing to their lives?

S.F.: I myself believe that such a person has a 'defective' perception of reality. I believe the person does not 'know the world' or know themselves truly. But I am not a person who loves to argue and persuade, not one who loves to prove himself the 'right' one in a dispute. It's simply not my way in mind.

Q: And this points to another of your many defects and inadequacies in service of God. You are not much of a Gemara learner, even though you 'learn' at a fixed hour every day?

S.F.: I believe with Prof. Ravitzky that it is impossible to expect all the Jewish world to learn in only one way. I am reluctant to define degrees of sanctity. But I believe that if the person learns with a will to serve God, and to contribute to the Jewish people and mankind, learns with a sense of respect and creative effort then there is no less holiness in learning Tanach than in learning pure Gemara, in learning Jewish history than in learning 'halachah.'

Q: By this you reveal yourself to not really belong to the 'orthodox world' which most of the people you have spoken within these interviews do belong to?

S.F.: Hashem created many different kinds of Jews, many different kinds of people. I would like to believe that those who truly will to serve God do serve God. But I am not the judge of this.

Q: But you are against those groups of Jews who turn completely inward, who will give no respect, recognition, no place to anything other than what they have within themselves?

S.F.: I believe our service of God means a sense of responsibility and obligation before the community, the Jewish community, and mankind. I believe those groups of Jews who withdraw into their own ideal purity are somehow defective morally. There must be responsibility for Clal

Yisrael, and this means too today before Medinat Yisrael, and Jews outside of Israel.

Q: But here you define your own circle, and think to exclude others.

S.F.: The service of God means on the communal level the service to Clal Yisrael. It means having a sense of the history of the Jewish people, above all of our relation with our covenant with Hashem.

Q: How is it you were so hesitant in defining the service of God on the individual level, and now bring forth with such great readiness definitions on the communal level?

S.F.: Perhaps my sense of how greatly Jews have suffered in the past is what leads me here to an effort at strengthening us. But though I believe such effort necessary, believe that we must act to help each other in history I certainly do not have absolute confidence what the short-range outcomes will be. I again am pointing to what I 'believe right for us' not what I know for certain is right.

Q: You seem to return again and again to the idea that the Jewish people by moving to extremes of assimilation on one side, and 'closed-off-fundamentalist isolation' on the other are diminishing their strength in the great moderate center where other worlds are met with and contended with.

S.F.: I know some of the teachers of Torah I have spoken with have a sense of imminent Messiah. And this leads to an extremism of one kind. Others seem to have withdrawn from history. I have the sense that our struggle is a historical day-to-day one. That just as the individual Jew must seek to serve God in each and every life action so must the people in its communal actions in history now.

Q: But to what end? Redemption? You do not seem so willing to talk about the imminent Redemption as you were a few years ago.

S.F.: I do not know the ways of God. If I have difficulty knowing what God wants for me as an individual how can I expect to know with certainty what God wants in each specific historical, situation for our people? To me it has seemed that we in the past few years have broken our covenant, retreated from the land Hashem promised us, endangered ourselves. But others argue our action is to bring what Hashem wants above all, peace and harmony, a new era of well-being for mankind.

Q: You do not have the sense of things going the right way, of being on the right path as you did a few years ago? You have lost the sense of 'inevitablity of' fulfilling the plan and promise, a few more steps after what happened in June '67?

S.F.: I am troubled. I believe the service of God is in following God's plan for redemption, returning of the people to the land, building of a society of justice in Israel. I see we have suffered a number of setbacks. And this when clearly I know it is mistaken to expect to all go in one direction, all go smoothly uphill.

Q: You are troubled not only by withdrawal from the land. You are troubled by withdrawal from a certain ideal. The whole motion toward becoming a typical Western consumer society, with all its imitation, low culture distresses you.

S.F.: We have served God by being a special people, special in holiness, special in our dedication to Hashem, special in our family purity, special in our love of and help of each other, special in our compassion and 'gemilut chasadem'.

Q: So you are not so tolerant after all. For those who have an idea of Israel as typical secular consumer society you have no patience?

S.F.: I believe we are a special people whose essential meaning is in our serving God. And that this should reflect in our walking as close as possible to the way God has given us. I believe when we do not do this we are alienated from our own essence, in contradiction with ourselves. I fear for us when we are others and cease to be ourselves.

Q: Haven't you after all the years in Israel seen come to know how 'not special, how ordinary' so many people are in Israel? How many do not make any connection with our being a covenant people, a chosen people, a people consecrated to God.

S.F.: Historically we serve God through our special relationship with God, through following complicated demands of God. Our living by the Torah is proof of our loyalty to God.

Q: You may deny it, but it is clear your 'program' is to make Am Yisrael return, and do Teshuva.

S.F.: This is of course a goal.

Q: And what gives you the authority to judge who is best serving God, and who not?

S.F.: I do not have authority. I am expressing my own thoughts, ideas, about the subject of *avodat Hashem*. These ideas are shared by a good part of the Jewish people.

Q: Wouldn't you be wiser to have a much broader idea of *avodat Hashem*? For instance HaRav Kook recognized the redemptive value of the work of socialist Zionist pioneers who in no way shared his religious vision. Rabbi Irving Greenberg sees that all kinds of people religious or not have the capacity to contribute to Tikkun Olam. Why don't you broaden your idea of the service of God to include those who are 'doing good for humanity' without having any God-related intention at all?

S.F.: It is God's task, and not any human's to judge what true *avodat Hashem* is. And this when I do have a sense that anyone who is improving the health, the well-being, the wisdom of mankind is 'serving God.' But I do believe Jews have their own special unique tasks in service of God. And this just as I believe each individual given his character situation goals has his own special way of serving Hashem.

Q: And yours once again has been in writing, including the writing of vast amounts of work which will never be known?

S.F.: Rabbi Steinsaltz talks about praying and not knowing what we have achieved in it. There are times we pray and we feel at the time we have done something, yet nothing of this remains. And other times when we might at the time feel we have done nothing, and yet have really achieved something. So I am reluctant to judge whether what now seems to be failure is failure in my work.

What I will say is that it is clear to me my own story, my own life, my own service of God has not been one steady uphill motion from success to success. In opposite it is filled with failures, breakdowns, mistakes. But of course brokenness, fragmentation, and their healing very often deepen our connection with Hashem. And there is a going down which may be necessary for a greater redemption.

Q: You once thought that the basic pattern of your life was a simple one of failure outside of Israel, and return to Israel which also was return to the religious tradition, creation of family, the turning of work to religious meaning.

S.F.: When I think of the setbacks of my own personal life, when I think of what I take to be the 'setbacks' the people of Israel have suffered in recent years I know how there 'failings' are connected with a deeper longing for God, a deeper need for connection with God.

Q: Why don't you say it more simply: 'Suffering helps us better serve God'. The once born person cannot know God as the twice born person can. Only those who have felt longing, loss, need for God's help most deeply connect with God. The suffering servant is the one who serves God best.

S.F.: I know the truth of this, and yet it strongly contradicts a fundamental truth many teachers of Torah, especially Hasidic ones live by, i.e. the true service of God is in Simchah. The joy of doing mitzvot is the highest service of God. Among others my holy teacher David Herzberg tries to teach this wherever he goes.

Q: But you yourself fall very very far from the mark? In fact you in your character show a certain love of sadness, longing, sorrow, perhaps even grief. Painful beauty, longing for God in sorrow is a strong element in your 'worship of God'.

S.F.: I believe we can serve God with all kinds of feelings so long as they are directed by a sacred intention.

Q: Again. Your own life is filled with failures, losses, sufferings, grief. People who you most loved and most wanted to help were not helped by you. In your childhood you strove to help your father, and could not. I will not make a list of all those you wanted to help, and did not. You are not exactly a good example of one who has 'served God' by helping others. This is also true in the realm of returning Jews to love of God. In the teaching of Torah you have no real accomplishments.

S.F.: I have never thought of myself as an 'ideal' servant of God, or even as a 'very good' servant of God. I know how small I am.

Q: You are with God now as you were with your father as a child, always striving to 'do good' and 'be justified' and never doing enough, never receiving the 'approval' and 'justification' you longed for. And this means you continually sin because 'you are not happy with your share,' you are always seeking more.

S.F.: There are times in my life, usually each day in prayer when I feel I am wholly where I am. There have been times in my life in my family life, in love, when I have had this sense of blessedness. But as a rule the truth is I am as a person always 'striving to do more.' I see this in my work.

Q: In other words you are ruled by the 'yetzer hara'. You are a person who is greedy for achievements, even if spiritual achievements.

S.F.: There is so much to do.

Q: But you have never been the kind of person who wars to right the world's injustices, who is striving all the time to correct society's wrongs.

S.F.: There are many kinds of the service of God which I myself have small part in. This does not mean I do not recognize their great importance. No one person can be expected to be strong in all areas of service of God.

Q: You have made greater efforts in the course of time of helping others. And you are involved in certain 'tsedekah' work. But it is not as great as it might be.

S.F.: I often give without knowing whether I am giving to those who have real need. I often give without knowing whether I am giving enough. I too often wonder whether I should not be working more for that ideal state where each one has enough, and does not need others, charity.

Q: You on the one hand admire greatly the Haredi world in which there is so much 'tsedekah' and on the other hand are repelled by so many who do not seem to want to work and earn.

S.F.: The whole question of whether the Jewish world demands more 'productive economic work,' or even more 'learning for learning's sake' is a real one. And I admit I do feel more comfortable in a world where most families make their 'parnosseh' through their own work. But again I cannot be a judge here.

Q: You too are far from realizing and living your own ideal in this?

S.F.: I have much to be grateful for. And if I have not been able to realize my own ideal I too understand that as a way of teaching my humility.

Q: You do make much of the idea that 'being grateful' to God for the good we have been given is essential to the worship and service of God?

S.F.: Every human being has 'gifts' in their life which they did not make themselves. Their own life is such a gift. And the world in its goodness when it is good. And whatever abilities they have. And the world of people who are with them. The search to find the good, to emphasize the good, to be grateful to the good is an essential part of the Jewish way of seeing the world. For we believe that God made the world, made life for goodness and blessedness.

Q: This means too being grateful and blessing for the evil we receive as well as for the good.

S.F.: I heard this from Rabbi Abraham Phelbin. People whenever some suffering comes to them ask 'why.' They do not 'ask' why for all the good they receive. The Jew is commanded both to bless on the good and on the evil.

Q: Does this mean that you have come to a position like Rabbi Leff's in which you believe that even the worst of evils has its Divine Reason which if not now but then at some point, perhaps in the eyes of eternity makes it understandable? Do you in other words believe the true service of God means this ability to take in deep and unshaken faith whatever happens?

S.F.: I know many people who have stronger faith than myself. I tend to put myself in the category of those who find it difficult to 'bless' on certain kind of evils. I often find myself, totally at a loss, filled with sorrow, confused. I say 'this evil which is happening now' is 'real' now, and nothing else, no other time or perspective can change this. In other words I find myself at times doubting God, angry with God, protesting to God, crying to God, simply confused. I do not have the kind of calm and strong faith that many others have.

Q: But here you connect yourself with a long tradition in Jewish life of addressing God in pain and question. And this out of the sense that what God demands is not false comfort and agreement but one's real Joblike heart and truth.

S.F.: So many things happen in this world. Living in Israel there are often events which cause great pain. Terror incidents, soldiers killed in fighting, traffic accidents, losses.

Q: And the service of God is in sympathizing with others, grieving with them as you so often do?

S.F.: It is often difficult to know what is right in this. Sometimes I blame myself for grieving too much, when I know in a few days those close to the person will still be grieving while I will not.

Q: But clearly the service of God is in loving and caring for others, showing compassion for others? For this is our going after the middot of Hashem one traditional way of truly serving God?

S.F.: I often wonder how Hashem can bear this world when it has so much suffering in it. I myself often resent knowing about the sufferings. I already 'have too much'.

Q: But perhaps this is another element in the service of God, learning to 'enlarge one's heart' so as to include caring for 'more' than oneself or one's own small circle?

S.F.: I don't know. There are too many examples of those interested in saving mankind who were most cruel to the people closest to them. That seems to me the very opposite of service of God. I believe the Jewish way is for us to care for those closest to us first. And then extend ourselves to more and more Jews in caring.

Q: Here you are again emphasizing the service of God in suffering? Where is the joy? Or is your speciality, the strength of your character more connected with the painful side?

S.F.: We all go through different periods of time in our life. I remember with special joy the period of time when my children were small, the first years of married life. But there comes a time in our life when the older generation begins to pass from the world. And then grief and loss enter our lives permanently. Sadness becomes part of our soul. And this when we are enjoined to always be searching out joy and goodness.

Q: You feel grateful for the goodness you have been given?

S.F.: I feel very grateful for having been able to know many good people. My parents, my brother, my sister, so many good members of my family. I often feel a love for almost each and everyone I have known. I thank God for this gift of love.

Q: You have not spoken of this cardinal principle of 'loving one's neighbor as oneself,' of this love as essential to service of God.

S.F.: I often feel 'Life is so difficult. Why not to help the person? Why not to make it better for them?' I think if each of us were guided by this fundamental principle in our relationships we would serve God better, and make it a better world.

Q: You often cite the Rambam's teaching that the greatest service of God is in the teaching of others to love and serve God. And wouldn't it be true to add in teaching others to love and help their fellow human beings?

S.F.: For many this element of loving and helping other human beings is central. My beloved teacher Rabbi Chaim Pearl *z"l* felt this strongly.

Q: But isn't this very love of others the source of great pain? Consider all those people who you 'miss' today who are no longer part of this world? Consider the pain caused when one of our loved ones is sick, or suffering and we cannot help them?

S.F.: I believe we cannot free ourselves of suffering and pain. And so when we can we should consecrate this in love of, and prayer to God. This may mean praying for the well-being for the soul of someone no longer of this world, in the world to come.

Q: Doesn't this lead to an idea that one conceivable ideal state of being is that one in which the person is continual connection with God, perhaps through prayer?

S.F.: Clearly this is one ideal, of living a continual prayer to God, of making our consciousness unending in its connection with God.

Q: And one's whole life-story should be a movement toward this?

S.F.: I know how far I am from this. And yet I sense within me often this deep prayer for God's help.

Q: You seem to place great emphasis on the child-parent model for our relation to God, when many today stress a more 'between equals' kind of relationship, the covenant of marriage?

S.F.: I know the historical interpretation which says God increasingly withdraws from history, increasingly restrains Himself so as to enable greater and greater human freedom and power. I know one whole school of thinkers, Rabbi Greenberg, Rabbi Gafni who make great use of this model. And I agree with the idea that we should not simply 'passively wait' and rely on God to do all for us. I do believe in the idea that our responsibility is to act, that Hashem demands this of us, historically. But I tend to believe that even our slightest action depends upon the help, the cooperation, the circumstances given by God. Our freedom is in action with God, not in our action free of God.

Q: So what does this mean for our historical communal action in service of God now?

S.F.: I do not make any new insight if I point to the same historical goals that Jews have yearned for for generations, i.e. a world in peace, a Jewish people living in the land of Israel in blessing in a society of justice, a mankind living in well-being and harmony, a world which flows to the house of the Lord in Jerusalem.

Q: Our service of God is then to help the world move toward the world of the Messiah, toward a higher and holier time?

S.F.: We have witnessed in the past generations the return of a great share of the Jewish people to Israel, the building of a Jewish sovereignty in the land of Israel, the creation of a Jewish society. The service of God is in our moving forward in realization of our people's traditional historical goals.

Q: And what of all the 'moments away from this mentioned before'?

S.F.: Rabbi Riskin has taught that we cannot expect the redemption to be one smooth process. There are motions forward and motions backward. We must strive to keep the overall goals in mind, and work to realize God's purpose in whatever small way we can. Serving God's goals for history in serving God.

Q: And how do you hope to influence in your service of God on the realization of this goal?

S.F.: "It is not for you to finish the work, neither are you free to desist from undertaking it." But also, I know how infinitely small a part anything I do will play. Still I must do my best.

Q: But if your service of God has no real influence, how is it service of God?

S.F.: I do not claim that my 'service of God' is great. However if it influences one or two people in a real way.

Q: You are admitting failure from the beginning?

S.F.: It is the Hasidic story of Hashem not asking Zusya why he was not Moshe Rabbenu but rather why he was not Zusya. I cannot ask of myself to be other than what I am.

Q: But do you feel you are striving hard enough, making enough effort, fighting for your idea of the service of God? Fighting for God?

S.F.: I don't know the answer. Perhaps I am not strong, aggressive enough in this. But I am not sure that being that kind of character is what God wants of me.

Q: So you are content to be a small servant of God?

S.F.: I do not know if I am content. But it seems to me that's what I at the moment am. If it turns out otherwise and my work has more influence I will understand God wants this.

Q: And you are content now with what you have done with this work on 'Service of God'?

S.F.: Not content. I do have a certain satisfaction that I forced myself to go out and meet with these people, that I learned from them, and that hopefully others will learn from this. And at the same time I know that the whole subject is vast, is as Dr. Daniel Shalit said 'infinite,' and that a person could give their whole life, and more to exploring it.

Q: You haven't finished the work then?

S.F.: I have done what I could do for now. And I pray it truly will be of help to some people in their service of God.

Q: But you know you could do much more. You have not even begun to touch upon all the ideas you have on the subject of 'Service of God.'

S.F.: I could force myself, but I am tired now. If I always have a group of worries on my mind it would seem this year they have multiplied exceedingly. The illnesses of other family members are what most concerns me now. My heart is more with them than it is with this writing. And it is proof if I ever needed it that there are 'other things' I care more about than this writing.

Q: Don't you suspect that these illnesses 'are punishments' for your arrogance? And ways of God's electing you out? Making you special in need and closeness?

S.F.: I so often have the feeling that in presuming too much for myself I have put myself in a situation which demands punishment. And the great punishment for me is to see those I love love hurt. On the other hand I find it also presumptuous to believe to know exactly how God works.

Q: Doesn't God always demand more, demand greater level of purity of those who God entrusts higher work to? Isn't the greatest servant of God Moshe, the one who is after all judged and punished most severely for the lightest offence?

S.F.: I know how poor I am in my everyday life as servant of God. I know how the average observant Jew is on a higher level than me. That is I think any comparison here between myself and 'gedolei Yisrael' is completely out of place. My life as a whole does not bear this kind of comparison.

Q: But in your work you pretend to be, or try to be 'higher.' And that is the 'self' your readers know. As 'servant of God' in the sense that you are known as servant of God you do presume. For after all you do have 'public name,' something most servants of God do not.

S.F.: Once I thought the meaning of being a servant of God was living a life of fullness and blessedness without great suffering. But there are so many examples of great tsaddikim, great prophets and teachers of our people who have suffered greatly, whether it be Rebbe Akiba, or the Kotzker, whether it be Rebbe Nachman or the prophet Jeremiah. Clearly only a fool would think the proof of being a servant of God is being free of suffering in this world. But I do not know that one can claim the greater the suffering, the greater God's love. This claim of Rabbi Hess z"l I find 'true' in some way, and yet not true in another. And I myself often have the feeling when a particular suffering comes that I would prefer to be without the suffering, rather than with the need for the longing for God the suffering evokes.

Q: There is a model of the servant of God's relationship to God in which human betrayal teaches that only the connection with God is of lasting meaning. Dr. Miriam Adahan expresses this.

S.F.: There is clearly the feeling "Your mother and your father abandon you, and only Hashem remains with you." And yet I want to see the true way is to so love others that this love is proof of our deep love of God.

Q: But you yourself have suggested that human love can be so great as to injure the one loved. A parent can love their children so much that they even wish to protect them from their 'duty.' A person can so love his own family that he puts the love of them before the love of God, and so sets up the dynamic by which there will be punishment.

S.F.: Tanach is rich with examples of servants of God who fail in their relationships with their family members. This failure may well give them a sense of need to repair. My problem is that in certain areas even though I understand the logic of tikkun, I do not make the tikkun.

Q: So really much of the time you do walk around with a sense of your own fault, failing, need to make repair. You do have a sense of being 'less' than you should be?

S.F.: The contradiction between what I am in my everyday life, and what I would be in and through my work is strong.

Q: You have always not been good enough in your own eyes. And this continues in your feeling of how God judges you.

S.F.: The Jewish people have historically had a sense of their greater burden, duty. They have had a sense that 'more' is demanded them. And this is essential to their chosenness, and their closeness to God. The people as a servant of God has been put to a higher standard, and on the surface this can be taken as explanation for the Jews having been the people who suffered the most. Now this when I imagine a certain part of our dream has been to remain chosen without having to endure the suffering. A chosenness for happiness. But apparently it does not work this way, and the people continues to demand more of itself in so many different ways (often wrong, and even evil ones) that it does more.

Q: Are you claiming that the Jews serve God even when they do not will to, simply through being who they are? Through suffering and living? And perhaps that all people 'serve God' in this way? But where is the merit in serving God if we, whatever we do, inevitably serve God?

S.F.: I have no answer which clarifies things logically, and without contradiction. I do believe the distinction should be made between those actions in which we suffer without effort, and those in which we are aiming to serve the will of God.

Q: As you are doing now?

S.F.: Back to the beginning. As I am trying to do now.

Q: And have you succeeded?

S.F.: I have said this before. I cannot be the judge.

Q: And yet in some way you feel you have succeeded? You have written these 'thoughts' you long thought to write.

S.F.: But it is not wholly as I want. There remains the sense that I have not done enough, that it is not good enough.

Q: So this is who you are 'the would-be servant of God whose service is never good enough.'

S.F.: Among others.

Q: And among those you have interviewed? Is there some priority in value?

S.F.: I do not believe it is right to look at it this way, rather to learn from each one. "From all my teachers I have become enlightened."

Q: And is there one who you look to as your own supreme teacher in this generation, as the great servant of God you have known?

S.F.: I in these interviews have spoken with many teachers of Torah, each one of whom has worlds of learning to give. When I understand that in the holy city of Jerusalem in Israel in the Jewish world such teachers of Torah are increasing. I am filled with a sense of hope for our future. The dream is of course that many whose parents and grand-parents fell away from the world of Jewish learning will return. And one reason they will return is that there are 'teachers of Torah' who know how to make the Torah relevant to their lives, to all which happens in the world.

Q: And your own contribution to this growing body of Torah knowledge?

S.F.: Very very small. But I take joy in knowing there are those like Rabbis Eisen, Gafni, Steinsaltz, many others addressing the issues. The sense which many had once that Judaism is backward, out-of-touch with modern thought has vanished.

Q: And yet you have the sense that there is no overall philosophical-theological work which does for our age what *The Guide to the Per-plexed* does for its age?

S.F.: One of the great blessings of this work of interviews was in meeting with those who are thinking of what our people can and must do to serve God. I have the sense that there will emerge new thinkers who will move our people forward. They will have a depth of Torah knowledge which I do not have. And they will have a breadth of learning in other areas.

Q: So the service of God is as you understand it also in the overall creative life of the people, most specifically here in the creative thought?

S.F.: To walk in the ways of the Creator, is to imitate Hashem by creating. Our creation, our co-creation with Hashem is the means of perfecting the world. It is the service of God in Covenant.

Q: And your story as you understand it is the story of a life in creation which moves away from creation for the sake of the creator to creation in service of God.

S.F.: I understand the story of the Jewish people and the story of mankind as stories of creation which are ongoing. I see the collective service of God as collective creation.

Q: But if we take the model of Torah learning as highest activity don't we see there that most 'learners' do not create any 'product'? Do not make great innovations they pass on to others?

S.F.: But they do make themselves over. Each great teacher and learner becomes himself a unique sefer Torah. And we cannot judge or know how this 'non-saleable product' is valued by God. Creation need not be a 'product'.

Q: Nonetheless when we ordinarily talk about 'creation' we talk about 'changes in the world' we talk about 'product' or 'works' which are 'used' by many. And when we talk about higher creation we talk about works which are preserved, which live generation to generation?

S.F.: I do not argue with this. I simply believe that we can see creation as connected to other kinds of action. I would contend that each person in a sense creates their own life and story. And that they help create that of others. And that our task in life is to create our lives, our stories in such a way that they serve God.

Q: And you regard the Jewish people as doing this now?

S.F.: If I cannot judge whether I am doing it by myself, how can I expected to be judge of whether this 'least of peoples' is doing this? I would however say clearly that those who are not contributing to the Jewish people, not connected in any way are not.

Q: I did not ask about the 'individuals' but about the people as a whole.

S.F.: In some ways it seems we are. The ingathering of exiles, the building of Israel in so many ways, the increased learning, the bringing back of many to Judaism. And against this the great assimilation, the 'dropping out even in Israel,' the turning away from our responsibility.

Q: You have in the past defined the service of God as a struggle. Here too it would seem that the people of Israel are in a continual struggle in regard to serving God.

S.F.: I do believe there is a struggle to turn our yetzer hara to good. And a struggle in other ways to truly create so as to serve God.

Q: And mankind naturally is also struggling. You see the role of the Jews as playing a special role in the struggle in bringing man closer to God.

S.F.: To bring mankind to worship and service of God, to bring us all to the living of moral life is the goal of Israel. And this involves tikkun olam transforming the world to one of harmony, peace, freedom so far as possible from evil and sickness.

Q: But aren't the Jews, and other people often involved in creating not for God, but for their own power? With mankind as the end?

S.F.: There is creation which is evil, or which can be used for evil. The vast forces of destruction unleashed in the modern world are possible only because of 'creative efforts.' Human arrogance and pride make the Tower of Babel a story continually reenacted. Instead of seeking to overthrow God we must subordinate ourselves to God's goals, and work to serve God.

Q: But there are many who claim that as God has gone into hiding generation after generation, Man has more and more usurped divine power. Consider the power unleashed by the possession of atomic energy, or the creative abilities acquired through genetic technology. Our human creative powers are enabling us to redefine ourselves as a species, and perhaps are preparing us to 'engineer' into being our own eventual 'successor' as 'dominant being' of earth and nearby worlds.

S.F.: I have my suspicions and doubts as to whether such a successor as rich as complicated as creative as the human can ever come into being. I do not see anywhere that God commands or needs this as part of divine service.

Q: But isn't this the point, our reality has taken us to situations beyond which the sources of the Tradition have insight into?

S.F.: I am not a posek, but I know a posek's duty is to be up-to-date on new developments in all areas. And I believe the 'posekim' of the future will have ways of answering the questions of the future through reading the traditions.

Q: So the posek will be the supreme Jewish creative figure of the future?

S.F.: Creation goes on in all areas of life. Our goal should be to direct that creation into being, service of God. And there are very clear parameters of what 'success' in this means in the social realm. A world more at peace, with less disease, less hunger, less human suffering, less envy and greed and crime, less cruelty and murder, less injustice, less hatred, less selfishness and meanness, . . . is one which we have to be striving for.

Q: So you view the process of creation, the process of service of God as a long slow continual process, of many many small efforts made each and every day?

S.F.: Clearly there are leaps ahead and breakthroughs. But I do believe continual intention and attention are the way to perfect our relationship with God. And again when I speak about creation in service of God I am speaking about a way of defining and perfecting our relationship to God.

Q: I thought the Jewish formula for service of God was simpler. We strive all the time as in our blessings, as in Kedushah to come nearer to God.

S.F.: And as Rabbi Steinsaltz points out, paradoxically the nearer we come, often we realize the farther we are away. There is thus I would say something always open, incomplete, not fully 'realized' in our relation to God.

Q: This is your definition and far from the Hasidic one where many of the greats in the joy of Mitzvot feel God wholly present.

S.F.: There are whole dimensions of the human relationship to God which I am not qualified to talk about. I simply have not had 'the experience' to do so. Consider for instance the whole relation to mystical realms. I do not know this. I strive in my life through my creation to improve my relation to God, to come nearer.

Q: But you by your character always sense an imperfect ability to 'please' God, to come close enough to God. And it is in fact this 'incompleteness,' this 'non-satisfactoriness' in your relation to God which drives you so much to seek correction.

S.F.: I think of a person like Rabbi Hartman who has done so much good in his life, created so much more than most. And yet in his heart one can sense there is always the need for 'more' and the feeling he has not 'done enough.' I am this same kind of duty-bound guilt ridden person. And I take myself to be one example of divine service, and not the single ideal example.

Q: But aren't there in your life 'moments' or times when you sense yourself truly serving God?

S.F.: Certainly I feel this way often in prayer. Certainly if I am writing in a certain way. It can be in a moment of helping another. It can be in a moment of blessedness of love in life. There are such 'times'.

Q: And perhaps in one sense the goal of life is as you have indicated before, to transform the whole of one's life into this deep sense of blessedness in serving God: to feel oneself always in the joy the simcha of serving God. And likewise to move to a world in which all are in this kind of ideal relationship with God?

S.F.: I am sure this is the ideal. The problem is life is so filled with sudden shocks and disappointments. I myself know how often I have failed to help the people I most loved. I often too; my own failure is much greater than that of most. So this large degree of imperfection in myself in my relation with others makes it impossible for me to be in perfect relation with God.

Q: There are even times you are angry at God, silent with God? Dumbfounded by God? Times when you protest to God? Complain at injustice to God?

S.F.: I could say I serve God with all my heart in honest and serious relationship to God.

Q: We return here to a point made earlier. You do not have the deep faith and resignation of certain people.

S.F.: I know. And I suspect one reason for this is that I do believe that my prayer, my protest can, paradoxical and impossible as it sounds, move God to change. And this so long as my prayer and protest is 'pure' in that it is for the greater service of God, for other people. It is possible to protest to God in the name of divine goals and ideals.

Q: There is the famous dialogue in Heaven after the Golden Calf in which Hashem does answer Moses, and does keep the people of Israel as chosen people. But you are not Moses. How dare you think that you can lead the eternal and unchanging God to 'change His mind'?

S.F.: Perhaps the word 'change' is not right here. Perhaps the right word is 'influence God.' I don't know. But I do know that a good part of my prayer is effort at making such influence. And this with the idea that God does reward those who obey.

Q: Your position here is not without contradiction.

S.F.: I believe God wants the truth of my heart, my soul. I am trying to give this to God in this writing.

Q: And you believe God will accept this.

S.F.: Perhaps this is the great change with the years. I do believe now God will accept it.

Q: So God loves you?

S.F.: God loves all His children.

Q: And you love God.

S.F.: I strive to.

Q: Imperfect creature still.

S.F.: Yes.

Q: Failure.

S.F.: Yes.

Q: And your service of God in these interviews in this writing, not good enough?

S.F.: Not as good as I had hoped.

Q: Yet something.

S.F.: Again I cannot judge. I have tried to do what I believe Hashem wanted me to do. I pray it will be of help to others and help make their lives greater in blessing and service of God.

About the Author

Shalom (Seymour) Freedman, a native of Troy, New York, is a writer on Jewish subjects who has lived and worked for many years in Israel. He has authored or co-authored five previous books, including the recently published *Living in the Image of God: Jewish Teachings to Perfect the World* (Jason Aronson Inc., 1998), a book of conversations with Rabbi Irving "Yitz" Greenberg. He is the father of two children, Yitzhak and Dina.